Nothing is Altogether Trivial

An Anthology of Writing from
Edinburgh Review

Edited by Murdo Macdonald

© the contributors 1995
Edinburgh University Press
22 George Square, Edinburgh

Typeset in Sabon by Koinonia Ltd,
Manchester and printed and bound
in Great Britain by Short Run Press Ltd, Exeter.

ISBN 0 7486 0698 X

Contents

Introduction and Acknowledgements: A Pattern of Writing

This anthology marks ten years since Peter Kravitz was appointed editor of *Edinburgh Review*, renaming the then *New Edinburgh Review*, and changing the format to that of a well-designed paperback book. Peter Kravitz's first edition arrived back from the printers in late 1984, and was launched in January 1985. Looking back at this issue, no 67-8 (the numbering was continuous with *New Edinburgh Review*), its contents prefigure the nature of the magazine to come. It's interesting to note that two of the authors represented there, James Kelman and Jeff Torrington, went on to win the Booker and Whitbread prizes respectively. No-one could have predicted that, but what was very clear was that those who appeared in that first issue – which included, as well as Kelman and Torrington, Agnes Owens and Tom Leonard – were writers whose work made a difference. Significant also is that Tom Leonard was included not as a poet, but for his pioneering research on the life and work of James (BV) Thomson, and this willingness of Peter Kravitz to print full length critical essays, is still very much a feature of *Edinburgh Review* today. Other qualities of the first issue should be mentioned, not least Jenny Turner's literary criticism which became a key feature of the magazine thereafter; in addition this issue showed the beginnings of what were to become enduring commitments to international writing on the one hand and to the discussion of the visual arts on the other. The final element of that first issue was the logo designed by Alasdair Gray which has given identity to the magazine ever since. In it are united images of industry, celticism, football, media, nature, and writing – all subsumed by the motto 'To gather all the rays of culture into one'. Few people other than the editors took this wording seriously at the time, but the generalist project of *Edinburgh Review* as it developed could hardly have been better expressed.

The next issue underpinned this generalist message with the publication of a major essay by the philosopher George Davie, whose ideas have had an incalculable impact on the intellectual culture of contemporary Scotland. In the preface to his book *The Crisis of the Democratic Intellect,* published by Polygon in 1986, Davie makes a point of mentioning Peter Kravitz and draws attention to his editing of *Edinburgh Review,* and this acknowledgment gives context to the mutual respect between writer and philosopher which led James Kelman to write an introduction to the first volume of Davie's *Essays on the Scottish Enlightenment.*

It has not, however, been possible to print here either of Davie's full length philosophical essays (issues 69 and 71) or Kelman's major essay on the relationship between the thinking of George Davie and Noam Chomsky (issue 84). Due to their length their inclusion would have severely restricted space for other material. Paradoxically, this editorial problem for the present anthology merely serves to underline the major significance of this philosophical aspect to the composition of *Edinburgh Review* as a whole. Issue 69 also contained an interview with Michel Foucault and this 'interview' aspect of the magazine (which later included Stuart Hood, Gianni Celati, and Christine Brooke-Rose) like the philosophical essays, deserves an anthology in its own right. A further component in the identity of *Edinburgh Review* was provided by Ann Ross Paterson who set a new standard for paperback magazine design with her cover for issue 70 and thereafter.

These comments only scratch the surface of what *Edinburgh Review* was and is. Peter Kravitz once said to me, when we were having particular problems of distribution and publicity 'at least *Edinburgh Review* is an archive'. This was a perceptive comment: looking back *Edinburgh Review* provides a unique insight into the culture of Scotland from 1984 onwards, whether through Janice Galloway's first published story, Frank Kuppner's art criticism in verse, Brian Holton's translations from Chinese into Scots, or R. D. Laing commenting on his attempt to synthesise Calvinism and Judaism in his writings. It would have been easier to compile a book three times as long as this, than to select the present book. Thus the work included here stands for something else. It reflects the thinking of a remarkable editor, who in addition to his work on *Edinburgh Review,* turned Polygon into a publisher whose name became synonymous with contemporary Scottish writing of the highest quality.

The original intention of this anthology was to mark the ten years since PK took over as editor with a selection of work from all the issues in that period, including my own editorship from 1990-1994. However the selection difficulties to which I've already referred led me to rule out my own contribution at an early stage. I regret this, but no more than some of the other omissions.

In addition to those mentioned above, there are many who should be acknowledged here. First of all, the present editors Gavin Wallace and Robert Alan Jamieson who initiated and gave their full support to this project. Along with them, Jackie Jones of Edinburgh University Press, whose recent advocacy of *Edinburgh Review* has been of great importance. Thanks are also due to her for the in-house editing of this book. Looking back over ten years thanks must go to all those involved with the magazine, not least the first assistant editor Kirsty Reid, and, during my own period of editorship, the essential contribution of Kate Eden. Thanks are due also to the staff of Polygon in its former existence as an imprint of Edinburgh University Student Publications Board, and in its present incarnation as an imprint of Edinburgh University Press: in particular, in recent years, Marion Sinclair and Pam O'Connor. It is, however, sad to record the debt of thanks due to the late Martin Spencer, Secretary of Edinburgh University Press, who is still greatly missed. There are others who deserve mention, not least Ed Baxter who edited the Encylopaedia Supplement for a period. But I must call a halt and simply thank all those who have made a difference to the magazine whether as contributors, on the editorial side, or on the production side, and in particular those who have given their permission for the reprinting of work in this anthology.

Finally thanks must go to the officers and Literary Committee of the Scottish Arts Council, for making survival easier for *Edinburgh Review* through the award of an annual grant. Without this it would have been very difficult for the magazine to play the part that it has in the encouragement of new writing.

Murdo MacDonald
Edinburgh
January, 1995

Note: The work is printed here in order of original publication. Year of publication and issue number are indicated on the contents page.

Commemoration Day

Agnes Owens

MOLLY STROLLED THROUGH the gates of the big city park possessed by a mild sense of adventure after she had cashed her giro and purchased twenty cigarettes instead of her usual ten. She walked over the grass to the pond and watched children throw bread at the ducks but the wind blowing over the water was too keen for comfort. She moved onwards, tightening the belt of her skimpy yellow raincoat clinging to her lumpy hips like orange peel. A stone, thrown by one of the children, skimmed close to her fat legs. Hurriedly she moved to the protective shrubbery of the gardens and allowed herself the luxury of a few puffs. She studied tags tied on to budding plants and was none the wiser. When she pulled on one about to bloom into some kind of mysterious flower, the stem broke. Guiltily she threw it down. Following a side path in the hope of finding someone to chat with, even if only about the weather, she almost collided with a young man running hard towards her. As they stood, nearly eye to eye, she saw he looked as startled as she felt, but when she stepped aside to let him pass he asked harshly, 'What's the time, missus?'

'Half-past two,' she said, glancing at her watch and not liking the word 'missus' or anything else about him.

'Is that all?'

'My watch keeps good time,' said Molly coldly.

'Got a match on you?'

'I have not.' A right ignorant one she thought, with his spiky hair and hollow-cheeked face. He stroked his chin nervously and she noticed a jagged cut on the back of his hand. She said, 'You've a bad gash there.' He looked at it. 'Must have caught it on barbed wire.' He stared behind him. She said, 'Better get it seen to,' and added, 'where does this path lead?'

He put his damaged hand in the pocket of his crumpled jacket. 'I wouldn't go up there if I was you.' His voice was threatening.

Molly retorted, 'I can go wherever I like. It's no business of yours.'

'Please yourself, but the north lodge is closed to the public. One of the upper crust, Sir Peter Carlin himself, is exercising his horses, as if the old bastard didn't have anything else to do.'

'Perhaps he hasn't. Anyway,' she added suspiciously, 'how come you were up there?'

'I wasn't. They chased me.'

She softened at the information. 'Oh well,' she laughed, 'no doubt the rich have got their troubles, like the poor.'

'Not quite the same though.'

'Trouble is trouble, no matter who you are.' She looked him over considering he was a poor looking specimen, but that was the style of them nowadays, seedy and ill-mannered.

'True.' He nodded his head.

'And I've had mine, I can tell you.'

'How's that?' he asked, twisting his head backwards.

'When you've lost a husband and a son in the space of a year, there's not much left to worry about.' She was aware this fellow wasn't totally interested by the jerky look of him, but she was glad of the casual way she could say this now.

'H'mm,' he muttered, then, 'God, I wish I had a match.'

She searched in her bag and threw him a box. He lit a half-smoked cigarette and returned the box, grunting something which could have been thanks.

'Better get that seen to.' She touched his hand.

'It's only a scratch.'

Fumbling again in her bag, she brought out a neatly ironed handkerchief, 'Tie that round your hand anyway. It will keep it clean.'

'It doesn't matter,' he said, backing away.

Molly shrugged and shifted about to ease her aching legs. The young man drew fiercely on the butt end of the cigarette then stamped it into the ground and shivered violently. 'Do you feel alright?' she said.

'I feel fine.'

'You look cold. I just wondered.'

'I had a dose of 'flu recently. It's left me dizzy. Is that OK with you?'

'It's no concern of mine,' she said coldly and made to move onwards. He tugged at the sleeve of her coat. 'Sorry missus. No offence meant. It's just that I've had a rotten day.'

She studied his thin, hard face. If Tommy had lived he would have been about this fellow's age, otherwise there was no comparison. Tommy had been fresh-faced and handsome, though not at the end.

'That's alright. We all have our off days,' but she kept on walking.

'You haven't a fag on you?' he asked, catching up.

She stopped and gave him one. He accepted it without any kind of thanks. His hand shook.

'Not in trouble, are you?' she asked.

'Trouble?' he repeated.

'It's not unusual nowadays.'

He regarded her with a blank expression, then smiled crookedly. He put the cigarette in his pocket.

'Aren't you going to smoke that?'

'Later.'

Like a mother and son on an enforced outing they continued to walk together back along the path leading out to the open park.

'Working, are you?' Molly asked by way of conversation.

'No.'

'That's the style of things nowadays –'

'I expect I'll get something soon,' he interrupted. 'I hate all this hanging about. It stinks.' He mumbled this as if he was speaking to himself rather than her.

'I can understand.'

'Can you?' he said bitterly.

Molly wished she was back home with a pot of tea on the boil. This young man's presence was worse than none at all. She'd be better off listening to the news on the radio, and that was bad enough.

'I don't think you do,' he added.

'Listen,' she said, stopping short, 'don't talk to me about understanding. I've had enough of that. My husband and my son used to say "keep out of our affairs – you just don't understand". Well, they're both gone. One died for nothing and the other from drink, and here I am, still not understanding.' She quickened her footsteps out of anger but he kept pace with her easily. 'Sorry missus,' he said.

'It wasn't only the drink though,' she said, turning to her companion, 'I've no doubt his heart was broken, my husband's I mean, after Tommy was gone.'

'Tommy?'

She sighed. 'I don't want to talk about it any more.'

They walked on in silence. Molly judged that in another ten minutes she would be out of the park and on her way home – a pity the excursion had done nothing for her at all and by the look of it, this one at her side was no happier than she was – poor sod, at his age too.

'I suppose you young ones have a lot to be bitter about – no work, no future, nothing to do,' she said giving him a sidelong glance.

He shrugged, looked behind him, then asked again, 'What's the time now?'

'Twenty-to,' she informed him, adding, 'meeting someone?'

'Maybe.'

She thought possibly he wasn't all there in the head. People like that sometimes had a passion for wanting to know the time as if there was nothing else to care about.

'They might be looking for someone in Maloney's bar. If you like I'll put in a word for you. I used to work there. Maloney would listen to me.' After a pause, she added, 'He liked my Tommy.'

'I've heard of Maloney,' he said without enthusiasm.

'It's good money and free drink, within reason.'

'I don't drink.'

'It's not a qualification.' Molly considered with the face he had, as sour as piss, he'd as much chance as a snowball in hell with Maloney, then she tripped over a stone embedded in the grass. 'Watch out!' he said, catching her elbow. She laughed to cover her distaste at the touch of him, saying, 'Swollen feet, that's my problem.'

'Hold on to my arm,' he offered.

Amazed at his decency she complied, but when she discovered she was being led towards the duck pond she said, 'I'd rather go home now, if you don't mind. I can manage fine.'

'Wait a minute. I've a fancy to see the ducks,' but he looked backwards as if he'd more of a fancy to see what was behind him. They reached the pond before she could think of the right words to allow her to head for the gate. It was deserted except for the ducks bobbing up and down in the water like plastic toys. Straightaway the young man turned his back on them and looked over to the park gate, breaking her hold. 'What's the time?' he asked.

'Nearly ten-to.' There was definitely something wrong. He was either mad or – her mind swivelled away from other possibilities as she knelt down and dipped her handkerchief in the edge of the water. Avoiding his face, she stood up. 'Wipe that cut. It's starting to bleed.' He wiped his hand carelessly and threw the cloth into the water as if its crisp whiteness offended him.

'Did you have to do that?' Molly asked, angered by the sight of the spreading piece of linen with the blue initial 'T' embroidered on the corner, attracting the ducks, who turned away fastidiously on closer investigation. His face remained pointing towards the gate like a dog that smells wind of a rabbit.

'I really must go,' she snapped.

'No, don't.'

'Why shouldn't I?'

'You're Tommy's Ma, aren't you?'

Molly held her breath. Her head swam and she felt sick, a sure sign of blood pressure. She closed her eyes until the nausea passed. 'My son is dead.'

'I know.' His thin face appeared less harsh, almost sympathetic.

'What has he to do with you?' She wanted to strike the insinuating look of him.

'I never knew him really,' he explained with his half smile, 'but we are keeping faith with him. You might say this is his commemoration day.'

A spasm of fury shook her. 'Commemoration day,' she shouted. 'Dear Christ, will it never end!' She looked upwards for a second then faced him steadily. 'I'll tell you something. I don't want no commemoration for Tommy from you or those others. As far as I'm concerned he wasn't my son at the end, dying the way he did – poisoned with hatred and half mad, just like you.' His face was hard again. 'I'm sorry you think that way missus, but it's nothing to do with you.'

'Nothing to do with me ? You knew who I was didn't you, else why have you clung to me like a limpet, talking about commemoration day?'

The young man's eyes swivelled to the gate then back to her. 'I hadn't a clue who you were. I only needed you for the time on your watch. I lost mine climbing over the barbed wire and I have to be at the gate on the hour to get picked up, otherwise I'm done for.' His voice harshened, 'So, what's the time now missus?'

In an exaggerated fashion Molly lifted up her arm and studied the watch.

'The time missus – the time.' He stepped forward as if to grab her.

She laughed. 'The time is it? I'm afraid I can't tell you that exactly, because you see my watch is always slow, I should think by quarter of an hour roughly. I should have got it fixed long ago but I'm never too concerned about what the exact minute is. It suits me, especially now Tommy and his Da have gone. Why should I care about the time?'

There was a space of silence during which Molly could observe the whites of the young man's eyes enlarge around the green and yellow flecked irises. She had always admired green eyes, yet Tommy's had been deep blue with long eyelashes. Probably this young man with the green eyes was going to choke the life out of her since he was done for anyway, but he just sighed then sat down on the wet grass, reclining on one elbow, staring over at the ducks still bobbing up and down like plastic toys. He looked exhausted. It was time to get going thought Molly. There was nothing to be done, but she couldn't resist asking, 'I suppose old Carlin won't be exercising his horses any more?'

'I reckon not,' he said with his lop-sided smile. He sat up and searched in his pocket and brought out the cigarette she had given him earlier on. It was crushed and bent. He threw it in the water. The ducks swam over. Before she left Molly handed him her cigarettes and matches. It was the least she could do. Now she dreaded going out into the street to hear the fearful whispers, the jubilant shouts and see the gloating eyes. It was all going to begin again.

In with the doctor

James Kelman

BY ONE OF THOSE all-time flukes I landed head of the queue at the doctor's surgery. Somebody nudged me on the elbow eventually and pointed to the wee green light above the door. I laid down the magazine and walked across. The doctor opened it and said, You first this morning?

Yes sir, I says.

Yes sir! It was really incredible I could have said such a thing; I dont think I've called anybody sir in years. But the doctor took it in his stride as if it was normal procedure; he ushered me inside, waiting to shut the door behind me. Then he walked side by side with me, leaving me at the patient's chair while he continued on round the desk to sit on his own one. He was quite a worried looking wee guy and it occurred to me he probably liked the drink too much. His face scarlet and his hair was prematurely white. He had on a white dustcoat, the kind hospital orderlies usually wear, but underneath it he was wearing an expensive three-piece suit. He sat watching me and frowned.

What's up? I says.

Aw nothing, nothing at all. Fancy a coffee?

Aye, ta, that'd be great. I sniffed and looked at the carpet while he rose to fill an electric kettle across at the sink. When he noticed me glance over he nodded. Aye, he says, this job, it's worse than you think. He grinned suddenly, he reached to plug in the kettle, then returned to the chair. I was reading that yin of Kafka's last night, THE COUNTRY DOCTOR – you read it?

Eh aye, I says.

Gives me the fucking willies … He shook his head: What about yourself?

Well, naw, no really.

It doesn't bother you!

Eh, no really.

He smiled. In this job you sometimes fall into the trap of thinking everybody's a doctor.

Pardon?

Naw, he says, you start talking to folk as if they're doctors.

Aw aye.

He frowned and turned to gaze at the electric kettle, he began muttering unintelligibly. Then he says, Probably I stuck in too much water and jammed the fucking thing! He shook his head and sighed loudly but it sounded a wee bit false. He got up off his seat and went to the window, he raised it and put his head out, and he whistled: Whsshhle whhssht!

The next thing the young lassie who works in the snackbar appeared. Her name was Brenda and she was roundabout 18, 19. Blonde-haired, but sometimes a bit sharp tongued for my liking. He says to her, A piece on sausage hen, and a cup of coffee. Then he glanced at me: What about yourself?

Naw, no thanks.

He shrugged. Hey I hope it's ready the now Brenda!

Aye it's ready the now! she says.

Ah you're a lifesaver, a lifesaver!

So they tell me, she says.

He left the window ajar while she was away. The snackbar was parked permanently in the waste ground next to the surgery and it wasnt long till she reappeared. When she gives him the stuff she says, You can hand me the money in later on.

Aye alright.

I could hardly believe my ears. And I was thinking to myself, Aye ya bastard! if you werent a doctor! Frankly, I was beginning to get annoyed. Here he was having a teabreak and ben the room a pile of folk was sitting there waiting. And then another thing started annoying me as well. How come he was taking me into his confidence like this? At best it seemed as if he was making a hell of a lot of assumptions about me, and I didnt like it very much.

The kettle started boiling. He says to me: You sure you dont fancy a coffee?

Positive. Look eh I'm in cause of my back …

He nodded; he sniffed, then he took a bite of his piece. What is it sore? he says.

Sore? I says, It's fucking killing me!

Hh! He continued chewing the food, gazing at me occasionally; he was waiting for me to say something else. I shrugged: I think maybe it's caused by the damp.

He nodded. His attention wandered to the window then he sat to the front and glanced upwards and sideways, and indicated a framed certificate hanging on the wall. I was a mature student at Uni, he says. And he fingered the lapels of his dustcoat. I came late to this … I started only about three years ago. He shook his head and sighed. Ah Christ, it has to be said; to a fairly big extent you've got to describe this as a young man's job.

Mmm.

Aye, he says, truly, a young man's job.

Well, right enough, it needs a lot of training.

Naw but it's no just that it's no just that. He grimaced at me and stared at his piece; he bit a mouthful and chewed, then drank a mouthful of coffee. He sighed again and he says: You married?

Eh, yes and no.

Separated?

I shrugged.

Ah – same as myself, I'm divorced. Hh! He smiled: Up at Uni I got involved with this lassie and *she* found out, the missis. Bang – out the door. More or less dumped the fucking suitcase out in the middle of the street man fucking terrible. Never seen her since! No even at all these family kind of business things. It's funny, when I dont go to one she does and when I do go to one she doesnt. And we never get in touch beforehand. It's a kind of telepathy or some fucking thing! He grinned at me: This auld uncle of mine, having a laugh with me, he says he never knows whether he's coming or going, is he going to see me or is he going to see her! Makes him dizzy he says!

I nodded.

Then there's the weans.

Aw. Aye.

You know what I'm talking about?

Aye.

Two I've got; how about yourself?

Four.

Four! Christ, aye, you do know what I'm talking about!

I shrugged.

But my two, he says, my two – aye, they're fine, they're alright. He began chuckling: Aye, they're alright.

I nodded.

Nice weans. I miss no seeing them. He frowned suddenly and leaned forwards. What was I talking about there?

Eh ...

He carried on staring at me, waiting for me to remember. To be honest, I was kidding on I didn't know because I was hoping if he never found out he would get ahead with the job in hand. But he started getting fucking really strained and you could see he was really intent on finding out so I says: Look eh, I think it was something to do with women.

Aw aye Christ aye so it was. He nodded ... Naw, I was just going to say, this job man, the way you feel at the end of the day it's well nigh fucking impossible I mean if you're wanting to meet the fair sex. You're just – you're knackered, simple as that; you just don't want to go out anywhere. I mean I've got this colleague and he was telling me I should join one of these singles' clubs. What he was saying, he was saying it would just save all the sweat of that initial carry on, the introductions and so forth …

He paused there, looking at me, awaiting my reaction. Then he says: I'm no sure but, to be honest, whether I fancy the idea. You hear these stories …

And he paused again, watching me. Eventually I nodded.

Okay, he says, so it's your back.

Well aye, sometimes it gets really achy.

Mmm … aches and pains, aches and pains … He lapsed into the sort of silence that lets you see he was miles away. There was one wee bit of bread left on his serviette and his fingers just picked it up and let it fall, picked it up and let it fall. Then he snorted and shook his head, he smiled at me: Kafka! From what I hear he was setting out to write this straightforward Chekov type doctor yarn. And what happens! Naw, he laughed briefly. I've had my bellyful of country fucking doctors!

Mm.

Aye, Christ, I was down in Galloway for a bit of my time. And I'll tell you something man I dont want to see another blade of grass. It was funny at first, all the gossip and the rest of it; then after a while you got used to it. Used to it! And I mean once you're fucking used to it your're …! Hh!

He shook his head and pursed his lips, dabbed at his mouth with the serviette, swallowed the last of his coffee. He gestured at the door: Many waiting?

Eh, quite a few. There might be more now right enough.

He sighed. To tell you straight, he says, they deserve better than me.

I watched him when he said it but he seemed to have spoken without any trace of irony whatsoever so I decided to reply in the same way. Look, I says, it isnt that so much; what it is, I think, really, is just that you dont seem to have the interest, I mean no really, no the way you should.

Mmm.

Well, you dont – Christ!

Naw you're right, I know. He glanced at the electric kettle: Think I'll have another coffee. What about yourself?

Eh aye, okay, fine.

Good. Heh I mean if you want a piece or something …? He indicated the window.

Naw, I says, it's no that long since I ate my breakfast.

I mean hh! He shook his head and laughed briefly, gazed away over my head to someplace, one hand balanced on the handle of the kettle and the other in his dustcoat pocket. To be frank with you, I only went to Uni to get involved in the ideas, metaphysics and so on, the history of the intellect, the past and the future and – aw Christ, fuck knows what else, no point talking, no point talking. Them out there in that waiting room man I mean, really, they dont understand, they dont, they dont understand. And it's no fucking for me to tell them, is it!

He patted himself on the chest to emphasise the point; then he came walking back round to sit down on his chair facing me. I nodded in reply to him but I was non-commital; there was a certain amount of elitism showing in his talk and I didn't appreciate it, not one little bit. And no just the thing itself but the way he was lumping me in the same boat as him. I felt like saying: What about them ben there man they're fucking sitting suffering!

And me and that lassie too, he was saying, me and that lassie. No kidding ye man we were just really interested in yapping on the gether – about all sorts of things, Kepler and Copernicus, and auld fucking Tycho! and we were relating it all to the painters of the period. Really interesting I mean, really. I was enjoying it Christ I've got to admit it. But that's how I fucking went there in the first place I mean – hh! Hey . . . He frowned at me: You ever read that HISTORY OF THE CONFLICT BETWEEN RELIGION AND SCIENCE by John William Draper?

Eh aye, aye.

Well I'll tell you for nothing, I think that's a great book ... And he jabbed his finger at me as if his suspicions had been confirmed but he was still saying it anyway and I could go and take a fuck to myself.

I didnt respond except to nod vaguely. But I kept my gaze matching his. After a few moments there was a rap at the door and he went to answer it immediately. He was scowling. He said loudly: Yes?

Eh, I was just wanting that prescription renewed ... It was a male voice.

Mm yes yes, yes, well I'm busy the now so you'll just have to wait your turn like everybody else.

Then he closed the door. He paused there for a wee while. And then he went over to the kettle and began examining it. He had forgotten to switch it on. This is why it hadn't boiled. He reached to the switch in such a way that I knew he was trying not to let me see. He gazed up at a pictorial calendar on the wall. After a moment he turned to me: You know something, he says, a few of them still act surprised because I'm weer than the average.

Honest ?

Aye, he says, smiling.

Well, I suppose that's because they're used to doctors being this and that, because they've got certain expectations about what doctors should and should not be.

Exactly. Aye. They think doctors're like the fucking Polis, you've got to be 6 feet tall to get in!

I laughed with him. I says, Aye but it's probably a class thing.

Probably, aye. He frowned and glanced back at the electric kettle. Then he sniffed. What d'you work at yourself?

I'm on the broo the now.

Aw are you!

Nearly eighteen month.

What! Jesus Christ! And he stared at me, a frown beginning to appear on his face.

What's up? I says.

Pardon?

Naw I mean how come you're no surprised? Is it because I've read cunts like Kafka and John William Draper?

Naw naw, not at all, not at all ...

I didnt believe him.

Naw, he says again, not at all, not at all, it's no that. It's your suit.

My suit! You kidding?

Naw, I mean, the cloth.

Ah well, aye, but I mean it's an auld yin man Christ I mean ... There's a lot of cunts walking about with better yins than this and they're on the broo as well.

So?

So! What d'you mean fucking so?

He stared at me.

Your fucking inference, I says after a few moments, it shows you're no really in touch with what's going on.

He nodded and felt the kettle.

Look, I says, if you want to know what I really think ... I think you're an elitist wee bastard – your attitudes.

My attitudes!

Aye your attitudes. Especially considering you were a mature student and the rest of it.

Hh! He shook his head at me, grinning sarcastically. Well, he says, that's a fucking good yin right enough. I mean dont tell me this is linked to that hoary auld fucking misconception that the vast majority of mature students are all good fucking socialists.

What ?

A load of shite that – Christ, you want to have seen the cunts I met up there! He made a face at me than laughed briefly: Tell me this, he says, how come you called me sir when you walked in that door? Was it because I'm a doctor?

Naw it wasnt because you were a doctor.

Are you sure?

Naw I'm no fucking sure.

Ah.

Well how can I be I mean Christ – anyway, I was trying to figure that yin out myself, earlier on. And I dont know, I dont honestly know. I was figuring it was because you're a doctor but that cant be right cause I've met stacks of yous in my time, stacks of yous. I mean I never call any cunt sir!

Mm ... The kettle began to boil at long last but he just switched it off and came back round to sit down on his chair, he was frowning at something and he looked at me, then smiled: Okay, he says, these folk ben the waiting room there, I dont see you rushing to let them in.

Pardon?

I said I dont see you rushing to let them in.

Aw well that's no fair, that's just no fair. Fuck sake I mean you've no even seen me yet!

Mmm ... He nodded. Sore back you said?

Aye, sore back. And it's fucking genuine and all so it is.

I didnt say it wasnt.

Naw, I know, but look it really is sore I mean ...

Okay, he says, sorry. I apologise ... for the wee dig and that.

Ah well. I shrugged. Aye and fair enough, I says, I'm sitting here chatting to you when there's a lot of folk waiting to be seen and eh ... There again but, maybe that's cause you're a doctor after all, relating it for instance to the way I said sir.

Expectations – aye, you're right, what a doctor should and should not be. That was one of the things in *The Country Doctor* I thought Kafka got terrific.

Pardon?

Ah, sorry, sorry, you'll no really know.

I nodded. Then I says, But what I was meaning there was you, being the doctor, holding the position of power, you've got to dismiss me, else I'll wind up being here for the rest of my days!

He laughed and stood up and came round to me. Just open your jacket, he says, and pull your shirt out your trousers, and your vest if you've got one on.

I did as he said and I also leaned forwards a little so's he could see properly. He used a stethoscope, and then began tapping about with something that felt like a steel mallet; and it was quite bloody sore when he kept it tapping on the same spot. Then he says, Have you got a lumpy mattress?

Even though I couldnt see his face I knew he must have been smiling, that he had been cracking a wee joke. And he says: Naw, I dont want to disappoint you!

I didnt say anything back for a minute. There was no point losing my temper. I heard him sniff and he began putting the stethoscope higher up my spine. Breathe in he says.

I did as he told me a couple of times and when he'd finished I says: Look, believe it or not, it is genuine; I did come in here to find out if there was anything up with my back.

Aw I know, I know, it's just ... He came round from behind me and put the stethoscope on the side of the desk. In my experience there's a lot of folk love to get told bad news about their health, it means they can lie down and die in peace, without being bothered by any cunt.

Pardon?

He only smiled in answer.

Naw, what d'you say there?

He shook his head but was still smiling. It was a really smug kind of smile and I didnt like it one little bit. I'll tell you something, I says, you're a smug wee bastard. I dont like the way you think you understand all.

Ah I know. He nodded. It is a bad habit I've picked up. He yawned and stuck his hands into his trouser pockets and he strolled to the window, swaggering slightly; and he gazed out for some time. Then he glanced round at me and squinted at his wristwatch. It's a digital, he says, you cant always see what time it is. Fucking useless as far as I'm concerned.

He continued looking at me; till it dawned on me what he was after. O pardon me, I says, you've finished.

Aye ... He yawned again and turned back to the window.

I was actually out the door before I realised the fucking situation, crossing the floor to the exit, tucking in my vest and shirt. Hey wait a minute, I says to myself, you're no letting the cunt away with that are you? Back I went – and I was feeling as fucking annoyed as ever I did in a long time. He was standing there just inside his doorway, ushering in the next patient. Hey you, I says, wait a wee minute, I've got something to say.

You've missed your turn, he whispers.

I have not missed my turn.

Aye you have.

Naw I've no. You dismissed me before I was ready, playing your wee class games.

I was not playing any wee class games.

Aye you were.

I was not. He frowned at me and then he glared to the side of, where I was standing, as though he had spotted folk trying to peer in from the waiting room.

And the other person who was to go in to see him said: Eh doctor, excuse me ...

The doctor shook his head. Sorry, he says, sorry, you'll just need to ... And he grabbed me by the wrist and took me inside, shutting the door.

I removed his hand.

He was already halfway round to his seat. Okay, he was saying, I've got no time for this sort of carry on. Just state your problem.

There isn't any problem. There's just facts, facts – statements of fact.

He nodded. He placed his elbow on the edge of his desk and dropped his chin to rest on the palm of his hand.

Okay, I says, it's all hell of a fucking boring, I know, I know. But what I really object to is the way you've made your assumptions about me, about what I am and what I believe man that's what I fucking object to, all these assumptions. But leave that aside; it's the way you've acted, no like a doctor at all. Christ sake I mean I shouldnt've had to sit here listening to all that crap when these poor cunts ben the waiting room are getting ignored, and for all you know are literally dying ... literally, dying!

He smiled and raised his head, straightened his shoulders and clasped his hands on the desk. Well, he says, you're letting me down now. I didnt expect you to come away with a chestnut like that for fuck sake I mean we're all literally dying.

Aw aye, very good.

Naw but ... He grinned. I truly believed you had a genuine interest in the whys and wherefores of this game, that's how I've been yapping on. I mean ... He leaned forwards: D'you think I go about offering every cunt a coffee?

You've no even fucking gave me it yet!

He frowned slightly.

I mean you offered me one two or three times but you never got round to actually fucking giving me it.

O, sorry.

It doesnt matter I mean I was only fucking taking it for politeness man Christ I wasnt even really bothered. Anyhow, I dont want this to detract from my main point and that is you, lumping me in the same boat as yourself. As far as I'm concerned you're an elitist wee shite and I fucking resent getting linked to you, to your beliefs. Okay? And the sooner we get a new doctor here the better.

Aye, and so say all of us.

Ah well you would say that wouldnt ye.

Maybe. He shrugged. It doesnt mean it's no the case. Actually I only came back to this city out a sense of duty. I hate the fucking dump to be perfectly frank about it. It was some sort of filial obligation, I wanted to impress my father – and he's fucking dead! That's the joke!

Pardon? What d'you mean?

He was dead. I was wanting to impress him and he was dead. How do you impress somebody that's dead?

You mean you knew he was dead like?

Aye. Just – one of these daft things you do. Too many fucking Hollywood movies! Naw, Christ … He got up and strolled to the window. Take a look out there, he says, it's a fucking disgrace. Here I am trying to run a doctor's surgery and I can hardly get fucking moving for dirt and dust and dods of garbage man blowing in the fucking door every time it gets opened for something I mean Christ sake man you're talking about that lot ben there!

And he was gesticulating at the door now with his voice raised quite high: Just tell me this, how come they dont go out there and build a fucking barricade!

What?

A barricade. They could fucking erect a barricade man to stop all the garbage blowing in the door.

I stared at him, then added: You should go and join BUPA ya cunt!

Aw thanks, thanks a lot.

Well no wonder.

Hh! He smiled. You know something? Chekov didnt even practise medicine; I mean no really.

Aye he did.

Naw he never!

He fucking did.

He didnt, I'm telling you, no really. l mean I dont even envy him because he was a brilliant writer I just fucking envy him because he got engrossed in ideas.

I dont believe you.

You ever counted up the number of doctors who became writers and artists, and musicians? Well there's been a hell of a lot, a hell of a lot.

Okay, fine, so you think it's better being one of them than the poor cunt who has to go about curing the sick.

He was about to reply but stopped himself and he says instead: The question doesnt even interest me. At one time it did but no now, no any longer. The way I see it I have to survive as best I can and sometimes that's bound to mean doing things that upset cunts like you.

Things like sitting about gabbing when you've a waiting room stowed out with patients.

Pardon?

You – when people're waiting to see you man you dont even fucking bother acknowledging them hardly, their existence, you dont even bother, you're quite happy just sitting here fucking complaining to me.

Who's complaining?

You are ya cunt ye. Since I came in here, you've done nothing else. You hate your job and you hate the surgery and you hate the fucking city and you wish you could spend the rest of your days just farting and gabbing like a bourgeois fucking intellectual. Well I'll tell you something, I think you've got a big chip on your shoulder and that's it, end of story.

Aw thanks, thanks a lot.

Naw, no kidding but, you're wee – at least, weer than the average – and you're a bit older than your contemporaries, the ones you went to Uni with. And you wear the wrong clothes and you drink too fucking much and your hair's prematurely white. And your wife's fucking threw you out the house for messing about with a lassie and you dont get seeing the weans as much as you'd like. And aye, also, from what I read into the situation, your sex life is nil, absolutely nil.

I stopped there but I continued looking at him. I felt it was necessary to do this because I also felt I had gone over the score in what I had said to him. But I couldnt take anything back. It was said, and that was that.

He smiled, then he put his right hand up to cover his face, as if he was trying not to break down in front of me. In fact it wasnt that at all. He looked at me very seriously and he says, I doubt if you've truly understood a single thing I've said.

Hh – well I think the very opposite. I think I understand only too well, only too fucking well.

Aw well then there's nothing more to be said.

Exactly.

If you would just tell the next patient to come ben on your way out …

Naw, will I fuck, do it yourself.

He smiled. I knew you'd say that, this is why I said it; in fact I've got a wee light I switch on, so you dont have to say fuck all – okay?

Aye, aye, great, that's great with me.

Good, glad to hear it ... He nodded then sniffed and glanced down at his desk.

After a moment I says: So what've you dismissed me or what? It's hard to tell.

He looked at me in an odd way, and I knew it was what to do next was the problem.

Mater Tenebrarum

A study of
James Thomson (1834-82)
'Bysshe Vanolis'

Tom Leonard

(1)

He told me once
The saddest thing that can befall a soul
Is when it loses faith in God and Woman;
For he had lost them both. Lost I those gems–
Though the world's throne stood empty in my path,
I would go wandering back into my childhood,
Searching for them with tears.

Alexander Smith: A Life Drama
London: D. Bogue. 4th ed. 1856, p. 198.

'THE CITY OF DREADFUL NIGHT' – the most pessimistic poem in the English language – is a poem written by a man, addressed to men, about a state of consciousness, indeed a state of existence, considered peculiarly masculine. It is also a despairing response to Saint Paul's First Epistle to the Corinthians, and to the Book of Revelations. It occupies a logical position in the output of a poet whose work constantly presents a male, guilty in body and in mind, looking for acquittal to a female – be that female a real woman, a dead woman, a celestial woman, a woman from a non-Christian afterlife, sleep seen as female, the muse seen as female, and last (but most certainly not least) oblivion seen as female.

From the outset, James Thomson's poetry shows a basic conflict: the conflict of a man with a deep sense of Christian guilt and sin – and a weak Christian faith. He was born in Port Glasgow when the place was alight with millenialist sects, and his mother – 'mystically inclined with Edward Irving'[1] – held all Protestant as well as Catholic churches to be in error, and the Second Coming to be at hand; as for the poet's father, it was only after a stroke had affected his mind that he began taking his son to private spiritual gatherings, which 'were not the sort of things with which he had anything to do in his days of soundness'.[2] With the death of his mother in 1842, the eight-year-old Thomson was placed in the Royal Caledonian Asylum, London, and reared thenceforth along orthodox Church of Scotland lines, having to learn off by heart the Shorter, then the Longer Catechism. In so doing he must have been obliged to unlearn those aspects of his religious beliefs his new mentors would have considered heretical. By the time Thomson was old enough in 1850 to leave the Royal Caledonian Asylum, he would therefore have been consistently grounded in the alleged sinfulness of men – but less consistently grounded in the nature of their alleged salvation. The poetry that Thomson subsequently wrote in his ten years as army schoolmaster from 1852, repeatedly describes a male looking to a female to restore his lost religious faith; this position is abandoned in the poetry Thomson wrote after he left the army and was staying with the atheist Charles Bradlaugh. These poems exchange the mariolatrous for more down-to-earth, naturalistic depictions of lower-middle-class urban courtship. But the transition is not made without some signs of strain, and the poems Thomson wrote after he left Bradlaugh's home and began living on his own in 1866, show the male still possessed by an intense sense of personal guilt. Neither does conscious rationalisation of this sense of guilt assuage it. The opening-words of 'The City of Dreadful Night' show the male confiding to the reader that he, as a writer, has arrived at an ultimate position of self-debasement: 'Lo, thus, as prostrate, "In the dust"'.

The reader following this process in Thomson's poetry will be struck, in the poems he wrote as army schoolmaster, by the number of poems in which a man seems to be talking to an absent or dead girl in his head – a kind of 'emotion recollected in insomnia' affair. The reader will also be struck by the banality of much of the verse: but it's worth reading, to follow the progress of the poet's mind. Three poems in this period 1852-1862 – 'Love's Dawn', 'Bertram to the Most Noble and Beautiful Lady Geraldine' and 'The Deliverer' – are examples of poems in which the guilty male shows confidence in the female's powers of redemption. The man in 'Love's Dawn' regrets that the woman will see through him to

> My heart's caged lusts the wildest and the fiercest,
> The cynic thoughts that fret my homeless mind,

> My unbelief, my selfishness, my weakness,
> My dismal lack of charity and meekness

but he has confidence in her gaze

> For, amidst all the evil, thou wilt find
> Pervading, cleansing, and transmuting me,
> A fervent and most holy love for thee.

Similarly, the 'torpid and defiled' Bertram finds that after he has met the Lady Geraldine, 'Numb Faith re-lives', and he is able to address her as

> Blessed Redeemer of my sinking mind!

The male persona of 'The Deliverer' is told

> Chastity, purity and holiness
> Shall shame thy virile grossness ...

> Till perfect reverence for her shall grow
> to faith in God.

But in other poems written in this decade, the male has less confidence. In 'Marriage' he requests that his long-absent wife return to him as

> Strength and hope and faith are waning

and the male in 'Tasso to Leonora' tells the female

> You are truer than my faith

and asks for 'some dear secret sign' that they will really meet after death. In 'Mater Tenebrarum' the female has died; and the male nightly cries on her to visit him from her 'Heaven above' that she might give him

> One word of solemn assurance and truth that the soul with its love never dies!

That she doesn't appear inclines him to the belief that she is 'utterly dead', which makes him despair:

> No hope in this worn-out world, no hope beyond the tomb
> No living and loving God, but blind and stony doom.

But still, contradictorily, he clings on:

> What keeps me yet in this life, what spark in my frozen breast?
> A fire of dread, a light of hope, kindled, O Love, by thee;
> For thy pure and gentle and beautiful soul, it must immortal be.

The truth is though, that the male in Thomson's poetry never shows any belief in a 'loving' God in the first place. At worst God is God the Avenger, at best he looks the other way. Unlike the female, he is not inclined to forgive, as this episode from 'The Doom of a City' illustrates:

> As one who in the morning-shine
>> Reels homeward, shameful, wan, adust,
> From orgies wild with fiery wine
>> And reckless sin and brutish lust:
> And sees a doorway open wide,
>> And then the grand Cathedral space;
> And hurries in to crouch and hide
>> His trembling frame, his branded face.
>
> ...
>
> How can he join the songs of praise?
>> His throat is parched, his brain is wild
> How dare he seek the Father's gaze,
>> Thus hopeless, loveless and defiled?
> How taint the pureness – though he yearn
>> To join such fellowship for aye?
> He creeps out pale – May he return
>> Some time when he shall dare to stay!

So it is to the female that the male constantly looks for moral strength and faith – faith in an afterlife which the male, purified of his guilty mind and body at last, can share with the female who has given him the faith entitling him to the afterlife with her in the first place. God himself is to be conspicuous by his absence in this Heaven of Thomson's; having arranged the eternal marriage, God can go and do his avenging somewhere else. Thomson seems to have been trying to construct an afterlife whose real God is Shelley; the tribute to Shelley in the first half of the nom-de-plume 'Bysshe Vanolis' is not simply a matter of style. But Shelley and a sense of sin do not mix. 'Reproach not thine own soul'[3] is hardly the motto of the Longer Catechism. So by the time Thomson left the army to stay with Bradlaugh in 1862, the male persona has been reduced – in 'To Our Ladies of Death' – to calling on Our Lady of Oblivion. But even in oblivion, it is hoped there might be some little consciousness of

> No sin, no fear, no failure, no excess.

In becoming closely associated with Charles Bradlaugh and his antitheistic *National Reformer*, Thomson was not mixing in circles whose criticism of religion was confined solely to disputing the truth of the Bible and the existence of God. The *National Reformer* attacked the adverse effects of the Christian religion in many areas, including on the status of, and on male attitudes towards, women. And when a regular contributor admitted that 'the passion of Love' made him hope to be reunited with his wife after death,[4] he was answered the following week by an editorial comment that he had confused reason with sentiment – and that the widowed who remarried might shrink from the complications of a polygamous afterlife.[5] Not surprisingly, the long 'Vane's Story' written between 1862 and 1864, marks a crucial shift in the attitude of the male from that in 'Mater Tenebrarum' of 1859. In 'Vane's Story' the male's monologue is set in a frame of defensive irony. Maybe the dead female *did* visit Vane – and maybe she didn't; maybe the poem is serious – and maybe it's a tall tale.

Between its satiric prologue and epilogue, the poem proper, 1,205 lines, can be seen as falling into three sections. In the first, Vane tells how his 'Rose of Heaven' visited him, and seriously discussed his lack of faith and his belief that Christians are hypocrites; in the second section he recalls how she started laughing at his concern with 'old bogey-tales of Hell', and how she told him that Shelley and Heine are alive in the afterlife. Vane then asked her to arrange, through Shelley's intercession, for the early despatch of 'Our Lady of Oblivious Death'. But in the third section Vane describes how after this lengthy dialogue was concluded, he and his visitor simply went off to a local dance-hall, for an evening's dancing together.

In functional terms, 'Vane's Story' quite literally describes the process of the male trying to bring his heavenly female down to earth at last; the way that irony and emotion sit uncomfortably together in the poem show though it's a pretty tricky business. Now that she has arrived, the male is next seen in a series of poems by Thomson describing, in vignettes sometimes quite pleasant, sometimes a bit arch, lower-middle-class couples 'stepping out' together. But 'The Naked Goddess' of 1867 – written when Thomson had begun living on his own – puts a stop to these.

In 'The Naked Goddess', the goddess of the title is seen on a hill overlooking a city, and the citizens of the place troop up the hill to marvel at her. Evidently challenged by her nakedness, a preacher offers to save her

> Spirit strangled in the mesh
> Of the vile and sinful flesh

whilst a 'sage' offers to bring her

> To full sovereignty of thought
> Crowned with reason's glorious crown.

But the clothes offered the goddess by the preacher are so constricting that her body bursts through them, and the gown offered by the philosopher is so baggy she dismisses it as suitable only for those with a body not fit to see. A little boy and girl whom she welcomes are the only two people in the city to benefit from the encounter; they eventually travel to a distant island where they found a state dedicated to her. The city goes to ruin and 'decay' on the other hand as soon as the goddess has departed, and the priest and the philosopher

> Died accursed in sombre rage.

The message of the poem is quite uncompromising: if the spirit of children is not to be 'strangled' by telling them their bodies are vile and sinful, or that their minds are much more important (being that which raises them above the animal) then to protect them they must be removed from the influence of clergy and intellectual teachers before it is too late. But where does this leave the adult male of Thomson's poems? The answer is found in the poem 'In the Room' which Thomson wrote the following year: in this allegory the male lying on the bed amongst the chattering furniture is dead – he has taken his own life. Cognition of the malaise – guilt of body and introspection of mind – has not been synonymous with its cure. That the condition affects males rather than females is suggested in the complaint

> The girls are better than these men
> Who only for their dull selves care.

As instance of this, the memory of a previous lodger, Lucy, is recalled in a passage of appalling but instructive sentimentality. Lucy apparently had been interested in all the room's objects, dusting and mending; 'fifty times a day' the mirror says, she would 'smile here in my face', adjusting her hair or tying a ribbon; she had got up early in the mornings, and opened the curtains; she hadn't sat writing all the time, apart from 'once a week a pretty note', nor had she read 'those stupid, worn-out books'; she had had her friends, too, 'blithe young girls' who had visited her – not like the 'glum and sour' man now lying on the bed, who had never had any visitors. Lucy, in short, is another of Victorian Literature's empty-headed dolls. But she is meant to be seen, in comparison with the male in the poem, as cheerful, extrovert, happy with her own appearance, and not a 'thinker'. But for the man, despair of mind and body has followed despair of spirit, into suicide.

The following year, 1869, Thomson wrote virtually no poetry. A diary entry for November 4th records that he spent five hours burning all his old letters and most of his manuscripts:

> Burned all my old papers, manuscripts, and letters, save the
> book MSS, which have been already in great part printed.
>   ... after this terrible year, I could do no less than consume
> the past. I can now better face the future, come in what guise it
> may.[6]

Two months later, in January 1870, he began work on 'The City of
Dreadful Night'.

(2)
The City of Dreadful Night: an analysis

> ... a man in himself is a city, beginning, seeking, achieving and
> concluding his life in ways which the various aspects of a city
> may embody if imaginatively conceived – any city, all the
> details of which may be made to voice his most intimate
> convictions.
>   William Carlos Williams: 'Argument' to Book One of
>   *Paterson* (1946) reproduced in prefatory note to *Paterson:
>   Books One to Five*, London, MacGibbon & Kee, 1964

IT MAY SEEM a paradox, given that the male persona of the
poems is now 'dead', that the poems – and he – should continue at
all. But this paradox, and this 'death', is precisely what 'The City of
Dreadful Night' is about. The narrator here, prostrate, tells the
reader that he is writing in the dust something that is not for the
religious, the hopeful, or the successful. Only those who know the
secret already will understand, no 'uninitiate' can divine the meaning of the message. The poem itself, in twenty-one sections, presents
a series of paradoxical images written, like the opening 'Proem', in
the present tense. These images are contained in the even-numbered
sections, two to twenty. On the other hand the odd-numbered
sections one to twenty-one give a series of accounts, in the past
tense, of aspects of a visit to this city made by the narrator himself.
These accounts function both as a guide, literally, to the place itself,
and to how people arrive there. The image contained in the 'message' fundamentally, is of a city-state, of 'Death-in-Life'.
    The only certitude that the living and sane have there is 'The
certitude of Death', the thing felt least strange is that 'Death-in-Life
is the eternal king', the hopelessness felt is at wonder as to whether
Death-in-Life can be brought to Life again; the men there are like

phantoms; the sound of traffic is most likely to be the sound of a hearse going by; the men live in the tombs, the 'wan and cold' reason in their central brain able only to watch their outward madness; people ordinarily complain that time passes too quickly, but the time towards death can't come quickly enough for these citizens:

> O length of the intolerable hours
> O nights that are as aeons of slow pain,
> O Time, too ample for our vital powers,
> O Life, whose woeful vanities remain
> Immutable for all of all our legions
> Through all the centuries and in all the regions
> Not of your speed and variance *we* complain.
>
> *We* do not ask a longer term of strife,
> Weakness and weariness and nameless woes;
> *We* do not claim renewed and endless life
> When this which is our torment here shall close,
> An everlasting conscious inanition!
> We yearn for speedy death in full fruition,
> Dateless oblivion and divine repose.

The images for 'Death-in-Life' continue: where, ordinarily, people affect one another socially in different ways, for good as well as ill, there each only infects the air the others breathe; where people usually attribute majesty and feeling to the heavens, in fact the stars are dead, the heavens 'a void abyss', the city does have a river – but it is The River of the Suicides: even if one does not seek death in it because of 'dear foolish friends', at least one can be sure in time of

> That one best sleep which never wakes again.

The first section on the other hand of the narrator's account of his past visit to the city, in which he watches a man endlessly circling round shrines to dead Faith, dead Love, and dead Hope, establishes the basis of the city as being a reversal of Saint Paul's First Epistle to the Corinthians: 'And now abideth faith, hope, charity, these three'.[7] The man engaged in circling round these shrines offers a metaphor for the meaningless of his journey:

> Take a watch, erase
> The signs and figures of the circling hours,
> Detach the hands, remove the dial-face;
> The works proceed until run down; although
> Bereft of purpose, void of use, still go.

A reference to Paley might seem obvious, but there's also an echo here of Waller's 'On the Fear of God'. This was one of the poems in the book set for 'repetition' lessons to be given in the army schools whilst Thomson was an army schoolmaster:[8]

> As clocks, remaining in the skilful hand
> Of some great master, at the figure stand,
> But, when abroad, neglected they do go,
> At random strike, and the false hour do show;
> So, from our Maker wandering, we stray,
> Like birds that know not to their nests the way.
> In Him we dwelt before our exile here,
> And may, returning, find contentment there:
> True joy may find, perfection of delight,
> Behold His face, and shun eternal night.

In fact a process in the poem, of as it were bitterly replying to specific books and passages of literature, runs through 'The City of Dreadful Night' from start to finish. And if the basis of the poem is a reply to the Bible, the source of the setting is most obviously Dante. But even though the inscription on the gate of Dante's Hell is used as a prefatory quote to Thomson's poem, the latter embodies within itself negative reversals of positive aspects of Dante's trilogy.[9] Section six of 'The City of Dreadful Night' for instance describes how the people in the city cannot even get *into* Hell – they have no hope left to abandon. And section four contains a reversal of the fortunes of the narrator in Canto Thirty-one of *Purgatory*, where Matilda drew Dante across the waters of Lethe towards Beatrice: Thomson's narrator is left on the shore, and his final

> But I, what do I here?

is a bitter echo of Matilda's 'Surgi, che fai?' when she wakened Dante in Canto Thirty-two.[10] Lastly, instead of the great vision of the Queen of Heaven in Canto Thirty-two of Dante's *Paradise*,[11] there is – Dürer's Melencolia. The references can be multiple: where the action of section four seems to have its source in Dante, the woman herself there seems reminiscent of the Lady in the 'Mask of Cupid' set in Busirane's enchanted palace in Book Three of *The Faerie Queene*. Spenser's

> dolefull Lady, like a dreary Spright,
> Cald by strong charmes out of eternall night[12]

has, like Thomson's figure bearing 'her own burning heart', a wounded breast, where

> At that wide orifice her trembling hart
> Was drawn forth, and in silver basin layd.[13]

And Spenser's enchanted palace, with its tapestries and altar to Cupid,[14] seems both the source and reverse image of what becomes in Thomson (section ten) a mansion of dead Love, wherein a young man, turning to stone, keeps a vigil by the corpse of the woman he loved.

But it mustn't be thought that Thomson, in these 'replies' to works of literature, was playing a literary game of spot-the-author. He wasn't writing for examination students, nor attempting to conceal his emotions behind a smokescreen of literary references. For as anyone who reads Thomson's critical essays will discover, Spenser and Dante – like Shakespeare, Burns, Whitman, Heine, Leopardi, De Quincey, Shelley – were people whose works Thomson cared about, passionately. He was always trying to persuade the reader of his essays to read them, and he always wrote with the basic given, that at heart any work of art is one person speaking to another. So his references to previous writers are not indications of his distancing himself, but are indications instead of the true intimacy of his address. He is as it were pulling out of himself those works of literature he loves, and stripping them of their innate optimism before the reader's eyes. But it is not 'The Literary Tradition' that he is lacerating in so doing – he is lacerating, in his despair, himself.

But of course not all the authors Thomson cared about show innate optimism. The pessimistic congruence of thought between Thomson and Leopardi can be seen in Thomson's translations of the Italian, section eleven of 'The City of Dreadful Night' with its paradox about the men who are 'most rational and yet insane' is reminiscent of a passage of Leopardi which Thomson translated for the *National Reformer* in 1869:

> For this is the miserable condition of man, and the barbarous teaching of reason, that, our pleasures and pains being mere illusions, the affliction which derives from the certitude of the nullity of all things is evermore and solely just and real. And although if we regulated our life in accordance with the conviction (*sentimento*) of this nullity, the world would come to an end, and we should justly be called mad, it is yet formally certain that this would be a madness reasonable in all regards, and that compared with it all wisdom (*tutte le saviezze*) would in deed be madness, since everything is done in our world through the simple and continual ignoring of this universal truth, that all is nothing.[15]

Where section nine, also, extends the metaphor of a purposeless mechanism (as the watch of section two, already quoted) from the individual to the universal –

> "The world rolls round for ever like a mill;
> It grinds out death and life and good and ill;
> It has no purpose, heart or mind or will.
>
> Nay, does it treat him harshly as he saith?
> It grinds him some slow years of bitter breath,
> Then grinds him back into eternal death."

– this seems an echo of Carlyle, whose work has many echoes in Thomson's, here being from the Everlasting No of *Sartor Resartus*:

> To me the Universe was all void of Life, of Purpose, of Voli-
> tion, even of Hostility: it was one huge, dead, immeasurable
> Steam-engine, rolling on, in its dead indifference, to grind me
> limb from limb. O, the vast, gloomy, solitary Golgotha, and
> Mill of Death![16]

Yet it's the prevailing refrain of dead Hope, dead Love, dead Faith which holds 'The City of Dreadful Night' together. After witnessing (section two) a circling figure visiting the shrines of these, the narrator (and reader) in fact then does likewise. The River of Suicides of sections six and eight can be seen as the shrine of dead Hope; the mansion of section ten, that of dead Love; and the cathedral of sections twelve, fourteen and sixteen, that of dead Faith. But the underlying references in the scene at the cathedral of dead Faith can hardly have been more immediate to Thomson, or to the poem's first readers. 'The City of Dreadful Night' first appeared in 1874 in the official organ of the National Secular Society, the *National Reformer*, edited by Charles Bradlaugh. Yet in section twelve, the congregation's ritualistic rejection of all political activity (besides art, drugs and religion) can be seen as a rejection of the National Secular Society's First Principle: 'That the promotion of Human Improvement and Happiness is the highest duty'.[17] And the atheist's sermon (section fourteen) which exhorts the congregation not to despair, as they have nothing to fear beyond the grave since 'There is no God' – this would certainly have been seen as an allusion to any one of the hundreds of such addresses made at the time by Charles Bradlaugh in towns throughout the country. So the congregation's reply (section sixteen) that oblivion beyond the grave does not compensate for unhappiness here and now, would certainly have been seen as a criticism of Bradlaugh's opinions, and those of the mass of secularists. No wonder there were complaints:

the man didn't even have faith in the National Secular Society. But with the completion, in section sixteen, of the narrator's visits to the shrines of dead Hope, dead Love, dead Faith, 'The City of Dreadful Night', with its interweaving sections of present and past tense, then introduces, in the extraordinary section eighteen, the image of a crawling figure trying to reunite his past with his present – not to go forward, but so that he can return to childhood, and the womb. The source of this would seem to be Alexander Smith, whose poetry Thomson liked enough to dedicate his 'A Happy Poet' to him in 1858. In Smith's 'A Life Drama' one finds these words:

> My life was a long dream; when I awoke,
> Duty stood like an angel in my path,
> And seemed so terrible, I could have turned
> Into my yesterdays, and wandered back
> To distant childhood, and gone out to God
> By the gate of birth, not death.[18]

And indeed, in the next section that continues the narrator's account of his visit to the city – the penultimate section in the poem – there is an angel standing before him. And the process by which this angel loses his wings, then his sword, then ends with his head between the sphinx's paws – this represents the process of spiritual, then physical, then mental despair, that parallels the death of faith, hope and love. And this is the initiation rite of the narrator himself.

But to readers familiar with Thomson's complete output, this angel with his sword, facing the sphinx, recalls a similar figure in a previous work by Thomson. In the prose fantasy *Sarpolus of Mardon* of 1858, published posthumously in *Progress* magazine in 1887, one finds:

> For the moon was high in heaven, and the stars were countless;
> – large, beautiful, golden, scintillant, eyes of triumph, strange
> to sorrow, all gazing down from their serene heaven into the
> Valley of the Shadow of Death. On either side of this rock rose
> two vast images, King and Queen; before it was crouched a
> Mammoth-Sphinx upon whose countenance gazed stedfastly a
> mightier angel, leaning upon his naked sword, his wings folded
> in marble patience....[19]

In this fantasy, the family of a dead queen carry her body to be installed on her throne among the thrones of dead kings and queens in the Valley of the Shadow of Death. They chant a requiem:

> We must toil with pain and care,
> We must front tremendous Fate,

> We must fight with dark Despair
> Thou dost dwell in solemn state,
> Couched triumphant, calm and brave,
> In the ever-holy grave.

The names of the three sons who carry her body are Roncel, Armon – and Vanolis.

And in the next, and last, section of 'The City of Dreadful Night', 'Bysshe Vanolis' has placed on her throne above the city the figure of Melencolia. This sad, thinking, introspective figure, who works on in her sorrow, has these qualities in common with one other woman in a poem by Thomson – the woman in the unpublished and untitled poem written, like *Sarpolus of Mardon*, in 1858, and beginning, 'The dice to play this dubious game of life'.[20] This final reference requires explication. The unfinished poem is in two cantos. In the first, the narrator relates how he was orphaned in early childhood, and taken into the family of a close friend of his late father; this man, a seaman, would often sit by the fire telling the children of the house tales of the sea. The second, unfinished canto describes

> The Mother – she was very good and sweet
> But always sad

– the reason for her sadness being that her father and her brother had both been drowned in one ship 'Upon the Goodwins'. The children didn't understand her suffering, wanting to say

> "You sadden us who want whole worlds of fun!"

Yet when she had received the news of the deaths, she had made no great show of emotion, but walked as if asleep

> With such a fixed & vacant stony gaze
> Doing her household work the while she went.

But she was inwardly 'frantic' with grief, as

> She and this brother loved each other so

until at length she filled the 'vacuum' in her soul 'with mystic love of God', and she learnt to welcome misery and 'life's thorniest paths',

> If she might only in pure trance rise
> To see her Lord – the Love ineffable

> Revealed in glory to her ravished eyes

If one compares this with the autobiographical letter which Thomson wrote a few months before he died in 1882,[21] one sees that

Thomson, the orphan son of a seaman, describes how his mother had 'a cloud of melancholy overhanging her; first, perhaps, from the death of her favourite brother, John Parker Kennedy, upon the Goodwin Sands'; again, Thomson notes how she was 'mystically inclined with Edward Irving', even 'following Irving from the Kirk when he was driven out'; that there was a portrait of Irving at home, and that he used to read 'for the imagery' some books of Irving 'on the interpretation of prophecy'.

It was principally the women who first amongst the Irvingites went into states of spiritual ecstasy, with or without possession of 'the gift of tongues'.[22] But more pertinent to the analysis here is that the Irvingites largely based their claims that Christ had bequeathed the spiritual gifts of healing, speaking in the tongues, and the power of prophesy, on their interpretation of Saint Paul's First Epistle to the Corinthians.[23] And the power of prophesy required the interpretation of the prophetic books of the Bible, notably, of course, the Book of Revelations.[24] And there, in the Book of Revelations, is the city of God, where 'there shall be no night', and 'no temple therein' (as God himself will be there); there will be 'a pure river of water of life':

> And God shall wipe away all the tears from their eyes; and there shall be no more death, neither sorrow, nor crying, neither shall there be any more pain.[25]

And yet, despite the bitterness of the reply to this, Melencolia works on. With her wings 'too impotent', her instruments which only bring bafflement and weariness, and with her expression showing that she understands 'all is vanity and nothingness', she embodies the same spiritual, physical, and mental despair embodied in the angel of the previous stanza. But still she works on. For what Thomson finally presents is an image of a practical, Calvinistic Madonna. Her name is not Melencolia; her true name is Our Lady of Work-on-Regardless, and it is to she that her subjects look up.

Notes and Acknowledgements

1 Letter by Thomson quoted in H. S. Salt: *The Life of James Thomson ('B.V.')*, Revised edn., London, Watts & Co. 1914. p. 4.

2 Salt, *ibid* p. 4.

3 Shelley: 'Revolt of Islam' Canto 7 Verse 22.

4 E. H. Guillame: 'The Existence of a Future Life' in *National Reformer*, July 16th 1864.

5

6 Quoted in Salt, *ibid*, p. 46.

7 Corinthians I. XIII, 13.

8 For a list of the books used by army schoolmasters whilst Thomson was employed as such, see *First Report by the Council of Military Education on Army Schools London HMSO 1862, ppvii-xiii; House*

of *Commons Session Papers* *1862 Vol. XXXII p. 400, 402.*
The book in which the poem appears is Walter MacLeod: *The Second Poetical Reading Book*, London, Longman, Brown, Green and Longmans's 1850. Lesson 12. MacLeod was Thomson's headmaster when teacher-training at the Royal Military Asylum, Chelsea.

9   Bodleian MS. Don.d.108 has large sections of uncredited translation of *Paradiso* in Thomson's hand, including Cantos 32 and 33 complete. This translation proves to be that by C. B. Cayley, Longman, Brown, Green and Longman London 1854.

10 *Purgatorio.* XXXI, 88-99; XXXII, 70-72.

11 Paradiso. XXXII, 109-125.

12 Spenser: *The Faerie Queene*, Book 3 Canto 12 Verse 19.

13 *ibid* Verse 20.

14 *ibid* Book 3 Canto 11 Verses 28-55.

15 Leopardi; letter of March 1820, trans. Thomson in 'Leopardi': *National Reformer*, November 7th 1969.

16 T. Carlyle, *Sartor Resartus*, Chapter 7 Book 2.

17 The Principles of the National Secular Society are reproduced in C. M. Davies: *Heterodox London*, London 1874, Vol. 2, pp 167-168 (2 vols London, Tinsley Brothers Ltd. 1874).

18 A. Smith: *A Life Drama*, London, D. Bogue 4th edn. 1856 p. 213.

19 J. Thomson: 'Sarpolus of Mardon', in *Progress*, Feb, Mar, April, May, June 1887. The extract is from Feb 1887.

20 Bodleian Ms Don d. 108.

21 Salt, *ibid* pp. 3-4.

22 The complex state of the 'Irvingites' at the time of Thomson's birth would require a chapter to itself. Such it has been given, in my critical biography in progress. Suffice it so say meantime that it seems highly likely that as a *follower* of Irving, Thomson's mother was one of those who experienced spiritual ecstasies while Irving was alive. (He died in 1834.) Whether, after his death, she followed the church he had founded as it progressed into the more ritualised Catholic Apostolic Church, or whether she joined with the group of Millenialists who rejected the rituals, or whether she just stayed at home and read Irving – this is impossible to say. A chapel for Irving's followers was opened in 31st August 1834 in Greenock, and this was described in the local *Greenock Telegraph*. The article was reprinted in the *Paisley Advertiser*, September 6th, 1834.

23 *Corinthians, Chapters 13, 14.* Irving's resting his belief on Corinthians for the authority of 'spiritual gifts' he often preached, e.g. in speaking on the authority of the 'tongues' he said: 'The strange tongue takes away all source of ambiguity, proving that the man himself hath nothing to do with it, and leaves the work and the authority of the word wholly in the hand of God. And therefore tongues are called a sign to the unbeliever, I Cor. xiv 22: 'Wherefore tongues are for a sign, not to them that believe but to them that believe not.'

E. Irving: 'Interpretation of tongues', in *Miscellanies from the Collected Writings of Edward Irving*, London, Strahan, 1866 p. 272.

24 See E. Irving: *Babylon and Infidelity Foredoomed of God: A Discourse on the Prophecies of Daniel and the Apocalypse*, Collins, Glasgow 1828. '... it is incumbent upon every Christian, especially upon every minister, to study and interpret the Prophecies' (p. 19).

25 Revelations 21.25; 22.5; 21.22; 22.1; 21.4. Chapter 22 Verse 8 'And when I had heard and seen, I fell down to worship before the feet of the angel which shewed me these things' also can be seen as obliquely referred to in the poem, section 20.

The Swinging Sixties

Sheena Blackhall

ALASTAIR GAZED INTO Morag's eyes. The sun was slipping
down beside the loch. He was looking at her as if he'd just seen her
for the first time. Love had come to Kirkintilloch.

'Annie!' Mrs Reid shook her daughter's shoulder impatiently.
'Annie, will ye pit doon that rubbishy magazine, an' rin roon tae the
bakers fur a loaf.' Annie set down the passionate saga of Alastair
and Morag with reluctance. *True Romance* was much more interesting than the collection of a packet of yeasty stodge. She took the
money sulkily, and mooned over to the mirror to pluck out some
offending eyebrows. Her eyebrows ran together like a thatch. It was
most unfair – between that and a preponderance of plooks, nature
seemed determined to blight her growing vanity.

Her mother groaned. Last year Annie had been happy to stot her
ball against the garage door, cheery in ankle socks. Now it was
constant backchat and a mini-skirt verging on the indecent. Besides,
Annie's thighs were far too fat to be improved by exposure; her
back-combed hair made her look like a frightened hedgehog. Her
mother took down a scrubbing brush and pummelled the mascara
stains on the virginal-white pillowcase. That was another thing – it
was inevitable that the girl would discover cosmetics – but did she
have to clart them on with a trowel? Now she was wanting to go to
the local dance – her wee Annie, that hated the sight of boys.

Mrs Reid recalled her own first dance; her father's words rang
ominously back over the years, doleful through the soap suds: 'And
mind an' be in by ten o'clock. I'll nae hae a dother o' mine ca'd a
whoor.' Aye, the same rules held good today, she thought. The lads
had all the fun. The Swinging Sixties were grand for a few painted
trollops down in London, but in the village, Calvin still reigned
supreme. An actress in Soho could drop as many 'love children' as
she liked – in Annie's village they kenned a bastard when they saw
one.

The bakery was practically deserted, but the handful of customers were enjoying their shopping. Annie scuffed her heels wearily
over the floor. She'd been to Aberdeen once, and had been amazed

at the speedy service there. The assistants had raced through the
queues like a dose of salts. Nobody asked how you were in the city,
or bored you rigid with the minutiae of last night's rural meeting.
Nobody noticed if your buttons were squint, or made you stand till
your feet went numb, while they discoursed with the person in front
as to the incontrovertible fact that Dr Masters smelt of drink when
he lanced Mrs Paterson's boil.

In short, the town was so chic, so high-powered, life in the fast
lane, where the action was.

'Onythin' new wi' you, Annie?' asked the shopgirl, flicking open
a paper bag with skilled precision. Ballooning with pleasure, Annie
stepped forward. Her turn for the limelight. She lingered over the
announcement, teasing out the small triumph.

'Could be, could be. As a matter of fact …' she paused to prod a
marshmallow, 'I'm goin' tae the dance the nicht.'

The shopgirl smirked, rather unpleasantly Annie thought.

'Watch oot for the guard, Annie. They're a gey faist lot.'

Annie rather hoped they might be … it added spice to the
anticipation. 'The guard' was a blanket term used in the village for
the lorryloads of uniformed youths who descended on the tiny
hamlet when the Royal Family came north for their summer vaca-
tion. Her Majesty always had a Scots regiment billeted near at hand
on these occasions, though it was not a favourite posting with the
men.

The barracks were too small to accommodate married quarters,
and if the scenery was spectacular, the entertainment (for the red-
blooded military male) was nil. Most had seen service in Aden,
Cyprus and Germany … but there were no exotic strip clubs in
Annie's village, just a fish and chip shop and the Saturday night
dance. No oriental lovelies to wink them on through henna'd curls –
just rows of fishnet stockings, amply filling chairs around the hall
like a trawling fleet in full sail, out to trap a sprat.

Surprisingly, given the circumstances, love did occasionally blos-
som, or rather, lust gone wrong. Every year at least one local girl
would lead a pimply, gangling Lowlander to the altar, stiffly
bodiced into her offwhite wedding dress, deserting the hills of her
fathers for squalid little married quarters. There, to be lost in a
labyrinth of faceless, cosmopolitan neighbours, who by promiscuity
and drunkenness, whiled away their grass widowhood.

Other local girls were less fortunate. They saw in these glib,
experienced soldiers the chance to break out of the village, before
the hills closed in and swallowed them whole – they threw themselves recklessly at every man in tartan trews or a kilt. Betty McPhee
was one such – twenty-four years old, with four bairns to bring up:

a Cameronian, an Argyll and Sutherland Highlander, a Gordon and a Black Watch. Village gossip had it that even the Boys' Brigade would not be safe – the lassie having such a weakness for uniforms. Annie had been aware of the guard for some time. Giggling convoys of her girlfriends wandered aimlessly back and forth outside the barracks, flirting with the sentry who stood sweatily to attention in full kit, or else they peered wistfully through the fence at so much pent-up manly charm, like penniless bairns ogling a tray of sweeties.

On Saturdays, the regimental band gave a display of piping on the village green. They marched out from their quarters, the pipe-major flinging a huge, sparkling mace high before him; pipes skirling, drummer fierce in leopard skin, swanking out in heavy tartan – all spanking clean, with belts and knives bulled to perfection, strong hairy limbs striding out in perfect symmetry. Small boys blew bubblegum and ancient curs scratched at pubic fleas as they passed, but Annie thought the military was wonderful. So noble – each like a real chieftain. You couldn't really blame Betty McPhee.

On Games Day the soldiers competed in the hill race, an arduous event, and to the chagrin of the local boys the soldiers always won, their long trained legs bounding up the tortuous scree to the summit, like mountain hares. Oh yes, Annie was ready for the dance.

It took her an hour to get ready, like a pharaoh being prepared for entombment. Her hair reached unheard of heights of lacquer, her skirt was hitched up so high it resembled a belt. A thin red line of cotton that stood between her and total revelation.

'Be back by midnicht,' her father warned. Safely out of earshot, Annie replied, 'Dis he think I'm Cinderella or somethin'? I'll come hame in my ain time – nae his.'

The hall was like a wedding where nobody's turned up. Jock Sim was at the door, guarding the wee tin takings box and the blue ink stamp that dispensed with the need for tickets – like a shepherd about to brand his flock. He rolled the date stamp over Annie's outstretched hand. Her palm was sweating – the inky numbers blurred. Tomorrow, she thought, it'll aye be there – proof positive I've been here at aa.

Jock looked tired – he'd had only two hours to sweep away the debris of the flower show. Two bookings in one day was too much – they expected miracles on the pittance they paid him as hallkeeper. Here and there, wet petals still clung to the floorboards. He ran his fingers under his white collar and hitched up the breeks of his best suit. Neil Reid's girl coming to the dance. Well, well. It seemed just yesterday he'd been at her christening. Suddenly he felt old. He was surprised that Neil let his girl out, tarted up like that, especially with the guard here – she couldn't be a day older than fifteen. But she'd aye been a wild lassie. He permitted himself a moment of lust, let his eyes linger on the firm, rounded haunch of her. If she dressed like that, she deserved all she got.

Annie circled the hall disconsolately, conspicuous in the isolation. Last time she'd been here, a sale of work had been in progress. Old lampshades and down-at-heel boots. The Blue Varmints were tuning up for the evening's performance ... the usual selection of eightsome reels, quickstep country and western airs, saving the waltzes till last. By the end, the couples would be paired off, would have arrived at the heave and squeeze stage, engaged in voyages of mutual intimate exploration, like surgeons feeling for bumps. Also, most of the men would be totally inebriated. Now, a drunk can wreak untold havoc in an eightsome reel, but in a waltz situation only slithers harmlessly to the floor, or wilts, doe-eyed, into the bosom of his beloved. The Blue Varmints always played *Danny Boy* at the end – by then the audience was awash with John Begg whisky and sentiment, and it brought it all to a soggy crescendo.

Annie was disappointed. No men had turned up at all, as the shopgirl could have told her ... none would, either, till the pubs closed. Jock Sim, taking advantage of the lull in admissions, dragged her round the floor in a furious Gay Gordons – a dance not suited to mini-skirts or girls with excessively large thighs. It was a relief when the music jarred to a halt. She ran for the cover of the ladies' lavatory, ostensibly to powder her nose.

The lavatory was a primitive retreat reminiscent of a log cabin, with an antique sink capable of bathing a baby rhinoceros. Suspended above it from a surly nail hung a large cracked mirror, and two Brasso tin lids sat on the window ledge, doubling as ashtrays.

Outside, three girls sat, smoking balefully. One of them was swigging whisky from a gill bottle. Annie stared at her, incredulous. 'Somethin' wrang wi' your face?' inquired the drinker. 'The dance should be licensed. God – ye'd need a drink tae look at the talent hereaboot.'

Annie knew the girl slightly – she came from a neighbouring village and only visited the place when the guard was in residence.

A sudden spasm of music from the Varmints announced that at long last the talent had arrived. The girls tensed, became predatory, affected poses. One or two managed a pout. Some of the lads were quite handsome – a few were Gaelic speakers, the soft seductive sing-song of the west. It wasn't etiquette to ask a boy up that you fancied – you needed brass neck for that. One by one the older girls, more experienced at giving a sly 'come on', were snapped up by partners. It was like sitting through a roup – all around folk were bidding, but somehow Annie couldn't master the signs.

Her mascara was running, and a splinter from the rickety bench had laddered her stockings. She had borrowed her mother's suspender belt, and it was digging into her crotch. Nobody asked her up, nobody at all. By eleven o'clock she was near to tears. The shopgirl was there, reeking of scent, ridiculously old-fashioned in a Vera Lynn frock with peep-toe sandals. Probably her granny's, Annie thought spitefully. Yet even she had found a lad – a gawky, leering farmer, with great raw hands, pawing her round the floor like a butcher manoeuvring a prime joint. He had an accent so thick you could break stones on it, acne, and jug ears, yet he held the shopgirl tight and she seemed to enjoy it. Monday morning was going to be horrendous – everyone would know that only Jock Sim, as macho as wet cabbage leaf, had asked her up.

Ten minutes from the end, Birkie McGregor came in to collect the crates of lemonade. His father supplied the soft drinks for the Saturday dances – he was about Annie's age, a shy, stammering boy, in Fair Isle jersey and grey flannels. The other lads called him a jessie. As he bent to hoist the crates, Annie seized a pinchful of flannel and nipped him hard. Birkie McGregor jumped up in alarm.

'Tak me hame, McGregor, or I'll tell yer dad I saw ye smokin' roon the back o' the chippers.'

Birkie went sickly pale, opening and shutting his mouth like a stranded salmon.

'Bit it's a secret ...' he stammered.

'A secret? In this place?' Annie was derisive. She began to wheedle. 'It's nae as if I'd asked ye tae mairry me – jist walk me hame ...'

Gallantly, Birkie obliged. As they reached Annie's door he began to assume the pose of a stalking heron, contorting his neck as if about to give her a quick peck.

'Bugger aff, McGregor – ye mak' me puke,' said the girl. He stumbled off down the road, totally confused.

On Monday, the shopgirl served up the loaf with a smile. *She'd* got a lad all right – she'd the love bites to prove it, strung round her neck like an African's baubles.

'Did ye nae fancy the guard, Annie?' she sneered.

'Oh aye,' said Annie, coolly. 'It wis a' yon Birkie McGregor's fault – pestered me aa nicht. Nae gettin' rid o' him. I didna like tae say no, wi' mam workin' part time in his faither's shop. Ye ken how it is.'

The shopgirl smiled. She rather thought she did.

Nothing is Altogether Trivial

Jenny Turner

IF I WERE only Superman, I could just say my responsibilities lie with Truth, Honor, Justice and the American Way of Life, believe it and have done with it. When Clark Kent got tired of trying to make conflicting reports hang together, he could always head for the telephone box and do a quick about turn. Telephone boxes are out now, since British Telecom went private; so the simple act of communication is further riddled with contradictions, hiccups, voices needing to be connected without a pure and simple way of effecting it. Mind you, Joan Didion did say that the feminist sweep from personal to political, from particular to general, was Emersonian in its naivety and thus an easy way into American books; would that it were so simple.

The three books gathered here are all by women and all interestingly un-American, which would suit me fine: we all applaud diversity so long as it leaves ourselves intact. Only it doesn't. Each of these books intercepts the reader, at a different phase of my personal and political being. Individual pleasure, social responsibility, hedonist, activist, benign appreciator of culture and all the permutations besides. If readers were all these things without contradictions, it should all fit together without problems; a never-ending story. An easy book for kids. Joan Didion also said that feminists were just silly women who couldn't face up to the responsibility of being adults. Maybe then it's a plus that we can't fit things together in a piece as slick and smarmy as Didion's *The Women's Movement*. The personal and the political only work well when you use the person as an excuse for politics, like Ronald Reagan, or Ms Superwoman's all-seeing ever-sensitive I. When a neater person sits down and thinks about the many ways they are, shouldn't be or can be involved in the world, it's the idea of sorting it all out with a rhetorical flourish that begins to look a wee bit irresponsible. But on with the story.

> 'I wanted to feed Lillian something delicious, because I knew that's what she was going to feed me. Glancing over the meat and poultry case at Key Foods, nothing spoke to the sweetness

of that woman. Maybe fresh pears stewed in brandy with orange chocolate sauce. "Mmmm," I sighed out loud ... Every other weekend for months now, she's been coming down on the Friday night express from Boston to wrap her legs around me.'

The Sophie Horowitz Story (Naiad Press, $7.95, distributed in the UK by Airlift Books, 14 Baltic Street, London E1) is the story of Sophie Horowitz, who is 24, Jewish, a lesbian and a journalist on a small feminist newspaper in New York City. She's in the supermarket, buying food to smear all over her lover Lillian. She tells her story in a butch Chandlerese, which means it's funny and subversive, which really means it depends rather heavily on good old male constructs for its effect. How powerful is womanpower if desire is still locked inside the butch/fem matrix, and pleasure in the ancient and rather manly-smelling food/sex one? I always hoped that the object of Women's Liberation was to free us all from being subjected to objectification – objectively speaking, maybe it's oversubjective of me to object to the facts.

I was getting confused. I turned to read my *Guardian:* less painful than facing up to facts. It was at the time when West Germany's Red Army Faction were trying to plant bombs on NATO buildings and the press was muttering cautiously about large-scale remobilisation of the forces of Euroterrorism. And there was a photo taken from 1981, a young woman bundled into a van by riot police. Sinister, very. By running an old photo, *The Guardian* subscribes to the myth that the RAF are only a shadow of their former selves, that whatever they do or think now properly belongs not to 1985 but to the space already allocated them in the dim and distant seventies. Like referring to them as the Baader-Meinhof Gang, when Baader, Meinhof and most of the gang have been dead for quite some time. For one thing, the powers-that-be don't help themselves much by this tortuous refusal to face up to facts, or so subsequent reports of European police caught on the hop seem to suggest. But what hit me hard, from our side of the Channel and our side of the fence, was this. Nowadays, normally, a ridiculous number of policemen looming, threatening, possessive, over a woman makes you think not terrorist but pacifist. How can two women look the same, in many ways think and feel the same, yet differ so diametrically on the most fundamental point of all? Is she my friend, but sadly misled on one or two rather crucial points, or is she in fact our own enemy within?

The best way of slipping round this one is to follow *The Guardian* and appeal to history, bottle the Euroterrorist away in a zeitgeist other than our own, labelling it with anything as long as it's different from our label, 1968, 1977, 1985. That way, we can go on admiring Fanon, Sartre, Malcolm X, whoever and not have to scrutinise their logical consequences too closely. In order for this to work properly, you have to split history into tiny, elaborately demarcated units: pedestrian time, tidy little steps one after another, smartly, narrowly avoiding the ethical clashes we'd have to face if Terrorist Woman ever caught up and made it to Greenham. The years manoeuvre on well-oiled hinges around one another (and who oils them?), a rather flimsy way of accounting for the fact that, out of all options, the non-violent one was the one I picked, yet for the German woman, terrorism was all that seemed open to her. Left, Right, Left, Left, Left: as we struggle to keep our act together, clinging to this hair-splitting determinism in order to avoid some awkward questions, sooner or later it's inevitable that someone's going to step on a crack in the pavement. When the woman of today and yesterday's girl meet face to face, will anybody's convictions be built on a strong enough base to stand firm?

At least old Sophie's my friend, though maybe a little misled in one or two respects. And a spot of internecine strife is always good for raising a laugh and a spot of conjecture: will she or won't she plump for the ripe avocado, the stone in its centre just aching to be plucked ? Or will it be the fat fresh fig, dripping with sweetness and rich red promise? These are options I can relate to at least.

Actually, she is rooted to the spot by a newsflash. Germaine Covington, glamorous urban guerrilla of the American New Left, has emerged from the underground and been arrested while trying to rob a bank.

Why should Germaine Covington matter to Sophie? She is everything Sophie is not: heterosexual, male-identified, a shikse, daughter of a millionaire, committed to violence as a purifying act. Her etymology is plain: the Symbionese Patty Hearst crossed with that woman of the Weather*men* whose name escapes me, a touch of the Meinhofs and, for the many feminists today to whom these names will mean little, Germaine as in Greer, that early and mighty sellout who betrayed sisterhood for the sake of a good fuck. An anachronism, yet a figure from Sophie's past, a childhood heroine since the day Germaine's first bomb rudely interrupted Grandma from singing her Yiddish songs. Tucked out of sight and mind as Sophie grows up and makes her own life along less controversial lines, abandoning dreams of international notoriety for a safe and cosy life as subculture cliché. To re-emerge in 1984, a clapped-out old has-been with leather miniskirt and greying temples: yet still a figure of quietly seeping potency.

Germaine only appears once in the story, but her shadow towers over every word and between every line. She's both receptacle and transmitter of all the shadowy facts and possibilities and logical conclusions which stalk around, pointedly ignored by most radical feminists today. That womanhood isn't a big enough answer to anything: exposed Western terrorist cells of the last fifteen years or so have contained more women than men, the women more visibly violent and fanatical; that a woman gained power in the sixties only by sleeping her way up the men; yet Germaine is the influence, so to say they were misled by blokes isn't really much of an answer either. No matter how pacifist, how separatist, how humane you are (and Sophie is all of these things), her perverse, discordant glamour has the power to disrupt the most sussed personal politics. And she has this power whether she wants it or not:

> Waiting, hoping, giving everything to build a movement and watching that movement crumble, leaving people's lives as hard as they were before. Betraying all their faith in the possibility of change ... does that sound romantic to you?

Single-minded, passionate commitment, hard, lonely living, anguish, pain – well yes it does, to be honest. And today's radical community – portrayed in gloriously rich accuracy – has nothing to stand up to it. *Sophie Horowitz* is packed with the sort of cosy in-jokes and cutting insights which make it well worth every lesbian, every feminist and every right-on person who ever has yearnings toward 1968 forming a Readers' Coop to buy. One-liners which deserve to be up in lights: 'Vivian was so familiar, like every character in every Marge Piercy novel'; of Vivian again (a straight broad, in love with an ex-Green Beret, with whom Sophie is also in love), 'The make-up on her face was applied by habit, not passion, and sat on her features like a fly'. There's a Lesbians Into S&M Conference ('no one who doesn't practice S&M has permission to speak'), headlines like ANTI-AMERICAN, COMMIE, LEZZIE, BLOODTHIRSTY PIG. Mrs Noseworthy, a dear sweet old lady, who is also King James, author of such classics as *Murder in the Missionary Position*. A Maoist fundamentalist group, Yellow Power, who led the masses by following them 'had short hair, didn't smoke dope, ate white bread with creamy peanut butter. They also lived in stable, monogamous heterosexual marriages, and didn't have oral sex'.

There's Women Against Bad Things, a group organised by Laura Wolfe, who was active with Germaine in the sixties but never made it to star status. Probably because she was a lesbian (and is, despite having been forced through brutal aversion therapy). The lesbian community treat Laura as a joke (though they take manly Germaine seriously enough) and who can swallow anything so idealistic and naive as Laura's Theory of the Big Lie?

It was based on the idea that everyone lies to themselves and abuses others to justify their lies. The goal of the revolution is to cut through that ... Your personal desire to fit in, in case the revolution doesn't happen, is precisely what keeps it from happening ... When most of us started readjusting our lives, going back to school, raising families, these women kept at it. They were afraid to go on with their lives ... Or maybe we were afraid not to.

Big joke, eh? The jokes are flying, the farce is spinning, the plot is thickening; the radical-feminist-lesbian-comedy-thriller-satire, in other words, is exposed as the bonny bristling bourgeois artefact it is. A busy busy world, cosy, nitpicking, interconnected, incestuous: you can only crack jokes about ideological squabbles and bitch over points if you see the struggle as a game, and there's no denying that for all the people who will bend up over *Sophie Horowitz* the struggle is often, from day to day, a game (you gotta laugh, or you might do something *reckless).*

But smiles freeze into cold shoulders the moment someone like Laura, or Sophie eventually, start taking things too seriously. Overstepping the mark. Straddled between a dichotomy (dyke-otomy) neither side of which holds up.

It all hit me even as I was bending up in glee over Sarah Schulman's caustic, affectionate caricatures. It hit Sarah Schulman even as she was making them up. Sophie, Sarah, everyone is left hanging on the cliff after the joke collapses. *Sophie Horowitz is* an unusual book because, although joyously positive about being a lesbian, it does not accept lesbianism as a way out of responsibility, guilt, bad faith and Bad Things. Lesbian is a noun, not an adjective, not a tendency but an entirely whole way of living. So lesbians have to live through all the compromises, mistakes and contradictions being, or trying to be, a whole human being in this world entail. And in rejecting patriarchy, the problems of living through it will encroach on lesbians' existence even more painfully than they do on women (and men) who lack even lesbians' warm solace.

From where she hangs, her friends bicker and support and condemn and bureaucratise themselves into irrelevancy, united only by the responsible fear of acting prematurely, or crippled by the self-preserving fear of acting at all. So much idle rhetoric, performed by a comfortable elite in the name of masses they have omitted to consult. On the other hand, the terrorist, who cuts the figure of Hero for people and politics which would rather not know, the rugged individual who pushes herself to the boundaries of self-destruction, seizes responsibility, acts on it and lives torn beneath the weight of the other lives she has destroyed on her way to finding her personal destiny. Yet the only institution even mildly touched by her tragic force is the media, which loves a hero it can stretch to tell its stories. So much idle rhetoric, actions louder and more terrible than words, performed by a vanguard too fraught to check and see if they had any followers.

Collectives collect in puddles and pools; individuals make rings but both sides are hopelessly estranged from life as it goes on. What, Sophie wonders, did the Jewish people do, in the lull between the first leaks from Hitler's Germany and the outbreak of war? 'Did they speak to each other about it? What vows did they make? What did they resign themselves to?' What difference does it make, and what difference would it have made?

What can I do? Sophie walks off alone into the skyline, wearing-two left gloves. I'm tempted to quote that poem you get on lefty postcards and which Arthur Scargill mouths on one of the Miners' Campaign Videotapes, the one that ends, 'And there was no one left when they came for me'. To end on a flourish.

But *Sophie Horowitz* never ends. I can spend so much time (and could spend much more) on a thin, easy, unelaborated little book because it has an economy born not only of a smart style but also because its every word leaps out of the page, grabs you by the throat, interrogates and addresses you on every point of your existence, finds you pointless yet gives everything you do after reading it more point. The story ends, the ball's in our courts, the rest, as they say, is silence.

Or would be, were it not that there are more stories, and stories like Rikki Ducornet's *The Stain* (Grove Press, $12.95; originally published by Chatto) which are radical in their own way without being responsible about it. Or so, in a bizarre way, *The Stain* seems to me.

Charlotte is born towards the end of the last century somewhere in some sort of France. She has a stain on her face in the shape of a dancing hare, the mark of Satan, in which she finds her destiny to be a saint. Growing up with frigid, awful Aunt Edma and idiotic but beautiful Uncle Emile, tender and brother to vegetables, she crosses paths with an Exorcist and Mother Superior who are nothing that they seem; she induces her first stigmata by eating her clock, her second arrives with puberty and comes every month after that until she gives up on mysticism and gets back to nature.

The plot, as you can see, is rich and fertile, with boundless opportunity to make connections, uncover old tendencies and grow new ones on top. Women's remythmaking – with brilliant excep-

Charlotte is lying in bed, considering her destiny of sainthood ... Charlotte's pale head, with its large, brooding eyes, is framed by a plump lace-edged pillow. She smiles to herself, knowing that in time a warm rice gruel, served in a porcelain porringer, will be brought to her; that a second equally satisfactory pillow will be fetched from the dresser to prop up her head, and that with much cooing, the gruel will be coaxed between her transparent lips. Eyes glued to the ceiling, Charlotte will accept this meagre dish, knowing that it is all she really needs to sustain herself.

Charlotte rolls her head to the side and examines her pillow. Experienced, she knows that within seconds a miraculous transformation will occur and it does: the pillow, rising gently away from her cheek, takes on the aspect of finely-grained snow that swells towards a distant horizon of frosted woods and towers. Leisurely she explores these mysteries with mind and eye, projecting herself as a minikin cavalier who - her trusty dwarf plodding at her side - confronts the lace border with equanimity.

Safe in bed she dares wonder thus; the plump coverlet, the bedside table with its ready water glass, the certainty that warm food will appear presently, all protect her: as does the time: five o'clock - that most tranquil of hours. A rosy light filters through the graceful curtains, and the linoleum, with its visions of speckled fowl amid florid branches, is faded and glossy.

Yes, thinks Charlotte, I am safe.

Her belly is empty. The gruel has not yet come and she, having vomited, is as clean as a whistle. And that means Death is far away. But is it? Is Death ever far away? Perhaps, like God, Death is Everywhere. Concealed in the

tions - is often a rather arid exercise, and I tried reading *The Stain* as allegory of guilt, family and sexuality but stopped because it was like making bonsais out of baobabs (a simile influenced by my second, more luxuriant immersion in the book). Instead of huffing and puffing at signifiers to subvert their insignifications, Rikki Ducornet (as I see it) rather cuts them loose from their social responsibilities altogether. And they go *wild*. The story oozes Roman Catholic iconography and belief, proliferating riotously, mischievous, sly, demonic, ready to play games. I can't think of a better way of describing it except that it's a proper story, yet also representation made abstract: like watching an impossibly brilliant animated film having knocked back a hefty dose of suspension of disbelief. Forests more teeming and metamorphic than even Disney or The Wizard of Oz; shapes and characters and things alter and dance through changing natures and potential significances moment by moment, frame by frame. Bosch is predictably on the tip of my tongue, because protuberances and gaps in particular have seemingly infinite capacities for doing strange things, but the tone is different, not cold and clinical (the psychoanalyst's dream artist) but earthy, brown, bucolic, to keep the metaphor going, a bit Breughel. And to further mix a garish metaphor: it's Dali too, the way things unpleasantly seep into life, life into frozen things. I always suspected that Dali's textures had something to do with the malleability and ambiguous fecundity of mucous membrane; whether so or not, Ducornet's certainly do. Words are warm, damp, rich and bloody, people are so brimming with uncontrollable life because they wear their stains on the outside; yet Ducornet is unlike all these comparisons because it seems to me that she's not probing what lies beneath; rather she is making a new world in which everything is on the surface, and it is this that she describes through the figure of the Exorcist.

> Unlike the Church Fathers, he (the Exorcist) did not argue that Evil was a lesser Good, a flaw festering like a boil on the buttock of Divinity. He knew Evil to be as methodical as the Good, and so just as true. The Universe was like a great pie cut into two equal slices one served up by Heaven, the other by Hell. And he stood in the middle....
> 'For,' as God Himself in the form of a great red leather boot had explained, 'the Word is the glue that holds the Universe together. It is what keeps the moon in the sky and the worms in the ground. Without it worms would fly. And shortly after, the Devil had appeared, disguised as a small glass slipper. 'Nothing,' the Devil had hissed, 'exists until it is seen.'

It is so radically heretical, so wickedly Manichaean that I think of (and apologise to) that other great American grotesque writer (and devout Roman Catholic) Flannery O'Connor. *The Stain* is the world of the Spirit, omnipotent, ambiguous, shifting, towers of an enchanted horizon, a silent bird of prey watching from the fabulous branches of rare trees. Or simply ticking away in a little green clock. And for the first time, Charlotte looks at her one and only playmate with suspicion. The dwarf's foolish face, the face she loves, troubles her. His smile, no longer playful and all at once ironic, is more of a smirk than a smile. The droll hat pointing to heaven is too pointed, almost sharp, as if hewn of metal, And the arms! Those beloved arms! The one so fat and squat is very much like the soldier's arm she had seen at the train station (its odd little sleeve tucked and pinned so neatly!); and the other, long and thin, is as thin as the arm of the organ-grinder who passes beneath her window on Saturday afternoons with a ratty, red-skirted lady ape, begging for apples and rags. Hadn't Edma called that man a Crafty Devil? And the ape a Thing of Hell?

Charlotte pulls herself up from her pillow and stares. Automatically, she puts her hand to her heart and wonders if she is going to be sick. But this thought is fleeting, for now all her attention is riveted to the clock. Yes! The swift arm, thin as a blade and as sharp, is very like the organ grinder's arm, and the other - why, it has been lopped right off! Have the two arms fought each other? If so, the fastest has clearly won. Where will it strike next? How ugly the little dwarf is! How rudely he grins! And Charlotte's heart pounds beneath her night-dress so loudly that the ticking of the clock is now imperceptible.

'I will show him!' Charlotte cries, frightened by the sound of her own high and quaking voice. And again, louder: 'I will show him!' She runs to the dresser to grab the clock and hurl it against the wall where it splinters into a hundred bits and pieces.

'There!' she sobs in terror.

'There! You see! I was faster!' And in triumph, she smashes the bits with her fist.

At once she pulls back, for she has badly cut herself. Fascinated, she stares as the blood drips from her hand in large, dark drops. She sucks hard, spitting out a shard that has caught to the flesh, and looks on stunned as the cleanly sucked wounds well up with new blood. She sucks again and again, discovering that her blood is warm and sweet; Charlotte thinks that she has never tasted anything sweeter.

'I am wounded!' she whispers, dizzy with excitement. 'This is my own blood!' And the sight of it affords her an insight into the terrible nature of her own intimate being: Charlotte has never been as clean as a whistle. Only dead things are that clean - old bones and empty bottles.

Holding her hand to her mouth she pokes through the pieces that lay scattered upon the floor. The metal parts she gathers together into a pile and hides under the mattress. The glass remains; fearing discovery but, above all, craving a thing that has always crouched silently within her, its face hidden, now visible, she, with the help of the near-full pitcher and her own drinking glass, swallows it all. And the feeling of glass going down her unwilling throat affords her a strange and terrible satisfaction. She thinks of the Princess who weeps diamonds, she, Charlotte, swallows glass. She knows her deed is the greater, more perilous by far, it is above all unprecedented. As Edma enters, the little porcelain porringer glowing like the Grail between her hand, Charlotte vomits blood, ropes of it, Exultant.

rewritten entirely in terms of the Flesh. The dull grey sludge of realism is split into its two fundamental polarities, Good and Evil, so splitting all other dualities and cleansing them all of their ethical content so they glitter, wink and dance, discrete shapes falling in brilliant kaleidoscope patterns. It's *because* this story is so entirely amoral and valueless that it is so funny, so liberated and so strangely liberating.

That's a hard thing to say and harder to justify; a comparison with Angela Carter (who has festooned *The Stain* liberally with rather elliptical garlands of praise, and who is cordially thanked in the acknowledgements) sets it in relief, for better or for worse. To my mind, Angela Carter's novels are dissatisfying because she wants to have her cake and eat it, be as decadent as Lautreamont and as worthy as the earnest socialist-feminist she always says she is at the same time. So she juggles her myths, legends and icons (ostensibly to reinterpret them for women), but in so doing she removes them from the historical context that gives them meaning. Then she panics, casts about for some sort of structure that is recognisably historical, and ends up in a most unworthy mess: bits of picaresque and fairytale, patriarchal fantasy and feminist analysis all patched together. As my old English teacher used to say: put new parts on an old car and you get a new banger far more potentially destructive than the one you had before which might've been bad but at least it didn't move. It goes lumpy and bits stick out. I remember my first impression of both Carter and Mervyn Peake were of coming up against highly decorative words, roadsigns pointing out that

'You Are Now Entering A Realm In Which Imagination Runs Riot', beyond which my imagination could not move. 'Lambent', it was, on page three of *Titus Groan;* 'pusillanimous' on page three of *The Passion of New Eve.* I got to like them, warts and all, but first impressions stick.

Ducornet's vocabulary, on the other hand, is even more extravagant, but the fiction never flags; rather than imposing a different world on the reader, or merely describing one, or bending this one to be tendentious, she has found herself a style and narrative that allows her to reveal her world, bit by bit, as a dynamic process of continuous creation. In this respect *The Stain is* like Christa Wolf's *Kassandra* which is of course a far more important novel than this one, and is certainly more historically penetrating than Carter ever is. So Rikki Ducornet does not have the commitment to history and ethics that would channel her gushing talent to the Cause; still, I can't help but prefer it to Carter's defeated rationale of sexuality is immanent force. (Patriarchy? Aye, aye, I feel it in my bloody chambers.) What good does that do? About the same as *The Stain,* but the latter is at least honest about it.

So it's like letting your socially constructed hair down and having a blissful wallow in mud, mud, glorious mud. Though it *isn't* much help for for cleansing the blood. I suppose this as much as any cultural determinism places it in the line of American Gothic, stretching from Poe to Capote and so on, embracing O'Connor when the effort of accounting for her mirthlessly twisting eye in the context of her cold theology becomes too much of a strain; only it doesn't leave you with quite the same empty cheated feeling afterwards. There is the same paucity of human and recognisably ethical content, but you're filled up with tangles of vegetable growth instead. Moral roughage for the jaded consumer of culture?

Not quite. So the sordid, guilt-ridden gloom of the Roman Catholic Church is given a good poke, the necrophiliac image of Dead Man on a Stick (as Mary Daly puts it) is defeated by the Tree of Life. But (to be pedantic about it) a tree is neither here nor there when it comes to our situation here and now. And moreover: I'm afraid Charlotte is led back to Nature by a man who tells sexist jokes. What can you say? I've never read a work of fiction as farfetched as *The Stain.* But fiction, it seems, cannot go far enough.

Louise Erdrich's *Love Medicine* (Andre Deutsch, £6.95) brings us back home to the homelands, or the 'reservation' as respectfully liberal, democratic and, needless to say, entirely unapartheid Americans prefer to call the frugal oases in which they have rounded up the natives of their fine continent and put them not to work. From my own limited knowledge and understanding of recent Native American writing, *Love Medicine* reads as a second-generation Indian story: that is, it has learned lessons from the work of Leslie Marmon Silko and Scott Momaday and others who wrote in the sixties and seventies. Maybe it's wrong to get prescriptive about a book just because it's written by a member of a wickedly oppressed and exploited ethnic minority; but, speaking from the outside as I do, it's either that or ignoring its cultural specificity in a wash of wet platitudes, like 'a book committed to certain true principles and a book of masterful expression', which is what some authority has grafittied on the back. Actually I missed the true principles, certain though they may well be; and I defy anyone to explain how a woman, writing from her experience as a member of an underclass, can be masterful. All the same, *Love Medicine* is a very good novel, on any terms. But it is so good because it is by an Indian, about Indians, and makes significant progress beyond the very good novels written before. It has learned lessons which had to be learned. Races condemned to one hundred years of solitude do not get a second opportunity on earth.

The heritage usurped from the Indians is the whole of Nature and the whole of America, which they once owned by default. Owned is not the right word, because ownership in the way we mean it did not enter America until the puritan Fathers arrived on the *Mayflower;* it was something more anarchic, more (with apologies) Edenic than that. When Third World Americans seized their visibility in the sixties, and to a lesser extent before, the Indians' position was therefore that much less tenable than that of the Afro-Americans who still had a spiritual home in Africa and had their sense of solidarity and identity less broken as a result. It is hard to mobilise effectively around sitting tenancy when you have been sat on so firmly for centuries. The Indians' loss is so great and so irrevocable that it is too easy to take it as given, Original Sin, which offers poor course for concrete action other than pangs of guilt (white America), blightedness (Native America) and elegy (both).

The analogy between spiritual and political guilt and oppression is clear in *Love Medicine:* on the hill beside the reservation there stands a convent. One character, Marie, goes up the hill, is subjected to God-fearing sadism and superstition, comes down again and ends up a typical Indian wife and mother, cuckolded, thwarted, empty, hoarding her secret past among the nuns. When the young Lipsha tries to bring Marie and her unfaithful husband Nector back together with an enchantment of frozen turkey hearts (it should have been hearts of wild geese) he uses an Indian recipe but tries to get it blessed by the priest. Neither magic works: Nector chokes to death because the heart goes down the wrong way.

In *Love Medicine,* the Indian myths and affinity with Nature
from which the novel derives its blighted poetry and limping power
have no regenerative capacity. How can they when white men have
seen to it that most Indians are halfbreeds, when the Great Spirit has
been recast for them in God's image, every element of their culture
thoroughly expropriated and colonised? As Silko and Momaday
wrote about young Indians rediscovering their tribal memory, hip-
pies were getting off on the souvenirs: open plains, lovebeads,
peacepipes and shamen. The sad Indian, destroyed by firewater,
rape, religion and disease, is repository of white America's Edenic
yearnings. From Natty Bumppo and Chingachgook in James
Fenimore Cooper's *The Last of the Mohicans* to strong, silent Chief
Bromden in Ken Kesey's *One Flew Over the Cuckoo's Nest.* From
well-meaning racism to cynical exploitation of a liberal trend:
Carlos Castananda's cleverly fabricated Don Juan, who took alternative mystics by storm until exposed as a charlatan.

Love Medicine is structured as one of those great American
dynastic narratives, like *The Sound And The Fury* or Jayne Anne
Phillips's recent *Machine Dreams* (reviewed in the last number),
changing voices, partial views, different times over thirty years up to
the present day. Unlike both these novels, *Love Medicine* doesn't
come to rest, finding itself one centre of consciousness big enough to
hold all the strands together. Neither does memory produce any one
central truth or comfort.

> Elusive, pregnant with history, his thoughts finned off and
> vanished. The same colour as water. Grandpa shook his head,
> remembering dates with no events to go with them, names
> without faces, things that happened out of place and time.
> Grandma and the others were always hushing up the wild
> things he said, or talking loudly over them.... Perhaps his loss
> of memory was a protection from the past, absolving him of
> whatever had happened. He had lived hard in his time. But he
> smiled into the air and lived calmly now, without guilt or
> desolation... His great-grandson, King Junior, was happy be-
> cause he hadn't yet acquired memory, while perhaps Grand-
> pa's happiness was in losing his.

Grandpa, Nector, actually stole land from his mistress in his
capacity as tribal chief, but the racial significance of his actions is
lost on him as he wallows in self-pity because this mistress,
unsurprisingly, breaks with him. When King Junior finds memory,
he uses it to try to escape from his father. When Lipsha finds out
that *his* father (life on the reservation is complex, interconnected,
incestuous: races condemned to one hundred years of solitude can

only avoid each other so long) is an outcast hero, a Red Power activist, his aspirations fly not to reclaiming his heritage but rather to escape it, live outside, away, anywhere, so long as it's not the reservation. Although the novel ends with Lipsha and his father speeding away, crossing the river, they are heroes only of a very partial sort: individuals can rise above the tribe (and, as Nector so rightly remarks, all the better if they can be seen to plunge afterwards) only in a mythical dimension, and to invest such qualities in an individual is impossible in the broken, enfeebled society Louise Erdrich portrays. Lipsha can maybe salvage his own life from the family's bondage, but he will save no one else's.

Love Medicine interests me not only because it's the most perceptive Native American book I've yet read and because it's a bitter and profound antidote to your typical bourgeois individual-family-nature-culture assimilation myth. As someone living in Scotland in 1985, I can't escape the parallels between life on the reservation: redundant human beings tucked away en masse, away from the industries that don't want to employ them, away from the proper facilities and privileges enjoyed by others at their expense, given instead a few hacked-up stories and a bottle of gin to keep them quiet, and ways of life that go on not a million miles away from where you are reading this. This I think is a valuable analogy because it reminds us that no matter how fetching any novel is in its melancholy, it is only part of the story and the other half, the bit still to be told and bits which are already being told in many different ways today tell of resilience, strength, the need, the will, the potential, and the possibility of change.

But *Love Medicine*'s whole production conspires against the revelation of this, the truly vital part of any tale. It arrived here in hard covers, highly priced, highly praised, with compliments, an award, an embargo and all. The national press have beaten it to a pulp with soggy appreciations of its poetry, humanism, ignoring, silting off, all its relevance to the here and now. *The Stain* has the sort of naff cover that makes you throw up your dinner and throw the book as far away as possible. Hard, too.

Sophie Horowitz is soft, accommodating and free from protocol. It would never have got here had it not been for a spot of transatlantic nepotism: call it samizdat, does the novel more justice. The way it is made and distributed only adds to how it refuses to call itself art and hide away from life; a book for you about you, if there were more like it maybe we would not have to sneak guiltily away to the *Cosmopolitans* and *Brooksides* we consume after finishing our homework. Not that the 'click of recognition' offers much comfort or escape; even as we empathise with Sophie's bitchy little thoughts

about her lovers and friends, her sidelong drool at a slab of chocolate cheesecake or wild dreams of world domination, Sarah
Schulman deftly lays bare the ambivalence in our very act of pleasure, the oppression on which our blithe freedom feeds, the impossi-
bility of ever having any innocent fun in this world. 'I remember one
day sitting with Laura over a tunafish sandwich, realising that every
bite we took, every cigarette we smoked, every step we made was
off the backs of most of the people in the world. It could make you
lose your mind. It could keep you glued to your chair.'

Sarah Schulman's book comes out of the feminist publishing
boom which brought spine back to our paperbacks, which in turn
comes out of the great insight which can never be repeated enough
and yet which must never be allowed to become a cliche, that

THE PERSONAL IS POLITICAL

which in turn means that

NOTHING IS ALTOGETHER TRIVIAL

which has its concomitant, there are an awful lot of things in this
world which are not half as important, relatively speaking, as they
(or their publishers) would like to pretend they are.

Here ends this syllogism. But the real problems, of course, are
only just beginning.

Alexander Trocchi: A Survey

Edwin Morgan

MOST OF THE critical writing on Alexander Trocchi – and it is not much in any case – has centred on his best-known work, *Cain's Book*. This is understandable, and no doubt that novel will remain his chief claim to fame, but it might be useful in the present essay to place it within a more ranging and comparative survey of his various writings, partly because there is not a greatly diffused sense or knowledge of these, even among the well read (a frequent fate of underground or semi-underground productions), and partly because he himself wanted all his writing to be seen as a continuum of communication, of self-definition, of modes of consciousness, rather than as a sculpture park of 'novels' or 'short stories' or 'poems' or 'essays'.

> It wasn't that writing shouldn't be written, but that a man should annihilate prescriptions of all past form in his own soul, refuse to consider what he wrote in terms of literature, judge it solely in terms of his living.
>
> (*Cain's Book*, p.131)

Such existential beliefs help to account for the formidable amount of energy Trocchi put into editorial and publicistic writing. When he began editing *Merlin* in Paris in 1952, he not only created a magazine which would be a vehicle for talents he thought important – Christopher Logue, Henry Miller, Sartre, Genet, Beckett, Nazim Hikmet, Ionesco – but also through his own thoughtful, persistent, and unshrill editorials was able to map out a new direction for 'Europe's independent minds', or perhaps more strictly a new non-direction, since so much of his argument was directed against directionism, against absolutisms whether Russian or American, against the Cold War which had piled such a mountain of bitter fruit in the very marketplace of victory. Meanwhile the first Russian sputnik went up in 1957, and the exploration of space and the Russian-American space race began. Without ever being anti-science, Trocchi felt the writer's complementary task was to become a 'cosmonaut of inner space'; the independent minds might well be nonconformist, alienated, iconoclastic, but whatever effect they had or wanted to have on society should have a psychological rather than a political mainspring. As co-editor (with Richard Seaver and Terry Southern) of the anthology *Writers in Revolt* (1963), Trocchi either wrote or underwrote the unsigned introduction, which asserted that both 'language and subject remain threatened by forces whose avowed purpose is to protect those unable to judge or think for themselves' and that what was needed was 'the deliberate avoidance of lip service to assumed values, and adherence instead to deeply personal impulse'. If this seems too inward-looking to justify the 'revolt' of the title, it should be pointed out that the anthology contained most of Allen Ginsberg's *Howl* and an extract from William Burroughs' *The Naked Lunch,* both works with strong contemporary sociopolitical implications, as well as Sade, Genet, Hesse, Baudelaire, Artaud, and the devious Malaparte. These and other names prefigured or were a part of Trocchi's 'invisible insurrection' as outlined in his article 'Invisible Insurrection of a Million Minds' (*New Saltire,* No. 8, June 1963; reprinted in America in *City Lights Journal,* No. 2, 1964; published as *sigma* portfolio No. 2, London, 1964).

This is Trocchi's most important single essay, and although written with his characteristic clarity and precision it belongs so much to the widespread and endlessly ramifying alternative-society millenarianism of the 1960s that it is hard to clinch a descriptive account of it. Briefly, the aim was nothing if not ambitious: not a Leninist *coup d'etat* but a *coup du monde* (his own phrase), a transformation of the mass of society, not from within the mass but through the influence of a 'nucleus of men', something like Plato's Guardians, who are 'capable of imposing a new and seminal idea' and who will work internationally and anti-nationally ('History will not overthrow national governments; it will outflank them'). Artists must have direct access to communities and 'eliminate the brokers', but there is a mild sideswipe at Arnold Wesker's ill-fated Centre 42 and its 'church-bazaar philosophy'. He envisages everything starting with the taking over of a country house 'not too far from the City of London', and the creation within that environment of a 'spontaneous university', a combination of Black Mountain College, Newbattle Abbey, and an Israeli kibbutz; and this repeated from country to country, building up a worldwide network of cultural and educational rejuvenation. In the sixties, these ideas did find some fertile ground, and the 1968 prospectus for the Antiuniversity of London, with its anticampus in Shoreditch, does indeed include among its antilecturers Alexander Trocchi, who will fortnightly 'describe in immaculate intellectual terms the spiritual attitudes and the new economic scaffolding which must be brought into play as the tactical bases of any possible evolution of man'. The severe deintoxication so many countries have had since these heady days gives such pronouncements the flavour of a document already historical. National governments, far from being overthrown or outflanked, have proliferated and will evidently continue to do so, and to gain or keep real power; psychology, inwardness, ideas of exile and expatriation now seem indulgent in a world which has so many immediate and basic problems and is again in the old Johnsonian phrase bursting with sin and misery; and who would not now be a shade suspicious of well-meaning phalansteries of potential commissars, even if all their cry was that they would leaven the lumpen millions into the light? Nevertheless, the whole antiuniversity movement, and Trocchi's thirty-odd *sigma* portfolios, attracted an impressive body of support, including Joan Littlewood, R. D. Laing, John Arden, Anthony Burgess, Robert Creeley, Kenneth White, Tom McGrath, Norman Mailer, Edward Dorn, Stuart Hall, Barry Flanagan, and Hans Magnus Enzensberger. Perhaps it is in the nature of things that such a dazzlingly loose congeries of idealisms must belong to a certain time and place and cannot be much extended or developed; which is not to say that an element of *exemplum* may not still linger, to tantalise later harder-faced decades.

These literary and paraliterary activities did not bring in much money, and it is usually thought that Trocchi's translations, and his pornographic novels, must have been potboilers. In a sense this is true, but by no means entirely so. The novels he chose to translate have themes that one can see must have appealed to him or offered him an attractive challenge, and they are well translated, in a manner that shows diligence and care. Jan Cremer's *I Jan Cremer* (1965; translated from Dutch with the help of R. E. Wyngaard) is the picaresque portrait of an outsider, a young hipster out of reform school who fights and cons and whores his way across Europe and North Africa, smuggling, selling drugs, painting pictures, bullfighting, even working in a slaughterhouse (a passage uncannily reminiscent of Archie Hind's *The Dear Green Place),* and finally being interrogated by the police for a murder he has seen but did not commit, in a sort of mirror-image of the end of Trocchi's own novel *Young Adam.* One central, self-observing, self-defining character is found in all the novels he translated: in André Pieyre de Mandiargues's *The Girl on the Motorcycle* (1966) the entire book recounts the leather-suited girl's thoughts and memories as she rides out one morning from her husband to her lover (and her death); René de Obaldia's *The Centenarian* (1970) is the sprightly and inventive monologue of an engaging eighty-seven-year-old, recalling his past and looking forward to his century; Valentine Penrose's *The Bloody Countess* (1970) is a fictionalized biography of the terrible sixteenth-century Hungarian countess, Elizabeth Bathory, who bathed in the blood of over six hundred murdered young servant-girls before she was caught, totally unrepentant, and tried; and in Jean Douassot's *La Gana* (1974) we have a blowzy, bizarre, Henry Miller-ish *Bildungsroman* of an unhappy and outrageously treated boy growing up into some sort of damaged teenage semi-maturity, the maturity of a solitary, hiding at the end like an animal in his dead uncle's room.

Whether tragic or comic, these are all studies in isolation, as are Trocchi's own two novels, and there are many incidental similarities. The motorcycle in *The Girl on the Motorcycle* has a function similar to that of the barge in *Young Adam* and the scow in *Cain's Book,* where movement in space sets off a displaced movement in the character's perception of time, so that he/she shudders or rocks or drifts through memories, present impressions, and imagined futures in a disorienting way. Or again, the old man in *The Centenarian* is not merely monologising for our benefit, he is writing his story down on a series of jotters he buys at the beginning, just as Joe Necchi in *Cain's Book is* actually writing *Cain's Book.* Hangings occur or are about to occur at the end of *The Bloody Countess* and *Young Adam,* and in *Cain's Book* the hero mentions his obsession with the image of a hanged man and actually suspends a doll in a noose from the mast of his boat, fearing that he has been living or writing in such a way that 'it can lead me only to the hangman'; to which one should add that Trocchi closes an essay on Orwell in *Evergreen Review (Vol.* 2, No. 6, autumn 1958) by contrasting Orwell's 'vulgar democratic unreflectiveness' and *passé* concern for sociopolitical factors at the expense of all others with the occasional far deeper insight into the individual human soul he showed himself capable of in his 1931 essay 'A Hanging' – and Trocchi quotes the passage where the wretched Indian on his way to execution steps aside to avoid a puddle.

In some of these translated novels there is a marked erotic interest, as there is also in *Young Adam* and *Cain's Book,* in his poems, and in the flamboyant and bitty *The Fifth Volume of Frank Harris's 'My Life and Loves': An Irreverent Treatment* (1958) (which is about 35 per cent Harris and 65 per cent Trocchi). Explicitly erotic writers like Henry Miller, Jean Genet, Allen Ginsberg, and William Burroughs were among the heroes of the 'revolt' with which Trocchi was associated, and there would therefore be nothing very surprising if his potboilers turned out to be pornographic potboilers. Without trying to insert a 'so-called' before the 'pornographic', one can still see a great deal more in these books, in the whole context of Trocchi's work, than the panting punter might suspect. In the best of them, *Helen and Desire* (1954, under the pseudonym Frances Lengel), there is again the isolated single central character through whose present consciousness and re-lived memories an existentialist, libertarian, anti-work-ethic philosophy of life is clearly formulated; and again the teller of the tale (a woman from Australia, held captive for sexual purposes by Arabs in Algeria) is herself writing it down, as her own novelist. The book is fairly regularly punctuated by her sexual encounters, both straight and gay ('I moved in the hot-house world of scented boudoirs, and flirted with the husbands whom I cuckolded') so that there is something for everyone, and the erotic descriptions are lush with the sort of metaphors that would have appealed to the later Metaphysical poets ('writhed on soft gimbals', 'the amorphous sludge of my breasts', 'sliding on soft graphite'); but on the other hand the main conduct of the narrative is nicely matter-of-fact in a Moll Flanders mode. As the book's title suggests, she is desire incarnate. Her narrowly religious father (a Scottish immigrant, one suspects!) had precipitated her adolescent reaction of complete amoral promiscuity, and as she travels through Asia and the Middle she comes to live for immediate, non-lasting encounters. 'What would I do with a man for twenty-four hours in a day?' 'All great lust is impersonal.' 'The western God, the Jewish God, was invented to make the hatred of life logical.' 'I am anxious to record everything, to break through the shameful shell of civilised expression.' At the end, fed for aphrodisiac purposes on honey, almonds, and hashish, and eagerly awaiting the next unknown evening visitor, she feels she is beginning to disintegrate, like Joe at the end of *Young Adam*, and her story ends in mid-sentence. Despite the fact that it has to meet the demands of its underground genre, this is far from being a negligible novel.

Thongs (1969) (and the title says it all) is a more broken-backed and unsatisfactory book from any literary point of view, but it has features that deserve mention. Like *Young Adam* and *Cain's Book* it has a strong Scottish, and specifically Glasgow connection. Like *Helen and Desire*, it has an isolated female figure as its central character. And like *Helen and Desire* and *Cain's Book*, it uses the device of the central character writing the novel which (maybe) the reader is reading. As in *Helen and Desire,* or more to the point perhaps as in Hogg's *Confessions of a Justified Sinner,* an 'editor' is printing the woman's own story as written in her personal notebook. Gertrude Gault (the same surname as that of Ella and Leslie in *Young Adam)* grows up in the Gorbals district of Glasgow and is the daughter of the Razor King. A violent and vicious environment is described, in terms almost parodically reminiscent of McArthur and Long's *No Mean City* except for greater literacy in the style, and the heroine's predisposition to being a victim, a willing one as it turns out, is traced back to a brutal father and a brutish society. At the age of fourteen she watches her father in a squalid sexual assault on his mistress, Hazel; he then thrashes his daughter with his black leather belt, and she discovers her masochism. Hazel, it emerges, is also a masochist, and introduces her to the owners and clients of a west-end mansion devoted not only to sadomasochistic pursuits but to the furtherance of a secret order whose headquarters are in Madrid. There is a Holy Pain Father, there are twelve Pain Cardinals, and a whole descending hierarchy of whippers and whipped. Although more than half of the book is set in Glasgow, the action finally moves to Spain, where Gertrude becomes Carmencita de las Lunas, is advanced high in the order, and dies as a martyr, scourged and crucified, and eventually a cause of pilgrimage. The theme of 'hanging', it will be noted, is here too, as well as the familiar self-isolation from society's norms, so the book readily finds its place within Trocchi's *oeuvre*. But it is virtually two separate stories, neither of them very persuasive, and the melodramatic Glaswegian mythology he falls back on is very different from the moving and beautifully observed Glasgow scenes in *Cain's Book*.

Erotic, but rather more publicly printable, are many of Trocchi's poems, collected in *Man at Leisure* (1972). He is essentially a man of prose and not of verse, but the verse is in some danger of being forgotten altogether, so a brief comment, at least, is in order. These poems, reminding us sometimes of Christopher Logue, sometimes of Alan Jackson, sometimes of Tom Leonard, seem to bear out a statement Trocchi (or the narrator) made in *Cain's Book*:

> I find myself cultivating a certain crudity of expression, judg-
> ing it to be essential to meaning, in a slick age vital to the
> efficacy of language. (p. 71)

Not all the poems have 'crudity of expression', but where it is used it is generally to underline sexual liberation or political satire. For the former:

> The stinking cauldron
> of inhibition soup
> had its lid lifted
> by Attacunt Peep
> the hairy mind-wrestler

the child with which
god blessed her
womb, and the sweet lust
by which it was irradiated....

('The Stinking Cauldron')

A characteristic political passage comes indelibly marked with the ampersands, contractions, and lowercase of the Beat era:

Concerning white geese of dover

now, the minister of aircraft production
the hon. john dracula
has just signed a contract fr a
progressive manufacture 'f
1,000 dreadnaught mk fck
tactical bombers
their eventual delivery
                'to procure
                peace'
                fr the geese
                in 1980

        &

in commending the governmental decision
brigadier general paralysis
                met with derision . . .

('Lessons for Boys and Girls II')

Probably the best poem is a long five-page piece, in a more straight-forward style, called 'A Little Geography Lesson for my Sons and Daughters'. It is about 'the east' and 'the west', and although it is not a dialogue it is rather like a medieval 'dialogue of soul and body', where strengths and shortcomings of two opposed subjects are set out. The wise came from the east, but 'its wisdom is dried up'. The wisdom of the west is a book of rules, 'not quite indispensable/for those who travel by Pullman'. The east is 'a dark uterus' waiting to be truly and fruitfully impregnated by the west, but artificial barriers keep the two apart.

If there is anything that isn't clear
I refer you to the chronicles of Zarathustra
or to the Chieh-hein of the Llama Swingitup. [sic]
if you can't get hold of these,
see me, please.

Trocchi's short stories and novels are the literary centre of his work, and bring together most of the ideas, attitudes, and themes already looked at. The four stories in *New Writers* III (1965) emphasise human isolation. In 'A Being of Distances' a middle-aged son who has been to his uncle's funeral returns by train to London and keeps thinking about his father, a widower now and a lonely man like himself; meeting his father at the funeral, talking to him, but not staying, has left him disturbed and empty, 'a being of distances'. 'The Holy Man' is a more grotesque, Hoffmannesque story about a dilapidated French residential hotel inhabited by mostly ageing and variously handicapped persons – a hunchback, two blind men, a dwarf, a dumb man, a one-legged woman, a one-eyed man. Interest centres on the man in the attic who has boarded up his window and never leaves his room; food is brought to him, excrement is removed. No one knows anything about him, but he excites much speculation. Here, the isolated man does not present his own case but is seen only through the eyes of others. In 'Peter Pierce', a man on the run from the police takes refuge in a room below that of an eccentric ragman. Before the narrator goes away at the end of the story, he has built up a tentative but never very illuminating relationship with the ragman who lives almost in a world of his own. The narrator feels he has been in touch with some mystery, 'face to face with the subhuman', and records the strangeness of the experience very much as Wordsworth relates his encounters with solitaries in *The Prelude*. 'A Meeting' is described elsewhere as being 'from a novel in preparation', and its characters appear also in the story 'The Rum and the Pelican' (*Merlin*, Vol. 2, No. 3, 1954). It makes little impact, and hardly stands by itself, but its unprepossessing hero, a thin, round-shouldered bespectacled clerk making desultory conversation with a female colleague in a bar, shares the lost, dislocated, aimless quality of life we observe in the main characters of the stories. The *accidie* that seeps into these tales makes us think of *Dubliners*, and Trocchi's style, low-key but precise, is a cousin of Joyce's 'scrupulous meanness'. A certain obsession with naturalistic detail – making cocoa, looking at a greasy fork, comparing old pen nibs – is strongly reminiscent, in a Scottish context, of James Kelman; in both cases it probably comes from the *nouveau roman*. The short stories are a mixed bag as regards quality, though two of them, 'A Being of Distances' and 'Peter Pierce', are worth anthologising. But Trocchi seems to have sensed that he needed to propel his figure of the outsider into the more ample space of the novel, give him adventures, give him enough time to allow a fertile interchange between present and past, give him also enough interaction with other characters to define the exact nature of his detachment (the classic pattern: being alone and desperately wanting relationships, having relationships and wanting to be alone; not Sartre's *Huis Clos* but 'L'enfer, c'est les autres/ moi-même/les autres/moi-même/les autres, etc., etc.').

The fascination of all this for a Scottish author is not hard to see, and although Trocchi learned from Sartre and more obviously from Camus's *L'Etranger*, we also cannot help noticing links back to Hogg's *Justified Sinner* and forward to Alasdair Gray's *Lanark*: the dislocation of time, the problem of the hero's self-identification, the tension between natural guilt and its abnormal absence, the story within a story, the prominence of father-son relationships, the presence of serious crime, whether real, imagined, or uncertain – all these aspects would be picked up even if a Scottish background had not been given to his novels by Trocchi himself, the actual setting of the Forth and Clyde Canal in *Young Adam*, the poignant and humorous recollections of the hero's early life in Glasgow in *Cain's Book*, the lurid Gorbals of *Thongs*. Whether Trocchi ever fully came to terms with his Scottish upbringing and early environment, in the sense in which Joyce and Beckett did in relation to Ireland, is arguable. Joyce managed it by compulsive memorialising and indeed re-mythologising of Dublin, Beckett by the occasional Irish setting, the flavour of Irish names and words, the marked un-Englishness of the tone of voice. But Trocchi, desperate to deparochialise, was swept into the new internationalism of the later 1950s and the 1960s, especially on its French-American axis, and it may be that decisions made too quickly at that time caused his difficulties in assimilating and using his own past. Nevertheless, it should be remembered that in his famous public clash with Hugh MacDiarmid during the Writers' Conference at the Edinburgh Festival of 1962 – an international event if ever there was one – Trocchi's claim was not a stateless or cosmopolitan claim: he was there on the panel of Scottish writers, and he claimed (if we strip off the colours of rhetoric) to have contributed more to Scottish literature during recent years than Hugh MacDiarmid had done. The argument was not so much a simple nationalism v. internationalism debate as it seemed at the time; it was rather an argument about how, in the early 1960s, a Scottish writer should go about his business, and whether a change of direction was due, whether it was time to take a closer look at what was happening elsewhere, whether openness of spirit rather than hugging of certainties would be good for Scotland. The significance of that moment in the McEwan Hall was that the evidence could not quite be brushed off by the largely Scottish audience, as it might have been if it had been given by one of the foreign speakers like Mailer or Burroughs; it was one of their own who was talking. With some, inevitably, he never passed the scandal barrier, the drugs-and-sex-rootless-drifter reaction, and despite his obvious intelligence, and the controlled style of his prose, it seems likely that his unjust neglect as a writer was not unconnected with various sorts of moral disapproval. In actual fact, *Cain's Book* no more proselytises for heroin than *Young Adam* does for murder. It is true that Joe Necchi takes drugs, both by himself and in the company of friends whose wild lifestyle is rendered fairly mercilessly; but he is also a writer, who vividly recalls and evokes a past and a present unconnected with drugs. When he was a boy in Glasgow his parents took in lodgers, at whose habits his father is always ready to explode:

> My father came in.
> 'I'm going out,' he said. It sounded like an ultimatum.
> 'You went out last night, Louis,' my mother said. 'I have nothing to give you . '
> 'I didn't *ask*, did I?'
> 'I gave you two shillings last night.'
> 'I didn't ask you for any bloody money!'
> 'Don't lose your temper, Louis.'
> 'I'm not losing my bloody temper! I didn't ask you for any bloody money! We've never got any bloody money because you're too bloody soft on them, the whole bloody lot of them! Pitchimuthu with his bloody fried sardines and that old bloody cripple in the blue room! Kept me out of the bathroom all bloody day with their bloody carry on!'
> 'Louis, you just stop this! Stop it at once! Go on out if you must, but don't begin that business all over again!' (p. 251)

In his present, working on a scow off New York, he records immediate detail, fixing a flux as it passes:

> When I woke up this morning around eight I found I was the last scow in a tow of four moving like a ghost-ship in fog. I say 'a tow of four' because last night there were four of us. Actually I cannot even see the scow ahead of me. I know we are moving because the wrinkled brown water slides like a skin past my catwalk. I threw an empty can overboard. It bobbed in the wake of my stern for a few seconds and then, like something removed by a hand, it was out of sight. I suppose I can see in all directions for about fifteen feet. Beyond that, things become shadowy and at the same time portentous, like the long swift movement of the log which floated by a few minutes ago. (p. 180)

In terms of plot and characters, neither *Cain's Book* nor *Young*

Adam comes to an end. *Young Adam,* a thinner and less impressive book than *Cain's Book,* but in some ways a preparation for it and a story that does stick in the mind, leaves its hero, Joe 'Taylor' as he calls himself, listening to a judge condemning a man to death for a murder he did not commit but which Joe did commit (or it may have been an accident, though he accepts responsibility for it). It is as if he is frozen, paralysed, totally unable to save the innocent man. 'I cannot remember how the court broke up. All I know is that suddenly Mr Justice Parkington was gone and the disintegration was already taking place' (p. 162). The novel closes rather powerfully on that unspecified 'disintegration'; more like the end of a film than the end of a novel. *Cain's Book* likewise refuses to 'end', except that its last two paragraphs are almost lapidary in their attentiveness to the problem of making a non-ending satisfactorily close the book. 'This, then, is the beginning, a tentative organisation of a sea of ambiguous experience, a provisional dyke, an opening gambit' (p. 251). We may be tempted to think that the man drifting and writing in his scow on the Hudson River is writing a drifting book about his scow on the Hudson River, but the 'organisation', the 'dyke', the 'gambit' all suggest control, forethought, shaping of material. At a second reading, the dramatic function of the 'embedded' scenes from his early life becomes clearer; there is a similar proceeding in Gray's *Lanark* and *1982, Janine,* and in some of the films of Tarkovsky. But was it written as novel or antinovel? Six years before he finished writing it, Trocchi wrote in one of his editorials in *Merlin* (Vol. 2, No. 2, Autumn 1953):

> In a literary climate in which we are exhorted to remember that 'novelists ought to write novels' – where accent, that is, is laid upon plot – we might point out that the imperative is redundant, that novelists, we suppose, and by definition, do, although serious writers, we feel, may not.

Hm. Well. No more is said, but the gauntlet comes down with a distinctly glittery clatter. It is surely time now for critics, admitting the force and range and originality of Trocchi's work, to take it up.

Quotations in the text are from the following editions: *Cain's Book* (Calder, 1963) (first published 1960). *Young Adam* (Heinemann, 1961) (first published 1954, under pseudonym Frances Lengel). *Man at Leisure* (Calder & Boyars, 1972). *Helen and Desire* (Olympia Press, London, 1971) (first published 1954, under pseudonym Frances Lengel). *Writers in Revolt,* ed. R. Seaver, T. Southern and A. Trocchi (Fell, New York, 1963). *New Writers III* (Calder, 1965).

Poetry in Translation

Aonghas MacNeacail

S tu mo chànan bheag sheang
s tu ga m'ionnsachadh
mo ghaoil àrsaidh òig

'You are my small slender language
and you are learning me
my young ancient love.'

THE STERN GRAMMARIANS of my schooldays would have rapped me on the knuckles for that translation. They would have inferred that I was using 'learn' where I meant 'teach'. In fact, I intended both. The Gaelic word *ionnsachadh* carries both connotations, just as 'learn' used to in formal, and still does in colloquial, English. Gaelic was my first language, for five years my only language. English was so alien to my infant ears I would only describe it as *bruidhinn bhuidhe,* the 'yellow speaking'. The concept of another language was totally strange to me. In the late forties, when I was an infant, we had no television in Skye. The radio, pre-transistor and battery-operated, was only listened to for the weather forecast and evening news bulletin. The inmigration of settlers from elsewhere hadn't yet begun, so Gaelic was still the everyday language of the community. School changed all that. Every monoglot five-year-old spent the first few weeks mastering a new language. After that, school was a totally English-language institution. In secondary school Gaelic would be chosen as a subject rather than French. The syllabus was geared entirely to native-speakers. A course which relied heavily on complex eighteenth-century verse and dry nineteenth-century prose deterred all but the most linguistically gifted learner, yet English was the medium of instruction. Our native language was presented to us as an archaic curiosity. Not surprisingly, any adolescent fantasies I had of following a literary career presupposed that the language of the living art was English. Perhaps it's also not surprising that I left school at sixteen, somewhat disenchanted, and headed for Glasgow.

My early attempts at writing were, therefore, in English. The

unpublishable product of the first five years – a solitary apprentice-
ship – was all in English. Even when I was beginning to develop a
voice of my own, and had begun to scan my background for themes,
I took it for granted that English was the only legitimate medium.
Not until my mid-twenties, when I resumed studies in order to enter
university, did it occur to me that I might have something to say in
my own language. At the time, I had begun working on a sequence
of poems, in English, on the theme of a Gaelic community breaking
down. This I regarded as my serious work. In contrast, the few
Gaelic poems I wrote then were of a more personal nature. They
were a kind of retreat from the commitment demanded by the other
work:

òran gaoil

ged sheòladh tu bhuam
cha'n urrainn dhomh snàmh
ach eadar braithlin
air fleodradh 'n ad cholunn
tha mi aig tàmh.

love song

though you sail from me
i cannot swim
but between sheets
i float in your body
my harbour.

an aimbreit

tha caolas eadarainn anochd,
mis air m'eilean, thus air d' eileansa.
aon flhacal bhuat, a luaidh, is buallaidh
mis, le rèimh mar sgiathan sgairbh, na tuinn
bi eòlas eadarainn anochd.

the contention

there's a kyle between us tonight
i on my island, you on yours
one word from you, love – I'll beat,
with oars like sgarts wings, the waves.
there'll be accord between us tonight.

It will be seen from the imagery that my preoccupations were
defined in coastal terms. Perhaps, naturally, as the first sixteen years

of my life were spent in coastal community. But these poems were written after I had lived in the city for over a decade. Even when I tried to come to terms directly with urban life, the images stayed absolutely rural:

neulag air fàire

anns a bhaile so, monaidhean
móra cloiche, cas is cruaidh. daontachd
cho lionmhor ri
gainmheach an fhàsaich.

ameasg a' ghrinneil, aon
lus beag grinn,
thusa mo ghaoil.

thu nas modha 'nam inntinn
na sìolmhorachd raointean
doimhneachd choilltean
farsuingeachd chuantan,

'nam chridhe mar
neulag air fàire
nach tig gus an deasgachd a dhrudhadh
'nam aite neofhasgach,

'nam chaolan
mar lilidh cho geal.
ged a shlìbinn do cheann
tha do bhroilleach cho fìorghlan.

cha ruig mi do chridhe.
aonar is eagal,
eagal is aonar.

small cloud on horizon

in this city great mountains
of stone, vertical, hard, people

numerous as
desert sand.

among the grains, one
fine little flower,
you my love.

greater in my mind
than fruitful plains

deepest forest
expanse of oceans,

in my heart like
a fleck of cloud on the horizon
that won't come to drench the sediments
of my shelterless dwelling,

in my gut
like the whitest lily,
though i caress your head
your breast is pure.

i can't reach your heart.
isolation and fear,
fear and isolation.

Biblical influences will be apparent in the 'desert sands', 'fruitful plains', 'shelterless dwellings'. Even the lily is an image recalled from an upbringing strongly influenced by the Word – with a capital W. Fear and isolation are products of a particularly rigid Gaelic Presbyterian interpretation of it. Jacob's ladder, another biblical image, is recalled from childhood as both comforting and disturbing. Man's twentieth-century ascent to the moon, so momentous a design, yet fundamentally banal in motivation, seemed like an adult version of my youthful fantasy.

an dràsda dà fhleasgach

an dràsda dà fhleasgach
a coiseachd air duslach na gealaich
a dhìrich o thalamh
        gu gealach
air rocaid   's a chabsuil
mar isean 'san ugh

a ghealach cho geal
anns an dubhair   gun streap
mi air staidhre 'nam inntinn ga
h-ionnsaidh 'nam òige   is nise

da fhleasgach a coiseachd a fàsach
bùrach son òr anns an duslach

is mise a coiseachd a chladaich
mo shùil air a ghealaich
mo phòcaidean falamh

at this moment two heroes
walking in the moondust
who rose from earth
                to moon
on a rocket   encapsulated
chickens in an egg

the moon so white
in darkness   i climbed
imagined stairs toward
her in childhood   and now
two stalwarts walk her deserts
probing for gold in the dust

and i am walking the shore
my eye on the moon
my pockets empty

There's a sense of alienation underlying the poems I've quoted so far. The exile does not readily celebrate society. The next poem was begun while I was still living in London (whence I had moved after fifteen years in Glasgow). By the time it had taken its final shape I was back in Skye, not this time to snatch a couple of weeks holiday, but to live there. Paradoxically, the images which were added to the poem in my native, thoroughly pastoral, land, included the least pastoral 'wharf', 'cloak' and 'parabolas'.

dol dhachaidh

seall na geòidh
a' siubhal 's
na gobhlaingaoithe

's fhad a dh'fhalbh a chubhag

seall na duilleagan dearg ag
éiridh air
sgiath sgiartghaoith
ag éiridh 's a siubhal

tha 'm bradan sgrìob mhór amach
air a shlighe

ghrian a dol na sineadh
ghealach ag éiridh
          'nam parabolan caochlaideach eòlalch

samhradh a siubhal
foghar air a dhruim

cleòc mor a sgaoileadh as a dhéidh

null 's a nall air cala
    fògarach anull 's anall
  null 's anall
    null 's a nall

going home

see the geese
journeying and
the swallows

long
since the cuckoo went

see the red leaves
rising on
the wing of a gust
rising and travelling

The salmon is a great stretch out
on his journey

the sun reclining
moon rising
    in their familiar changing parabolas

summer journeying
autumn on his back
    a great cloak spreading behind

back and forward on the wharf
    an exile back and forward
  back and forward
    back and forward

This exile made it back, after nearly twenty years, to a writer's fellowship at the Gaelic College. The college is located in the south end of Skye but, although I grew up in the north among different surnames, it was, in more ways than one, a homecoming. The topography was familiar – civilisation represented by a tattered ribbon of cultivated strips sloping down to a stretch of water, beyond which the dark serrations of a mountain ridge sliced at clouds. Behind was moorland, sparsely treed and peaty. Within the cultivated littoral, the people, most of them anyway, still spoke my language and sang songs that were familiar to me from childhood. After so many years of urban living, readjustment was neither

immediate nor easy. Hardest to come to terms with was the fact
which had brought me there, that I was a Gaelic writer. It mattered
a great deal, of course: but I *had* spent most of my adult life
surrounded by the English language, and had devoted most of my
creative energies to working in that language. The need to let Gaelic
dominate the creative imagination required that I change habits of
thinking which had become ingrained. It was the songs that provided the link which reconnected me to my native culture. I wanted,
in any case, to bridge a gap which I felt had grown between modern
and traditional Gaelic poetry. The best way to do it, I felt, was to
bring the melodic intensity of song into the irregular structures of a
modern prose, while marrying imagery that had stood the test of
time with contemporary preoccupations. In the first poem to pursue
these objectives, I took the physical details from my surroundings,
but the central image arose from a coincidence of sources. Francis
James Child's collection of Border Ballads has a reference to the
White Hind as an 'international folk motif for love'. About the time
I made that discovery I also came across, in Dwelly's Gaelic Diction-
ary, the phrase *'eilid ag iarraidh a h-annsachd'*, translated as 'a hind
in search of its mate'.

          mi gabhail ràd na beinne   àrd
          ameasg nan tullach liathruadh   toirt
          fainear na h-éilde
                    'ag iarraidh a h-annsachd'
          tha ghrian gun chùram
          'san iarmailt cheana agus spealtag
          na seann ghealaich
                    dol na sìneadh air chùl
          an da sgurr 'san fhireach thall a tha
          smèideadh ri chéile mar a bha iad riamh

          'se dh'iarrainn an àite bhi siubhal
          bhi dlùthchomhla riutsa
                    m'eilid bhàin
          's mi gun dùsgadh fhathast

          chan eil sin ri bhi san tràth seo
          agus reul dheireannach na h-oidhche dol bàs
          tha thu fada bhuam anise 's mi siubhal rathad na beinne
          gun chinnt a bheil thu na d' dhùisg
          no gu bheil àit agam na d' bhruadar

          'b'eòlach do sheanair' ars na feallsamhna
          mar gun cuireadh am briathran stad air an t-sealgair
          's mi falbh a shuidh air chùl deasc

far an tig thu eadar mo pheann is am pàipear
falachfead ameasg cholbhan chraobhach mo leabharcunntais
cuindh do mheallthighinn bhuaireachail maill' air a chleoc agus
mo mheasrachadh buileach air seachran
bi mo dhiathad gun tuar no seagh
agus nuair a tha mi ag òl tha fhios a'm
nach fhaic mi an cupa
bi thu na d' reul air chùl m'aigne
cho dearrsach's gun cuir thu a ghrian air ais

ach 's ann air an t-sealg eile bhios m'inntinn
far am bi na buillairm choma gan giùlain
air guailnean luchd-faghaid a tha
gun aithne dhe d'ailleachd
chan e du chniadachd a tha dhith orra
ach an t-sealg
          an t-sealg is
          a bhuille sgoilteach

               o m'eilid bhàn
               o m'eilid bhàn

The white hind

i take the mountain road   high
amid the grey-red knolls
observing the hind
               'seeking her love'

the carefree sun
is in the sky already and the silver
of the old moon
               goes to rest behind
the two peaks in the ridge which
beckon each other as they always have

i'd wish, rather than travel
to be close to you
               my white hind

and not wakened yet

that's not to be this time
as the last star of night goes out
you are far from me now as i travel the mountain road
uncertain whether you are awake
or whether i have a place in your dreams

'tell us something new' say the philosophers
as if their words could stop the hunter
as i go to sit behind a desk
where you will come between my pen and the paper
hide-and-seek among the branched columns of my ledger
your distracting illusory visit will slow the clock and
completely unbalance my judgement
my food will be without appearance or essence
and when i'm drinking i know
i'll not see the cup
you'll be a star at the back of my mind
so bright you'll extinguish the sun

but my thought will be on the other hunt
where the indifferent weapons are carried
on the shoulders of stalkers who
don't know your beauty
not your caresses they want
but the hunt
  the hunt and
  the gutting blow
    my white hind
    o my white hind

Although personal themes have been a constant, indeed dominant, feature of my Gaelic writing, poems I've written since returning to the Highlands have been increasingly public in their concerns. 'The White Hind' is intended to be more than a simple love poem. Land and language are commemorated as much as lover. Taking further the development toward a public kind of poetry, a poem called *Amadan* – 'fool', or 'madman' – is in the form of a dialogue between an old woman and her errant husband. Strong drink and its effects form the background to their discourse. It's a story complicated by economic conditions but also by a straitjacket of religious puritanism which has to be broken out of occasionally. It's an old story in the Highlands, and it continues. *Cailleach* is the Gaelic for 'old woman'.

  ach fois a bhi agam

 ach fois a bhi agam
 cha toirinn siud dha
 ars a chailleach
 a guidhe sìth na fàrdaich
 's a céile tighinn dhachaidh
 air a phòcaid a tholladh

anns a phràban bhinnteach
ach cha bhiodh e balbh
– an ainmich thu na reultan
  's an coisich thu nam measg
  an seall thu *betelgeuse* dhomh
  co miad de theaghlach
  tha leantainn na gréine
  (clann is oghaichean)
  faic a ghealach bheag chruinn
  cailleach òg na gnùise gruamaich
  dìleas ri traill-shaoirte
  riarachadh na cruinne seo
  cà'il ar mic 's ar nìghnean
  cuin a fhuair thu bhuap
  eil guth air tilleadh,
  ma tha thu searbh dhén ghealaich
  ma thrus thu a naidheachdan
  tiugainn a choimhead nan reultan
  theid sinn air chéilidh orr' –
amadain ars a chaillich
amadain amadain
an tug thu bonn
dhachaidh leat
is màl ri phaigheadh
– chunnaic mi drèag ars esan
  os cionn an tigh mhóir
  samhla bàis do reul uaibhreach
  de shìol an duine
  a reir na sgeòil ars esan
  's am fear ud shuas gun shìol –
b'fheàrr naidheachd chruaidh na gréine
na faileas gun cholunn ars ise
tha màl ri phaigheadh
– tiugainn a choimhead nan speur
  a bhean mo ghaoil
  nuair a tha màl paighte is sinne
  air fuadach gu talamh eile
  bi na reultan a tionndadh
  's a tionndadh 's bi amadain
  'g an amharc leis an aon duil
  gu bheil saoghal ri lorg
  taobh thall na gealaich
  far am bi amadain a seasamh
  san dubhair gun léirsinn air ceum

a coimhead nan speur
gun uallach
ach a cheist cheudna –
ach eadar na reultan 's a mhisg
mo cheile
de th'agad dhòmhsa
– mo làmh, a ghaoil
suarach 's gu bheil i
is éibhleag de dhòchas –
amadain ars ise

were silence assured me
i wouldn't give tuppence
said the cailleach
wishing peace in the household
her spouse returning
having burned his pockets
in the curdling tavern
but he won't be dumb

– can you name the stars
will you walk among them
show me betelgeuse
how big a family
follows the sun
(children and grandchildren)
see the little round moon
young hag of the surly face
faithful as a freed slave
serving this planet
where are our sons and daughters
when did you hear from them
any word of coming back
if you're sick of the moon
if you've garnered her news
come and look at the stars
we'll pay them a visit –
madman said the cailleach
madman madman
did you take one coin
home with you
and rent to be paid
– i saw a meteor, he said
above the mansion-house,

sign of death to a haughty star
of the seed of man,
that's the tradition, he said
and sir would leave no seed –

better hard new from the sun
than a shadow without a body said she
there's rent to be paid
– come and look at the sky
    wife, my love
    when rent is paid and we
    evicted to another earth
    the stars will be turning
    and turning madmen
    watching with the one hope
    that there's a world to be found
    on the far side of the moon
    where there will be madmen standing
    in darkness unable to see a path
    and watching the sky
    with no burden
    but the same question –

but between the stars and intoxication
my spouse
what do you have for me
– my hand, love
    mean though it be,
    and an ember of hope
madman she said

The poems I've quoted so far have tended to close on an unresolved note. Even where the question remains unanswered, the interpretation which suggests itself is unlikely to be a brash affirmative. Given that the place I grew up in was the well from which I drew all my imagery, and most of my themes, perhaps it is natural that poems written elsewhere should carry a certain undertow of estrangement. There was the fact that my native culture was steadily and, it seemed, inexorably, eroding. I was apart from it, and watching it die. One thing I was tiring of was restraint. So much contemporary English poetry is characterised by, and commended for, its detachment, its understatement, its gentle ironies. It is fashionable to be uncommitted, to see, from the seclusion of the parlour, intricate metaphors in the kitchen garden. I wanted, particularly after I had returned to Gaeldom, a wilder creative terrain. The language might

be dying but it wasn't dead yet. For that itself, it would still sing a
jubilant song. I began by quoting from the poem I want to end with.
It is unashamedly exultant, an epithalamic song addressed as much
to words as to woman:

> thug thu dhomh samhradh

> *de los lenguajes humanos el pobre solo sabria tu nombre –*
> *pablo neruda*

> ghabh an geamhradh buaidh air an earrach
> bha e fuar, bha e nimheil
> gheàrr sgeinean an reolhaidh a céitean

> chum na craobhan an guirme
> duint'
> an a rumanan caol an geugan

> thréig smeòraich gaoil na raointean
> thriall camagan ciùil as gach linne
> sgap a ghàire 'na neulagan anail
> thar fhirich chrion àrsaidh ar dualchais
> air gaotan geur neo-aireil
> thuislich danns' a mheudaidh gun dùsgadh n-anam
> leig sin bhuain a bhi sireadh
> cuach òir na gréine torraich

> chaidh teanga na treubha balbh
> ach osann gann bìgeil fhann
> fad chruas mhall an earraich

> gun shamhla againn
> a shuaineadh ar spiorad 's ar gnè
> ann a' rop soilleir daingeann
> _____

> bha misc, 's mo shannt gu tràghadh,
> a dh' aindeoin, sìor shireadh
> fiu 's gaoireag a fidheal
> no fannal a fànus.
>   is choinnich mi riutsa
> mar lasair bhlàth ròis as an domhan
> nochd dhomh blasad dhe d' bhinneas

> na d' ghnogadh gun fhiosta 's do thighinn astigh orm, is
> thug thu dhomh samhradh
> _____

> cha ghabh d' àilleachd innse, mo luaidh, chan eil air mo theanga
> de bhriathran, ach teine falaisgreach.   seinneam

òran dhut is tuigidh mo chinneadh e, tuigidh
m' aiteam am fonn.   tha thu beò
rùbain ruaidh m' fhala
a dhùisg mi le brùchdadh deargleaghte
do ghaoil a 'buillsgean na cruinne
's tu m' iarmailt's mo thràigh, m' reul-iùil tromh gach dochann
's tu mo ràmh air a chuan thoirmsgeach
nuair a tha na stuaghan ag éigheach *dealrachd dealrachd*
        thubhairt fear eile ri t' éil' ann a' suidheachadh eile
'anns gach cànan a labhras daoine, na
truaghain amhàin a dh' aithnicheas d' ainm'
ach m' aideachd àigheachsa
anns gach canan a labhras daoine bi
d'ainm air gach teanga, proiseil, priseil
's tu mo chanan bheag sheang
's tu ga m' ionnsachadh

                mo ghaol àrsaidh òig

you gave me summer

'in all the languages of men, the poor alone will know your
name' – Pablo Neruda.

winter prevailed over spring
it was cold, it was bitter
knives of frost cut may

trees kept their green
enclosed
in the narrow rooms of their branches

the songbirds of love fled the fields
ripples of music abandoned the pools
laughter dispersed in vapours of breath
beyond the crumbling ridges of our history
on sharp indifferent winds
the dance of growth stumbled without wakening in our soul
we gave up our search
for the golden cup of the fertile sun

the tribe's tongue went dumb
only a rare sigh, a whisper
through the slow hardness of spring

we had no symbol
to plait our spirit and kind

into a bright durable rope

i, desire all but ebbed
still continued my search for
even the mewl of a fiddle
or the merest breath from the void.
              and i met you
like the flame of a rose-blossom out of the universe
a taste of your sweetness was given to me
in your knocking unnoticed and coming in on me, and
you gave me summer.
your beauty can not be told, my love, there are not
                 on my tongue
enough words, but a spreading heathfire, let me sing
a song for you and my clan will know it, my people
will know the melody.   you are alive
red ruby of my blood
who woke me with the molten eruption
of your love from earth's core
you are my sky and my shore, my pole-star through
                every hardship
you are my oar on the turbulent seas
when the waves are crying *glitter glitter*
an other said to another, in other circumstances
'in all the languages of men, the
poor alone will know your name'
but i proclaim exultantly
in all the languages of men, your
name will be on every tongue, proud, priceless
you are my small slender language
and you are learning me
             my young ancient love.

A Torn Piece of Pringle Tartan

(Reflections on the life and work of the Scottish artist,
John Quinton Pringle, 1864-1925)

Frank Kuppner

1. After a few weeks heavy with contemplation,
    The artist stretches out his brush towards
    A sombre landscape of grass, slope, water, and shingle,
    Now judged insufficient, and begins

    The slow delicate tentative process
    Of adding to the forbidding, rocky foreground
    A young girl half in motion; backwards and forwards
    His hand moves through a succession of sunlit mornings.

3. The waves regularly scraping out to sea;
    The waves regularly scraping into the bight;
    The hand dragging less regularly
    A less necessary, less wild fluid.

    Real water cavorts before the eyes;
    A real house stands, bored, by the distant hilltop;
    The light scuffing of unreal children
    Sends a shiver through the autumn air.

5. An old woman is bending over a pump;
    Behind her curve some worn out steps;
    Why this strange absence of other people?
    Surely, in the more fashionable areas of town,

    A relative blatantly admires a young passing woman;
    A relative sits, listening to a boring art teacher;
    A relative bends low over her sleeping child;
    Water makes a gurgling sound in the background.

7. A line of shops beneath the diagonal railway-bridge;
    In twenty-odd years, how many overhead journeys?
    In eighty-odd years, how many journeys overhead?
    I think we may safely assume a great deal of overhead journeys.

    And always, such a variety of walkers beneath the bridge;
    Reflections in shop windows, glancing in shop windows;
    Ah, the unrecorded postmen; the buyers
    Of suddenly stale bread; the perishable goods

    Always on display; they steal a look through
    An open door they will never encroach within,
    And catch sight of the small neat head of a workman,
    Labouring at an infinitesimal task.

10. How could one imagine that the (I suppose) small man,
    Deferentially helping one in the (I suppose) small shop,
    Should turn out, without warning, to be an artist of genius?
    As easy to assume him to be a murderer.

    Perhaps we are more awed by his immediate neighbour:
    A robust and possible butcher, worryingly unworried
    As he transforms unwieldy lengths of corpse
    Into neat slices, capable

    Of being carried in a hundred hands,
    Each so subtly different, towards
    Somewhat more different houses, and
    Into a few dozen of tomorrow's citizens,

    At present dispersed impressively through the city;
    From a pregnant woman walking beside the Kelvin,
    To the unresponsible, unassuming neighbour,
    Grinding more dust from a spectacle lens,

    Through which, in a day's time, there shall look out on the world
    Who knows what paragon, as he or she
    Hurries or does not hurry, towards or away from
    A person who will die or will not die in France.

15. All days the trains pass by overhead;
    Taking happiness and unhappiness
    Predominantly to the South-West of Scotland;
    A few moments inside a lower shop

Concern themselves with household objects
Which mystifyingly stopped functioning
In room after room nearby; a few adjustments
And a pair of clock-hands start to move again.

17. Again, I take out from a heap of books
    The catalogue of a recent exhibition
    Which I work with; the best compilation known to me
    Of Pringle's pictures; those fifty thousand

    Hand movements, preserved from a million or so,
    (Really, I have no idea how one might count them
    With greater accuracy); I turn the pages,
    And one familiar image after another

    Returns to the sight. A few more weeks have passed,
    And I am roughly the same; but if, for instance,
    That car which stole through changing traffic-lights
    Two or three days ago, whispering past

    That person, who was myself, who was already
    Crossing the road, had instead made forceful contact,
    Then whoever next had picked up this book would also,
    I suppose, have turned the pages with the same results.

21. The old woman bends over the pump;
    Ah, forty years ago that attitude
    Largely resulted in the mature woman
    Who now, at the top of a curving stairway nearby,

    Unbends from a full shopping-bag, astonished
    By the man who hurried out of the neighbouring door,
    Pushing her roughly aside, and running
    Downstairs towards the recently demolished houses.

23. Green river; green trees; green sky;
    A boy in a bright blue coat is standing beside the river;
    In one arm, he holds out a long black stick;
    With the other he points to a watery divergence;

    The green sky drifts down to the level of the fields;
    Quietly he slips out of his bright blue coat;
    He reaches down to the orange coat on the riverbank,
    And, wearing it, walks back to the white path.

25. Smoke rises from tenement chimneys;
    Impossible to say exactly which;
    Some broken panes of glass reflect light
    From a normal star above a normal scene of poverty;

    A young girl walks down a winding exterior stairway,
    Proud of her new boots, towards
    Inscrutable lines of unbroken windows,
    Behind a few of which burn small local fires.

27. This temperamental window usually favours
    A plain green expanse leading down to the sea;
    And a small road somewhere in the middle distance,
    Usually empty or nearly empty;

    But on every thousandth morning or so,
    Nothing but a sudden palace satisfies it;
    Hidden, for reasons of discretion
    Behind a changing cover of fog.

29. What shards and scraps lie about the courtyards;
    A few leaves from unobservable trees;
    A few crumpled papers from hands
    Which could be anywhere by now.

    A young girl walks down a winding exterior stairway,
    Proud of her new shoes, towards
    A calm doorway through which she disappears
    Causing a slight flutter of local details.

31. After all, young children played beneath
    Equally bright warm skies, before
    Words existed for them to shout,
    In what seemed youth, absolute youth too;

    As ferociously – perhaps more ferociously –
    Perhaps less ferociously – as the small group
    On either side of a peeling door marked 'Private',
    Which creaks a little as it swings shut.

33. An old man's head on one side of the sketch;
    A young girl's on the other; if the ageless artist
    Holds the paper up to the light, he will notice
    Places where the carefully chosen lines

Carelessly intersect. This should tell him
Something about the nature of the universe,
Or something about the thickness of his paper,
Or something about the thickness of the universe –

I'm afraid I am not sure. But, in the end
When he has locked the sheet inside some folder
And gone out, the direction of the street
Will not lead him equally towards both.

36. She throws the knife once more into the drawer,
Not going mad, like her chorus of neighbours,
Or rushing towards her immediate offspring,
Brandishing a lethal weapon; the children

Advance irregularly towards the table
In every second house in the street, towards
What a few misplaced lethal cuts produced,
In rooms full of shut or nearly shut drawers.

38. Inside the riot of ill-built sheds, what broken
Corners of the nineteenth century lie abandoned;
Some of those who will die in future famous wars
Chase each other over the rubble; what patterns

The mud takes between falls of rain; revealing
That two people have wandered into that outhouse,
That someone has climbed a dangerous fence, that someone
Has walked through the edges of that wide puddle.

40. Four birds in the sky, and three children
In the small back yard surrounded by high walls;
They giggle as they share a secret; the clouds
Drift among spaces which the birds have left;

Ah, how the scent of future perfume floats
From the windows where their parents argue, finding
The small gaps between them, standing beside
Planks precariously leaning against a wall.

42. This is where the great artist then lived;
And we assume that of the hundreds and thousands
Of momentary visitors to the city
During his occupation there, scarcely

One in any month ever saw these buildings,
Except by pure accident, perhaps
Strayed off course in the aftermath of seeing
The Cathedral, the Obelisk, the Infirmary;

But not likely to have come deliberately here,
Unless deeply committed to the exploration
Of acute urban poverty; when, turning
Into this dilapidated street

From another street, equally dilapidated,
His or her heart is staggered by another
Cause for anger; the intelligent eyes
Sway and focus on a single figure

Walking solidly towards one of the houses,
Obviously a tired man. Our kind visitor
Turns away from the scene, hoping
To put this pity to later use,

Imagining another wasted evening,
Doubtless involving drink, in a life too troubled
To be fuller than it is, and walks back towards
A more fashionable area, never knowing

What a cruel trick statistical probability
Has just been playing; as the tired man
Climbs his curving stairway, opens a door or two,
And walks, smiling, past an unfinished painting.

49. The same heavy uninteresting curtains
Hang across his windows, as across
The windows of his neighbours; with what purposefulness
They are flung back to intercept

Another bright shared morning; the sun floods
(Perhaps) onto a variety of faces,
Some of which, speaking, turn away at once
Towards whoever they are speaking to,

And some of which look down into the street,
For the street, incredibly, is again there,
And the morning light has recently decided
To give a walking figure a sharp shadow.

52. We shall all disappear, but this architecture
    Will remain motionless behind us; another sunset
    Will witness the usual crowds, and the sunrise
    Illuminate a silence that remains unbroken

    As the morning slowly proceeds. The empty buildings
    Will continue to posture elegantly through turning space,
    And the sudden clatter of footsteps in the corridor
    Will disappear in ignominious retreat.

54. These streets seeming so stripped bare, these venues
    Of too much sudden noise, which force
    Discomfort on the passer-through, not equal,
    It might appear, to the discomfort of staying –

    It might appear, one should watch these people closely;
    Thinking, the next of them, for all I know,
    Could be another great artist; which is true;
    But I have found it does not quite work like that.

    He locks the shop door, and hurries away;
    He will not reappear for a few days,
    Having travelled off to see an exhibition;
    A few figures carrying stopped clocks

    And other such impedimenta, stare,
    Baffled, at the shut door, curse, and retire defeated;
    But, if they come back in a day or two, discover
    That the quiet affable man has returned to work.

58. Slowly the carpet becomes substantial;
    With what precision the weaver co-ordinates
    The huge ungainly machine; in a month or so,
    The shining naked feet of the accountant's wife

    Will hesitate, then pause languorously
    On the sensuous soft fabric, before carrying
    Over towards the bed, whatever it is
    She is carrying; after a brief pause

    He treads a cigarette end underfoot,
    Looks left and right at the activity of the street,
    Then returns to his place of work; a few seconds later,
    His hands and feet are moving in complex patterns.

61. 'I quite like Pringle's paintings. All those little dots ...'
Said the man in the Hunterian Art Gallery,
Uniformed and humorous, as I was buying
A postcard of one of them to send to my sister.

When I left, I found it had started to drizzle.
A few students hurried close by, to the library.
An undecided rain, covering the slabs
Down which I walked, with lots of little dots.

63. My grief is earlier than this sunlight;
These cars are parked in a later arrangement
Than my perfect memories; that gentleman
Who appears to wander unconcernedly

Down a subsequent version of a street
Once painted by a great artist, in a world
Of people quivering after personal disasters
Seems not to know how slow his watch is running.

65. A girl in white walks down the road;
The steam swirls from a passing train
And returns slowly to the reappearance
Of absence; unseen passengers

Disembark at the nearest station,
And rush invisibly up a clanging stairway,
Reach the street, and disperse across it,
Leaving it, within a minute, utterly empty;

Utterly empty for two minutes;
Utterly empty for three minutes;
Until the girl in white walks round the corner,
Moving a little more quickly than before.

68. The man who almost invented television
Leaves the shop, and, an hour afterwards,
A man who left some fingers in South Africa
Breezes in for a minute's conversation.

An hour after that, he locks the shop door
For nearly the 9,000th time, crosses the busy road,
Walks at a normal pace into a sidestreet,
And walks along a sidestreet at normal pace.

70. The dog barking on the street corner
    Does so irrespective of whether the passer-by
    Who has suddenly turned into his territory
    Is a hopeless drunk, a great artist, or one

    Of the very many who work in the neighbouring shipyards;
    It barks on, for longer than it needs to,
    And the noise disturbs an unseen arrangement
    Of figures hidden by a none too thick wall.

72. Perhaps a small sign goes up in the optician's window;
    Shortly afterwards, the shop closes;
    It may be one in a thousand passers-by
    Think this significant enough to comment on.

    And though the forgotten optician dies
    Not too long afterwards, it is long enough
    For the new grocer who has taken over the site
    To now seem an inevitable part of the street.

74. We will all disappear, but this architecture
    Will remain motionless behind us; another sunset
    Will light up the usual crowds, and the sunrise
    Illuminate a silence that remains unbroken

    As the day slowly proceeds. This is only
    What happens anyway, with the element
    Of renewal removed. How unforgettably
    The next sunset will reflect from our old windows.

76. The same heavy uninteresting curtains
    Hang across his windows, as across
    The windows of his neighbours; with what forcefulness
    They are flung back to intercept

    Another bright shared morning; and returned
    In an echoed volley at night, to shut off
    Such secret rows of interiors, in most of which
    The usual unremarkable night follows.

78. Darkness again cohabits with windows;
    This pebble hanging in infinite space
    Has turned out of sight; a few travellers
    Briskly use the dark street, accompanied

Each to his own door, by a favourite need;
A few different travellers float among them,
Unsure, orbiting, intoxicated,
Confused by the unfaithfulness of light.

80. The haphazard collection in the streets
    Has such an impression of permanence about it
    That its eternal momentary shifting
    Seems a betrayal of its potential. The horse plods

    Through a thousand or so perfect untaken photographs
    Amid the noise of children, halts at the corner,
    Then disappears; returning on the next instant,
    Being dragged back by an obviously angry Deity.

82. A net seems to hold back the sky; sometimes
    It seems peculiarly evident
    That such a device is useful; the creeping suburbs
    Hurry, laughing, over the crest of the hill,

    Then freeze in an attitude of permanence;
    The girl leans down, watched by five pairs of eyes;
    The suburbs snigger and race to the next hill,
    Effortlessly slipping through the gaps in the net.

84. A few figures move in the shadows; the eye
    Cannot quite make out who they are, beyond
    A suggestion of two people; this leafy canyon
    Which so improbably connects

    A pair of major city streets, providing
    The perfect venue for disconnected utterances,
    Following a small river, about
    Educational questions, or the sinuousness

    Of an absent third party – the argument
    Drifting from one to the other with little strain –
    In a place which one frequents far less often
    Than one wishes to, through sheer forgetfulness.

87. After a few weeks heavy with contemplation,
    The artist stretches out his brush towards
    A sombre landscape of grass, water, slope, and shingle,
    Now judged insufficient, and begins

To add to the stony, granitic foreground
A young girl, slowly beginning to scamper
Over the rocks; beginning to scamper,
A little more, a little more.

89. Looking out the window for the 10,000th time,
    Or the 8,000th time, or the 9,000th time,
    Onto a still unfashionable street
    And the moments disposal of passers-by,

    Then turning back into the room,
    For a few more unrecorded words,
    And a laughter not quite loud enough
    To cause a pause in the neighbours' talking.

The Last Shift

Jeff Torrington

AT SEVEN IN THE EVENING the cleaning gaffer's whistle called me to what turned out to be my last firing turn. There was an ironic cheer from the rest of the cleaning squad as I pocketed my book and stood up. 'Hope it's the Garbage Train,' the hare-lipped Kershaw shouted, and the card players laughed.

Outside the bothy, puddles were tautening with frost.

The cleaning gaffer came up to me. 'You, is it, McRae?' I nodded. 'Right,' he said, 'team up wae Matt Dolan – a relief job at the Central.'

Dolan was waiting for me outside the Rostering Hall. He was built like a Toby-jug and his face had the complexion and texture of poisoned veal. 'Christ,' he grumbled when he laid eyes on me, 'that's all I need on a Friday night – a bloody jaicket.'

I frowned. 'I've had loads of turns.'

Dolan sniffed: 'Still a strong smell of paraffin on you, son.' He clapped my shoulder. 'C'mon, there's an engine about due off the shed.'

We went past the oil store then the lamp room. Ghosting out of the wall of smoke and steam, and looking as if he was composed of the same vapours, came McCourt, the motions-man. As he passed with his smoky collier's lamp and his oil cans he gave us a grey nod.

The Shed roads were packed with locomotives, 'the clapped-out tools of Capitalism', as a commie driver had once described them to me: in long rows stood decrepit Jumbos and Pugs, N.B. 'Coffee-Pots', gaunt Austerities that, double-headed, worked the ore trains, Stanier Black 5s, B.R. Standards, Scots, Britannias, Moguls, Clan Class locos and a few toylike Barclay diesels. Still more engines were steaming down from the firedrop grids and, out in the dark, we had to pick our way carefully across the rails to the shed signal. The engine that was to give us a lift to the Central Station was still coaling-up, so we went into the guard's bothy to wait.

In the bothy, Dolan watched the guards playing at brag but cocked an eye in my direction the moment I slipped the paperback from my reefer pocket. I sighed as he craned forward to squint at the title. 'Walt Whitman,' he said with a smirk. 'Who's he when he's at hame?' I grunted a reply and his smirk deepened. 'He's a poet, is he? Imagine that.' He turned to the card players. 'Awfy intelligent firemen aboot these days, so there is. Couldnae keep a fire going in Hell, mind you, but you should hear them spelling their names!'

The guards laughed and this encouraged Dolan to start telling jokes.

When the engine, a Stanier Pacific, came to the Shed signal we clambered onto the footplate. I found a corner against the hand-brake while Dolan stood on the driver's side. The open firebox gushed heat into the cab and steam rose from the newly hosed floorboards. Using a rag, the fireman was wiping the glass faces of the vacuum and steam-pressure gauges. Dolan, with the toe of his boot, nudged a large lump of coal towards me. 'Hey, John,' he shouted, 'fling this off – but don't forget to haud on to it ...'

Both Dolan and the driver laughed then the Shed signal dipped.

The powerful engine clanked past the signal box, went under the bridge, then hacked leisurely out onto the mainline. The fireman, whose senior position in the links was indicated by his bleached overalls, began to scatter some coal around the firebox. I watched him, admiring the fluency of his movements, the rhythmic strokes of the shovel as he skimmed its blade from bunker-lip to firebox, knackily placing each throw of coal exactly where he wanted it on the glowing bars, then the expert way he built up a 'heel' behind the firebox door, tucking each shovelful neatly into the corners.

I was watching a flame-master at work and I knew at that moment, though I'd long suspected it, that I'd never achieve such dexterity, such fineness of manual balance. No matter how many firing-turns I logged I would always be a jaicket, the railway slang for a green shovel-walloper. Fires died on me; it was as simple as that. I had only to look into a firebox and a healthy fire, lying on the bars like a purring lion would, within minutes, roll over and die. As a driver put it to me once: 'John, when you kick it, don't ask to be cremated – the bloody fire'll go oot!'

The fireman took a key from the tool bucket and chapped on the injector steam handle. Next, he jerked the water-lever to and fro until he had made the connection between tank and boiler. I gave him a cigarette. We both stood looking up at the lit windows of a passing tenement. 'It's a swine this Friday night working, eh?' the fireman said.

I nodded, then astounded myself by saying, 'This is my last one.'

The fireman looked at me. 'You wrapping it, then?'

I took a heavy draw on my cigarette. 'Aye, definitely, this is my last shift.'

The fireman turned to knock off the injector then he gave the blower-handle an upward nudge.

At the Central Station we discovered that the train we had come to relieve was forty minutes down. Dolan cursed at this for he had obviously been hoping for a quick scamper back to the Shed with the engine and for an early lowse so that he could get in some elbow-bending; not that he was going to be denied. 'C'mon,' he said, 'there're better places than this tae kill the time.'

After he had bought me a pint of beer Dolan and me had a long chat about Walt Whitman. That'll be right! All he said was: 'You keep tabs on the board, son, just in case that train makes up time. I'll away for a blether with the lads.' And with that he took his whisky and chaser over to the other side of the pub where two drivers from his own link were seated.

It's funny how working people find it hard to talk about the arts. Class hostility, I suppose. In my cleaning squad I was known as 'The Professor', and quite a few drivers scoffed at my reading habits. There was an exception, though, Nat Curran. Nat was a dreamy sort of bloke. He had, on one unforgettable night-run, for instance, allowed our engine to drift by a stop signal while he was pointing out a star system. You could talk to Nat about almost anything: Zen, existentialism, flying saucers; he could rap about Camus, Sartre, even Bergson, and a little Jung too, although, in his self-effacing way, he claimed that pride in such smatterings was equivalent to 'a wee boy rattling his pocketful of jorries to prove how smart he was'.

I grinned. Imagine, for instance, Ma saying over breakfast, 'I was reading Chekov last night. He's ever so incisive, isn't he?' And, from ben the room, Grandpa shouting: 'Away you go – he's no' a patch on your Dostoievsky!' Ma, if I knew her, was more likely to be yelling: 'You've done what, you eedgit? Chucked your bloody job!'

I took a sip of beer. In the bronze gloom of the gantry mirror I could see the man who had given up the railway. The decision had surfaced on a sort of mental reflex, the activation of a nerve-loop in the mind. There'd be no going back. Not that I was kidding myself that I'd found freedom. I knew I was only swopping cages, for it's the working man's condition to pace to and fro behind the bars of his class, to be part of the capitalist menagerie. 'Roll up! Roll up!' Whitman had cried, juggling language like luminous hoops. 'Come and see Homo Sap – the Working Man.' A shameless barker for the nobility of toil, old Walt. He had you almost believing that the cage was an illusion until you rammed you head against the hard prose of reality.

The engine we were due to relieve, a Britannia Class, swept into the station and came to a halt against the hydraulic buffers. Almost at once, doors began to swing open in the frost-streaked coaches. Soon the platform was thronged with people as they converged on the ticket-barrier. The train's crew were Carlisle men and while the fireman washed his hands in the scummy tool-bucket his driver explained the reasons for his late arrival. Dolan couldn't have cared less, his expression suggesting that he wanted shot of them. The driver handed over his sheet then he opened his locker and began to gather up his gear.

I got down onto the platform again and going forward to the engine's smokebox transferred one of the lamps to the central bracket then took the other to hang at the base of the tender. I dropped onto the track between the engine and the leading coach. This would be the last time I would ever tie-off an engine. The thought, as I shut off the steam to the heater-bags, didn't excite me all that much. When I was ready for uncoupling I gave Dolan a shout and with a great fussing of steam from its cocks the engine squeezed back onto the coach buffers. Well, at least the next time I boarded a train it would be at the civilized end. I flung the coupling clear of the hook and clambered back onto the platform.

When I got back to the cab I found Dolan having a ding-dong with a station official. There was to be a change of operations. From what I could gather we were, instead of going light-engine to the Shed, to follow the coaches out once they had been withdrawn by the pilot engine then reverse and tie-on to a set of coaches at an adjacent platform. We were to remain there until signalled then draw the coaches to a nearby marshalling yard before returning light-engine to the Shed. Dolan argued the toss but, nevertheless, lost the argument and the official swept away to attend to more important matters.

'The boozers'll be shut afore we're by,' Dolan moaned. 'Could be nailed to they coaches till midnight.'

I nodded as if in sympathy but I wasn't all that bothered. When it's your last shift what does it matter if you have to go the distance? I glanced into the firebox. The blue flames told even a chancer like me that the fire was badly clinkered, or 'poxed' as they say on the railways: the firedropper wouldn't be chuffed. Maybe I'd be able to get a dart through it once we'd got shot of the coaches.

Dolan muttered another curse.

'What's up?' I asked.

'My lighter,' Dolan said. 'Must've left it in the pub.' He worked his way through his many pockets. 'Expensive, tae. Wife got me it.' He rose from his seat. 'I'll nip across and see if it's there.'

Twigging that Dolan was less interested in his lighter than he was in tossing over a few more goldies, I volunteered to go. 'What's your lighter look like?' I asked.

But Dolan had already quit the cab and was standing on the platform. 'I'll no' be two shakes.'

I hooked a thumb at the coaches. 'What if this lot's away before you're back?'

Dolan shook his head. 'The pilot's no' even on top of them yet.'

'You'd better be back on time.'

He nodded. 'Don't be daft, I will be.'

Before I could argue he was off his mark. I watched him pass quickly through the ticket-barrier then scurry across the busy concourse.

I admit that at any other time I'd've had the wind-up: big Britannias and jaickets just don't belong together. Even the hare-lipped Kershaw who was always boasting about how drivers let him do yard-shunts would've been in a flap had he been left on his tod on one of these jobs. But tonight was different. I was on my last firing turn and nothing about the railway bothered me anymore. If it came to the bit and Dolan didn't make it back in time I'd maybe make excuses for him, say, for instance, that he'd been caught short and was at the toilet. But that was it, nothing more.

After knocking up the blower-handle a little I shovelled a light scattering of coal around the stale fire, switched on the injector then hosed some water into the toolbucket. Next, I opened the tender door and sprayed down the depleted coals for we'd be travelling tender-first and an eyeful of coaldust wasn't funny. I hosed the floorboards too, a searing steamy anger that thrashed layers of muck from the buckled and branded planks and spat silvery scores along the oilcans.

I washed my hands, enjoying the wet rasp of the sand-speckled soap between my palms. While I was doing this the engine gave a slight shudder and I knew that the pilot engine had come on top of the train. I leaned from the cab to confirm this; yes, the small pug had joined buffers and a shunter could be seen jumping down from the platform to tie-on.

I looked across the station concourse. No sign of Dolan.

About five minutes later there was a lurch then the coaches began to draw away from the engine. I stuck my head out of the cab window. With sparks volleying from its lum the pug made off with the coaches into the darkness outside. Right away an officious-looking platform inspector came running towards the Britannia. 'C'mon,' he yelled, 'Get a move on – there's a train due in!'

There was a lot of whistling and flag waving. 'My driver's in the toilet,' I said lamely but the official didn't hear me. Anyway, the noisy arrival of a Cathcart circle train wiped out all chance of being heard. I could still see the flag waving and the angry looks of the platform staff. Taking a deep breath I crossed the cab to screw off the handbrake. This done I confronted the controls. Gingerly I released the vacuum brake then nudged open the regulator. There was a great up-pouring of steam from the cocks then the engine began to crawl towards the platform signal. Men were still urgently waving for me to get a move on but keeping the regulator well notched down I drifted along the track.

I got the right-of-way almost at once. Taking my time I took the engine past the signal and out into the darkness beyond. The overhead gantries blazed like Christmas trees. When I was clear of the points I stopped the engine and began to wind back the reverser. What the hell was I supposed to be doing? Looking after a mate, was that it? Since when had a sarcastic bastard like Dolan become a mate of mine. Good old McRae, helping out a mucker. So what if I broke my neck or scalded myself skinless? I'd stuck by a comrade, hadn't I? That's what counts.

I stared up at the signal, willing it to greenness.

What's the last sound heard by a man being hanged? Is it the crash of the sprung trapdoor? Or, maybe, the crack of his rupturing backbone? Yes, that'll be it, though as a sound nothing dramatic – a faint click perhaps, much like the one I heard behind me at that moment. I turned to gape at the gantry above the massy bulk of the tender. A signal was at green. Whose? Mine? Definitely not. Couldn't be. In the nearby tall signalbox a window slid open. A man appeared with a loudhailer. He began to pour angry words down on me.

'We're supposed to be going on top of coaches in the station,' I shouted up at him. (Note the 'we're' – the mad bravery of it!)

The loud-hailer cleared its throat then spoke the worst news I've heard in my life. 'That's been changed. You're light-engine-to-the-Shed. Get a bloody move on ...

I've faced death only once in my life, a long-range affair with a hospital bed for the arena, an almost abstract engagement drama-tised by charts tracing the enemy bug's encroachments and a proces-sion of medics who like weary infantry scouts came with terse messages from the war zone. But this was different, here was collision with the brute energies of the thing, impact with its bloody awfulness.

Was I for a rat like Dolan really going to charge like a blind rhino into that orchard of lights? Not likely! But there I was altering the controls for a tender-first run, releasing the handbrake, taking over the controls, opening the regulator ...

('Do I contradict myself? Very well then I contradict myself.')

My old Grandpa has a war story which he likes from time to time to take from his head and show to people for the wonderful lie it is. You can't help but admire the way he has taken an ordinary lump of experience then imposed his vanity on it, how he has pared away the grey layers of truth to expose the far more interesting grain of dramatic possibility. I don't have his gift. When talking about this incident on the footplate of the Britannia I hear myself taking from my verbal prop-box gimcrack phrases like: 'My heart was going like a steamhammer' and worse still: 'The night was alive with incoming train ...'. Creeping rhetoric too: 'Could this be my signal?' 'Had I taken a wrong turning?' 'Was this express train heading straight for me?'

But when I press into my memory for the real facts I find that I'm like the fear-bedazzled child emerging from his first ghost-train ride, the tender walls of his mind seared with the phantoms that had leapt at him in the dark, the ghosts and gargoyles that flared in dark corners, the eerie shrieks of wraiths and ghouls, but little at all remembered of the train itself except maybe the colour of its wheels or the way it shuddered when it took a bend.

From the journey of my own particular 'ghost-train' I too carry away such scraps: the water beginning to bob in the gauge-glasses; the sound of coal shifting in the tender; a woman glimpsed at a tenement window watching television while carnage of horrific potential passed her by; the stink of fear coming off me; and my own voice yammering, 'You'll be alright, John ... Don't panic ... Take deep breaths ... of course you can make it ...' – the sound of a semi-hysterical little-boy-lost. When even these impressions fade there'll still remain with me the brutal images of those black-jawed engines that pounced at me in the dark, the terrifying constellations of lights and, worst of all, those coachloads of complacent humans who raced past so certain of their destination, totally oblivious of this rogue force loose in the dark with a jabbering monkey on its back.

I only knew I'd a chance of making it when the gantries began to thin out. I'd seemingly blundered through a complex signalling system it took experienced drivers days to learn and – At the window of an oncoming signalbox a man was yelling something through a loud-hailer. 'Get back for God's sake! What d'ye think you're doing?' But no he was shouting something quite different: 'Hurry up – there's a bloody train at your back!'

I nudged the regulator wider and the engine fairly spanked into the tunnel.

The signals proved no problem now, a kid could've read them. I'd even time to rattle some coal into the firebox and after a struggle get the injector going. I passed another box. Its signalman waved to me as if in congratulations. I felt chuffed with myself. Something to tell the squad, especially Kershaw. 'Did you hear about McRae? Dolan did him the dirty at the Central and he brought back a big Britannia on his tod ...'

The Shed signal loomed.

I sounded the whistle in acknowledgement as it gave me the come-on and took the engine at a canter up the loop line past the coaling plant to the turntable. Old Eddie Slater came from his bothy to fling the points. He offered to turn the engine for me but I grandly waved him away. 'Do it myself' – the new motto. Another bonus – Kershaw was in the vicinity of the turntable knocking around on an old umbor shunting dead engines. I nodded smugly to him as I took the Britannia onto the turntable.

With the engine turned head-out I took it down to the coaling plant. It was deserted. The coalman must've sloped off for a pint. I lined up the engine's tender with the coal-chute then stepped into the controls cab. Carefully I tilted the chute then pressed the coal-release handle. The coals thundered into the tender. They continued to do so for a long time – too long a time; by now the tender should've been topped up at its front end. Puzzled, I left the controls cab to check. The first thing I saw was Kershaw and his mate standing in their engine cab laughing and pointing with their fingers. I soon learned why. The cab of my engine was choked up with coal – I'd forgotten to shut the tender door.

Baited by Kershaw and his driver I shovelled off as much coal as I could but I had to move on when another engine came in to coal up. My position was ludicrous. I had to sit on the heap of coal in a crouched position, my head only two feet from the cab's roof. Only because I'd howked out a space near the faceplate was it possible to operate the controls.

To the sound of Kershaw blowing the Jumbo's whistle and waving derisively I took the engine down to the fire-grids. I didn't bother to stop at the watering column but rolled on to come to stop with a clang against the buffers of an ancient 'Beetle-Crusher'.

A firedropper had been waiting for my engine to finish his quota. He was covered in grey ash and looked knackered. He propped his irons against the cab then climbed up.

'What the hell's this?'

Abjectly I squeezed past him then dislodging lumps of coal got down from the engine. 'I'm sorry,' I mumbled.

'I'll bloody sorry you, china. You'd better shovel this lot clear ...'

I walked away between the stationary engines. Most of them were raddled with rust and water pee-ed quietly from the sprung rivets in their tenders. My eyes were smarting from the blowing ash. Tongs, pokers, drawbars, and buckled darts littered my path and I had to step carefully over them. A long-handled clinker shovel hanging on a metal pole chimed in the wind.

Standing by a glowing brazier the Shed-Arranger watched my coming with curious eyes. As I drew near him he asked: 'What's he shouting about?'

I shrugged and kept on walking.

James Kelman Interviewed

Duncan McLean

The first conversation took place on the morning of March 1st 1984, a couple weeks after the publication of *The Busconductor Hines,* James Kelman's first novel. He was working at the time as Writer in Residence for Renfrew District Libraries, and we talked in the office he had use of in Paisley Central Library.

The second conversation took place near the end of July 1985. After reading an advance copy of *A Chancer,* (which wasn't actually published till September 26th), I visited Kelman at his home in Cumbernauld. We talked in the afternoon, and again late in the evening.

The idea was that our conversations would record something of the way Kelman was thinking at the time of publication of his first two novels.

DMc: Here's an extract from an article Neil Gunn had published in the Glasgow Herald *in 1941: Glasgow needs 'a working class novel written from the inside.' This would show 'not a catalogue of horrors, but a revelation of the higher virtues, of periods of hardship bravely endured, of the usual human ills, flashes of irritability, of happy times and good nights, a whole lot of gossip and not a little sentimentality.'*
JK: That's very good, you know. I haven't read Neil Gunn at all. At one time I would have been surprised at that but not really now because I was reading an article by Naomi Mitchison about her relationship with Neil Gunn, and I didn't realise he was a good socialist, you know. I read that because I didn't know anything about him, you know. But yeah, that's a good kind of statement to make. (Pause). Refer it to me though.
DMc: Well is Hines *'written from the inside' of the Glasgow working class? And is it a 'revelation of the higher virtues'?*
JK: Eh, the second part of your question is political right. You see if I start to reply, in a way, it's rather as though, well, it comes from the outside and relates to the first part of your question. It's from the inside, of course, aye, because it's told, eh, well it's written in the

form of a sort of interior monologue in a sense, right, you know, it's not written in the 'I' voice but it may as well have been written in the 'I' voice, so in that sense it has to have been written from the inside, otherwise it would have been found out too easily, you know, eh, you know. So I think that would answer the first part of the question OK. Now the second part of the question. If I was to start to discuss it now in those terms I would be discussing it from the outside of that culture anyway, which I'm not. Eh, you know, it would be a mistake for instance to assume that because someone was a writer therefore they're no longer a part of that culture. Cause that would assume that culture, or rather the culture of art, is somehow divorced from working class culture, and that isn't true. I think for instance that that quote of Gunn's would, eh, assume that. Well, from what Gunn says ... 'a revelation of the higher virtues' ... in one sense the higher virtues would be art, art and culture, and in that sense art and culture is obviously just a part of working class culture.

DMc: You mentioned a wee while ago that Hines *is written in a sort of interior monologue. Isn't it actually closer to an interior dialogue?*

JK: There's a couple of technical things going on in the book, you see. I can't really describe it as an interior monologue, nor is it a dialogue, because either the character could be schizophrenic, or else the narrative voice could be schizophrenic, or else the narrator ... contained in the narrative voice is a dialogue between narrator and central character. And that isn't happening either. Eh, I don't think any of those things is happening. I mean, I just said 'interior monologue' as a quick description of what can happen with the 'I' voice. But everything eh ... There's different kinds of writing as you know, eh, there's different forms of writing. It's hard to ... eh, what was that question again?

DMc: Well if it isn't interior monologue or interior dialogue what...

JK: Those things are occurring within ... there's a lot of different things ... there's different business going on, you know, eh. The only thing that doesn't go on ... well there's an 'I' voice about three times in the book ... eh ... in reference to the main character, or perhaps it's the narrator, I don't know. There's nothing technically for instance that would disassociated ... It's very possible, you see, that Hines could be writing that novel. I mean that it is technically possible within the framework of the novel. Nothing that happens happens outwith the perception of Hines, for instance, absolutely nothing. So Hines could have written every single thing. In a way. I'm starting to refer to myself in the third person, you know: 'Kelman had two cups of coffee between half nine and ten o'clock this morning.' You know. A lot of people refer to themselves in the third person. I could describe it as a first person novel written in the third person. There's a lot of tricks you can do in prose. You find when you're doing a short story there's a lot of things you can do, you know you don't realise perhaps you're so powerful until you start getting involved. A lot can be done in it.

DMc: I suppose another side of it then is when Hines is 'no longer able to tell whether he was speaking or thinking.'

JK: That is another side of it, yeah. That is a technical thing. Eh aye, it's an illusion, aye. Difficult to do that! I mean just in a very practical way in my prose there's not for instance any quotation marks to distinguish dialogue. Now if I had used quotations – inverted commas – for dialogue, it means I couldn't have done that the same. It would have been impossible because the transition has to be done through the narrative, right, and it has to sort of switch from one sort of dialogue into narrative voice without the reader being precisely aware of where it happened, OK? But I mean you couldn't do that with quotations because rightaway you'd see where the quotation ends and where the narrative begins, wouldn't you. It just wouldn't be possible. One of the reasons why people would think 'Oh look at that, Kelman doesn't use quotations! Gallus!' it's not that at all. There's a very technical reason why a lot of writers don't. But it doesn't matter what they use. It doesn't matter. I mean there's no technical reason why they do or don't use quotation marks at all. Beckett, for instance, doesn't use quotation marks for a reason. He works between voices quite a lot. But it's a hard thing to do. Like all good illusions or tricks, it's hard to do, you know. It's not easy.

DMc: Lewis Grassic Gibbon put his speech in italics. He didn't use quotation marks either ...

JK: My knowledge of Lewis Grassic Gibbon is too slight, you know, I don't read Grassic Gibbon. I haven't read his novels. I've kinda glanced at them. I've read a couple of short stories by him, a long long while ago. So I don't know enough about his work to talk about it technically although I know he was doing some good things.

DMc: I've got here that famous bit of his essay where he explains what he's trying to do in his prose, technically. He tries to 'mould the English language into the rhythms and cadences of Scots spoken speech, and to inject into the English vocabulary such minimum number of words from Braid Scots as that remodelling requires.' Now, that sounds to me pretty much like what you do.

JK: Yes, I've no grumbles with most of that. I think it's fine. I knew that quotation before. I can't remember where I read it. I read a biography of Grassic Gibbon, and as I say I read some of the things out of that *Scots Hairst*. So that's good. I think that he was a man of his time, Grassic Gibbon, cause that was going on. He was a near contemporary of Joyce and of Kafka. That kind of thing was going on throughout literature, and it's good that somebody in Scotland was aware of it too and working in prose you know eh. Only a good socialist could make that statement.

DMc: So you didn't get involved in that kind of experimentation with prose through Gibbon at all.

JK: No no, I mean eh no. It's a tradition. It's part of a tradition in literature, you know. It isn't always something you get at university. You get the other tradition there, the mainstream tradition, eh, probably because of politics, you know. I don't think I'd ever read any Scottish writers at all when I started writing. I'd read very few English ones either. I usually read eh – I'm talking about when I was twenty – in my twenties for instance, I only read European writers and American writers. Russians are part of Europe. You know, Russians, Germans.

I didn't go to uni. until I was 28 eh. I used just to write when I was on the broo and things like that. And I really didn't like literature at all. Or English literature. It's not even a question of it boring me, because I hated it, you know, I hated the class assumptions that were being made by anybody who was involved in English literature as I thought of it, and still think of it, to some extent. You know. Because some of the reactions that my novel will get because of its language, for instance, show real class prejudice, you know. The prejudices can be quite phenomenal. People who think they're critics, you know, and probably are critics, until they're met with something below the belt.

DMc: How would you have reacted to a novel like Hines *when you were 20? Or what are 20 year olds now, like you were then, going to make of it?*

JK: Eh I don't know. Depends on what their background is to some extent. Eh I mean for instance if they're growing up ... that English literature can contain stories ... working class culture may be a part of literature, and that literature can be a function of ordinary life. Cause normally it isn't. The things I like to read about, and that I was interested in when I started to write, you know, like snooker, going to the dogs, standing in betting shops, eh, getting drunk ... all these things weren't part of literature, you know, apart from Russian, European and American literature. It didn't happen in English literature. In English literature the working class were always servants, and you never saw anybody apart from, say, in Scottish literature, where there was gillies, you know. But they didn't actually live any lives at all, because they were all stereotypes. So I mean,

I hope – no, not I hope – the stories I write, I hope, eh, well, in my opinion they're about things that aren't usually found in literature. Or if they are, it's great, you know. I'm certainly not jealous about it in any way … 'My wee area … my wee …' It's the largest area in Britain! But as far as literature's concerned, it's dead, and has been for a long while. There may have been people who've done this without me noticing. For instance Grassic Gibbon, Neil Gunn. I'm glad to hear that. It doesn't mean I'm going to rush and read them, as a matter of fact, but eh, I think it's smashing. One of the things that set me back on my heels was to discover that I wasn't alone. You know the short story of mine 'Nice to be nice' … I was in a pub with Anne Stevenson, an English poet – an American who writes English poetry – she'd assumed that I'd read Tom Leonard's poetry, but I'd never even heard of Tom Leonard and it was really good to get Tom's poetry, which was the *Six Glasgow Poems*. And I mean I stopped writing phonetic transcriptions of dialect after that because he was obviously much better than me, and much more involved, in ways different from me. So that was great, you know, to meet someone like Tom who was involved with that. To meet Alasdair Gray and people like that who were involved to that extent, you know, who were treating literature as though … just assuming their own right to do it, you know. Eh, Tom's poem where it's perfectly fine just to be watching Scotsport and drinking a Carlsberg Special Brew and listening to Neilson in the background. That type of thing … that poetry being possible for anyone who has a standard upbringing in literature is just impossible because people who watch Scotsport don't fucking read literature! So that type of thing was good. So it's good that those type of writers … American writers, eh … I can't think of any American writers, although eh … Sherwood Anderson I used to like a hell of a lot, you know. I liked stories like 'I am a Fool'. Those type of stories which I thought were great. I remember reading that when I was twenty or something and really being knocked out by it. A story about a boy who goes away to work in the stables. At that time I had still … well I had just given up the idea of being a jockey. (Laughter). Those kind of stories. I remember reading 'The Cincinatti Kid' for instance and being knocked out by that; the idea that a story could be written about a poker player, you know. I mean again this is totally … this doesn't happen in literature! Those kind of things I found really good. Eh and that led me on to say Kerouac and people. Takes you into literature.

DMc: So was it after reading those people that you started to write your own stories then?

JK: Eh.

DMc: *And was it because of them that you started?*

JK: I don't know really. No honestly I don't know. I can't think of any motives or causes except that having time, you know, having time to do it and being involved in it and eh ... I don't honestly know. Cause at one time I would have preferred to have been a painter.

DMc: *How did you get into the 'other tradition'?*

JK: Through eh ... mainly Tom Leonard I suppose, because Tom was very influenced by Carlos Williams, which took me into ... I mean the only people I ever read were prose writers, I never read poetry at all – still don't read very much poetry, you know – but the people I was reading, Sherwood Anderson for instance, and those great American woman short story writers – Katherine Anne Porter and people – who are tremendous, as I say are doing something different with language that you don't get in English. Anyway, I found out Carlos Williams, who had consciously fought against, say the Eliot influence, who was wanting to make the most important thing in literature the voice – something that Eliot was totally opposed to. Because for Eliot there is The Voice of Literature, right? And that voice isn't of course our voice; that voice is the voice of Radio 3. And that would apply in America as well, and throughout the Commonwealth, throughout the English speaking world there is the one voice, the voice of English literature, and it's not your voice, unless you've managed to go through uni. and start to speak as if you came from Hampstead Heath, you know. But writers like Carlos Williams fought against that, so that language becomes involved with ear. Do you read Charles Olson at all?

DMc: *No.*

JK: An American poet who was one of the tutors at the Black Mountain thing, you know, with Creeley and all them. Olson – who's poetry I find difficult – but I like a lot of wee things he says in essays, you know. Talking about the pulse, for instance, the rhythms of the writer being the pulse, and the way the blood goes through your head, that is your syntax as a writer, I think that kind of thing is total anathema to mainstream English Literature, but it is the only good side of literature. The rest is all rubbish. I mean the mainstream writers, it's total rubbish. Just look at the stuff that's produced, take the great contemporary English writers of say the last forty years – they're all fucking hopeless! – I mean they're embarrassing, people like Golding and that, they're total second-raters, Waugh and Graham Greene and all them, they're fucking second rate, you know. You'd be laughed out of world literature if you were to put forward things like Philip Larkin and all that: it's junk, total second rate junk. And yet that is all that the Voice of

Literature has produced – Eliot's stuff. It's barren, totally barren, because it gets rid of people and produces culture, the voice of A Culture.

DMc: And like we were saying earlier, that is the voice that isn't relevant to most folk, the culture of the universities.

JK: Aye, all it does is prop up. Jobs for the Literary Boys you know. It plunders literature. It's not only barren creatively, but it plunders the whole of literature. I mean all the resources belong to the unis. I remember in my honours year writing an essay on this. The whole of the resources of literature belongs to, say, university critics, more or less, you know libraries, stationery, every single thing belongs to people who either work for, within universities, or else who have degrees in English Literature, and they're the people who own literature, who own its resources, they own, for instance, Tipp-Ex. I mean I've got to take a job like this ... writers for instance like Alasdair Gray, and people like that, they don't have typewriter ribbons! They don't have fucking paper, they don't have anything! I mean the people that have that ... go into any university department or any bookshop, the people who have access to stationery, none of them have anything to do with ... they're all fucking vultures on literature! I remember Bernard MacLaverty and I going down to London for the launch of the first *Firebird,* and the bus gets in early to Victoria, you know, say about half five, and so we're walking about, and so we went to the British Museum, and you're only allowed into that place ... you had to have a certificate or a letter from somebody from university saying that you were worthy of entering it. I mean you could have gone along there with six books and said 'Look, my books are in this fucking place, and I can't get in.' And they'd say, 'Oh sorry, you've got to have a letter from a university authority.' They actually ... the same with ... I mean, look at Glasgow University library; that's probably the best library ... well as far as I'm concerned, there are things I'd love to get my hands on. I can't get into that library; I mean you've got to be a university person to get into it ... to use their photocopiers ... Say I want to ... If I finish a novel, right, what do you do with it? I mean it's going to cost you ten pence or twelve pence a page to get it photocopied; if you're in the university you can just get it done for nothing. Now on a basic economic ... It sounds petty to anyone who has access to the stuff, but it's everything to someone who doesn't have it. That is a class thing: people don't understand what to-be-without is. They don't actually understand things like ... eh ... I did an interview on the radio, which was hopeless, the other day there. Anyway, the thing is, the guy who was interviewing me was a nice fellow, a nice middle class fellow, but he didn't understand certain basic facts of life; number 1: that somebody like Hines doesn't have any choice. He's not on the broo because he's a masochist – or on the buses because he *wants* to be on the buses, that if he wanted he could always be a university lecturer and get twenty grand a year. He couldn't really appreciate – and this is one of those class things that people who are economically secure and stable don't understand – what not to be secure means. They don't understand what it is to be on the broo for instance; they don't understand these things except as temporary phenomena – they don't realise that it can be a permanent situation from which there is no get-out. You know, your prospects won't improve next year, you can't borrow money on the strength of it because it's the strength of nothing ...

DMc: You were attacking the uni there, and the class thing within it, and I would join in with you on that but I mean you've been through uni., I've been to uni., so aren't we being hypocritical or cutting our own throats or something ...

JK: No, there's a very important distinction here. It's an important one to be aware of, otherwise you're in danger of giving literature away to the people who think they own it already anyway, you know. It's like... you know the kind of Stalinist Communist point of view that would say 'Fuck all art because it belongs to the bourgeoisie,' now usually the people who say that are themselves bourgeois anyway, and it's a real kind of condescending patronising thing to do because in a sense it's as if they don't want the proletariat to be contaminated by art, as if somehow it didn't belong to them anyway in the first place. So even though such people can be sort of well intentioned, in effect what they're doing is saying to the people who think they own literature 'Oh aye, it's yours.' And it's important to realise that literature doesn't belong to any one class at all, literature just belongs to mankind – it's a universal, you know. You see, one of the things that I know has been said about the way I use language is that it's a kind of attack on literature or somehow a negation. But it isn't at all, it's just an attack on the values of the people who own literature – or the people who think they own literature. So when I use the word 'fuck' all the time, that is in fact attacking their values. They think it attacks literature, because they assume that they own literature, but it's not, because literature doesn't belong to anybody at all. It's important to recognise that distinction ... If you're studying literature ... When I was at uni I was studying literature, but that doesn't necessarily mean that you become a part of the establishment, only if you want it to be. Anybody who wants to study literature is entitled to do so, because it doesn't *belong* to anybody, you know. So when you're going there, you're not going to study what it is to be one of the middle classes – not unless you want to do that. I think part of the trouble is that when you go there you suddenly realise that you're almost being forced into assuming certain attitudes and values. I mean, they force you into saying that Eliot's a good writer, and if you really hate everything he stands for, you want to be able to say 'If he's a good writer that means that writing is fucking rubbish; I don't want to study the concept of literature at all.' I mean I spent four years trying to find an argument for that really; ultimately what I wanted to be able to do was to say 'Right, Eliot is a good writer but he's a bad artist.' I wanted to get to some kind of position like that, you know. I wanted to be able to define things and say

Drawing of James Kelman by Alasdair Gray from *Lean Tales*.

'Right, what does it mean to say that this is a good poem.' I don't accept all the criteria of the Great Critic who can look at the words without looking at – well I don't know, without looking at what? Eh ... Can a fascist write a very good poem? Is it possible to say that Eliot's a great artist? Or someone like Evelyn Waugh for instance; can he be a great artist? Can he be a great literary artist. To me the university system in this country, or the university literary system hinges on that. And if it can't answer that question ... well I don't really think it can. Well I think it can, but not satisfactorily, because I think the answer is 'Yes, he's a great artist.' I mean how the fuck anyone who is a total fascist can be a great artist, eh, I don't want any part of that art. Well, I say I don't want any part of that because ... the Stalinist point of view, which is to deride that, you know. I mean a lot of great upheavals, say, cultural revolutions, is because people have recognised that, or rather they've recognised that this is a logical extension of a certain kind of argument that art is rubbish; and they've accepted that so therefore they go and burn books and burn paintings: 'All artists are fucking bourgeois wankers' you know, and fair enough, but the trouble is that in doing that they're giving art away ... it's so stupid ... it's a stupid thing to do. Because I'm involved in writing, I don't want to do that, because I know that writing can be great, and can be the most honest and truthful profession, you know ... I mean, I don't want to give Kafka away to people who live in Morningside, or give Joyce away to Bearsden ... or Sherwood Anderson or Carlos Williams or all the great ... They're welcome to keep Eliot if they want, you know! It's important to realise that, that literature does not belong to a class, it doesn't belong to the universities, it doesn't belong to schools, although the schools like to think it does. Like Tom Leonard, when he was asked by the *Glasgow Herald* why he uses 'Fuck' in his poems, he said he uses 'Fuck' just so's his poems wouldn't be given out in classrooms. (Laughter).

DMc: Aye, I remember thinking as I was reading The Busconductor Hines *that this was the first time about, or one of those rare times, when there was a realistic amount of swearing in a piece of literature.*

JK: Well, even in the way that question was said. For instance, what makes you think it's swearing? You see when you use the term 'swearing' it's a value; I don't accept that it is swearing at all you see. How can you talk about it? 'The use of the four-letter word'? That's not satisfactory. You actually have to be really specific and say 'Let's have a discussion on the use of fuck and cunt and bastard and shite,' because there's no way of really talking about them in any kind of objective sense. Because it's *not* swearing. There are so many different parts of the argument. I mean basically it's a linguistic argument, it's an argument about how language is used, and I'll give you an example that I've heard used myself: 'Swearing is an act of verbal violence.' Now this comes from a teacher who had these two wee lassies in the class, and suddenly one turns round and batters the other one. And the teacher calls up the lassies and says 'Right you, what did you do that for?' And the wee lassie says 'Please miss, she called me a fucking C.O.W.' Now the thing is that 'C.O.W.' is the swear, it's not 'fucking' that is the verbal violence, that is the swear word there. So when you grasp that point ... the argument has somehow altered already so that the use of four letter words, eh – fuck, cunt, bastard, and shite – they're part of language, and they have to be treated in the same say that the study of language treats other words. You can't sort of separate them off and say 'Well these are swearwords, they're outwith the argument.' They're not, they're part, you know. So when we talk about language, we include them, they're part of language, so we have to talk about things, verbal acts, you know, things like ... an action ... we have to be much more systematic, we have to be really serious about it and say ... Obviously if I say 'Look at that sun, it's fucking beautiful,' obviously I'm not swearing, I'm doing the exact opposite, you know. So in that sense I object to taking part, for instance, in a discussion that hinges on the use of swear words in literature, because right away you've begged the question of what those words are, you know, and you're involving me again in a value system that *isn't your own to deny*. I mean I deny this fucking thing, but suddenly you find that you've affirmed it; the very fact that you're talking about swearing means that you've affirmed it, you know. It's like, if I'm a good atheist, which I am, and you say 'Do you deny God?' and I say 'Oh aye, I deny God,' well that's that whole business of how can you deny it without affirming it. You want to be able to use Russell's way out by saying 'I deny there is an object such that it ...,' you know, the existential quantifier: 'I deny the existence of a being such as that existence called God' or whatever the hell it is, you know. There's that way of doing it and that's important.

Another thing is you see, usually the use of those four letter words – I'll call them that – is a really middle class way of using literature because... say about 15 years ago you had this stupid carry on where you weren't allowed to use 'fuck' unless you were talking about the act of screwing, you know. Now, it was never ever used, I never ever heard it used that way in my life until I started hearing Kenneth Tynan talking on television about D. H. Lawrence. I'd never ever heard that. In my experience no one ever used the word 'fuck' in that way. But suddenly people would say 'I don't mind you using "fuck" as long as you use it properly' which is an absurd way to talk about language altogether. It's almost the type of thing that someone involved in Scottish Literature would say, you know! It's totally absurd. But that became the way of talking about swear words, you know, which again was a real class thing – a real cultural thing. I mean, with four letter words the same applies as with any words, and it's the same rule that any writer has which is: 'Don't repeat yourself unless you can get away with it.' And if you're using the word 'fuck' which most people would three times in each sentence, you can only do that if you're going to do it very well, so that people don't notice; the same applies to the word 'and' or the word 'wall': you can't use the word 'wall' in successive sentences unless you want the second one to be very emphatic, you must have a reason for doing it. Well the same applies for four letter words as any other words. Eh, aye.

DMc: Anyway, I just thought I'd mention that I thought you had the eh four letter word proportion about right, for the first time.

JK: I don't think it's usual to meet books written from a working class experience that is total. Total in the sense that the character can be at the same time an intellectual and still be a *bona fide* member of the working class. In other words, not a writer... though I'd argue with that; but isn't someone who's been to uni necessarily, but it still might be – I'd even argue about that. But somebody who is working on the buses, and the possibility of uni doesn't arise really. In fact it has and he's rejected it on another level, cause the bus driver's wanting to do his highers, and there's the possibility that he might manage to do that, but the character Hines won't manage to do that, and there's no possibility of him doing that. So it's still possible to be an intellectual and, say, to read black Penguins, to read the Classic Series, and to remain a busconductor. That is possible. And because of that, it makes life total. It means that his mind, in a sense, there are no pockets of it within our culture that haven't been opened in a way; you can't work round the character because it's written from the inside, and also because it's written from the inside of our culture. Usually it's self-conscious, but it isn't self-conscious in that sense, that form of irony doesn't exist; usually you get a form of irony where the working-class-ness of the character is shown as an irony between the writer and the reader. Or the other form, which is the worst form – I don't want to mention any names – eh there's a novel that's been published recently, written by a Scotsman – I shouldn't even have said that – anyway the thing is, you know the situation of working class novels in Great Britain from the fifties onwards, which includes people like Sillitoe and John Braine, and all that crowd, where the hero is a working class character who finds the education system and becomes a member of the middle class. Now what happens – and you'll see this quite a lot – is that when this character goes home, for instance on a holiday, he goes home from uni to visit his parents and his friends and his mate – usually he'll see his mate and he'll see his old girlfriend, you know. Everybody except him, of course, speaks phonetically, he speaks standard English. Nobody else does, even his parents don't, he's the only one that speaks standard English. Apart from everybody he knows at uni – they all speak standard English. Now that happens a great deal in north of England novels, plus Scottish novels, and it's really terrible. Now in that type of thing, usually it's well intentioned too, people think they're being true to their roots, but of course what they're doing is the very opposite. It's a terrible thing to see. And so many writers who could have been good writers have done that. And they're forced into that situation to some extent, you have to actually fight your way out of it.

I'm actually very influenced by American literature; there you can get away with it, you don't have to get involved with that situation. I mean a lot of young British writers that want to write, they look at American writers and must be really amazed at the freedom they find, you know, those kind of anthologies you see. You can swear and talk about sex and anything you like; how can you do it? It must be really amazing, you know. They don't have to fight their way through this big paper bag of English Literature of How Do You Talk. We actually have to discover how to talk before we're allowed to write about subjects, and then we think it's surprising that we can't write about certain subjects because we don't have the right voice! They obviously don't realise that language is the culture – if you lose your language you've lost your culture, so if you've lost the way your family talk, the way your friends talk, then you've lost your culture, and you're divorced from it. That's what happens with all these stupid fucking books by bad average writers because they've lost their culture, they've given it away. Not only that, what they're saying is it's inferior, because they make anybody who comes from that culture speak in a hybrid language, whereas they speak standard English. And their language is the superior one. So what they're doing, in effect, is castrating their parents, and their whole culture, and saying 'Right, that's fucking rubbish, because it's not the language of books. I speak the language of books, so does everyone I meet at uni, so do the lecturers and so does my new girlfriend, who's father is a fucking book millionaire or something, and they all speak the real way.'

DMc: How long have you been writing Hines *for?*

JK: I started that years ago. I keep finding old versions of that in the house. When we moved house I found old versions dating back years. Certainly ten years ago I started at least a couple of pages of it. But I did the bulk of it one time I stopped smoking, I did a lot of it then. Then I had to start smoking again to finish it. My first story was published in 1972 when I was 25; I must have written that when I was 22 or something. The first story in the collection, *Not Not While the Giro*, that's the first one I had published. Even now there are old stories lying in a drawer that I can't finish; I take them out every now and then and try to finish them, but they don't always work.

DMc: Have you got anything planned to go on to next?

JK: Aye, there's a long … I've started a … I kind of stopped writing for ages because ... I chucked smoking last June and I find it impossible, well almost impossible ...

DMc: What, to write without smoking?

JK: No, to exist without smoking. (Laughter) But I'm finding it slightly easier now you know, cause it's eight months. But I'm involved in this long thing just now, and it's difficult, because if I'm involved in a long thing I want to be able to sustain it, and work on it at all hours, work through the night or whatever. I just find I work and sleep; that suits me down to the ground. I love that really – never leave the house, you know: stay in the house for three or four weeks and then maybe go out and get drunk for four days. You can't beat that way of living, it really is good, you know. I can't be bothered doing this job, but I have to for the cash, because we need the money, you know. Contrary to what people ... when you've no money what it means is that you've no money. They don't seem to grasp that, you know. Sorry, sorry; but I am in the middle of quite an interesting piece, because I'm trying to handle a universal situation; the trouble is that the present keeps bursting in; it's vaguely a fantasy, anyway. I'm quite well on with it as a matter of interest. Well, I've finished page 43, plus there's another 20 or 30 pages of former drafts that can easily be incorporated, so that would take it up to about 80 pages, you know, and there's no signs of it stopping. And I'm enjoying doing that. There won't be one single 'fuck' in it ... well I'm saying that, which I maybe shouldn't be doing, because you're cutting off possibilities; at this moment it seems unlikely, because it's very sort of ornate language it's using, you know. But the present day bursts in, linguistically. But it's about ... well it's trying to do a kind of university thing, you know; because I felt I should do that.

DMc: Just to show you could, like?

JK: No, I think that it's important to use that experience, and if I don't I'm falling into the trap of what I was criticising other writers for, thinking that somehow the university experience isn't mine, or isn't part of the culture as a whole, but is only part of the middle class or upper class culture, whereas it shouldn't be: you should be able to go to university and still be a member of the working class in quotes, if you want to be. In a sense that's like literature: all learning should be available to anybody, you know, you shouldn't necessarily have to come out of there getting one of those 15 or 20 thousand pound a year jobs, you know, for the rest of your life, unless you want to do that. So in that sense I think it's important to be able to write about university without being coy and without writing in sections, but being able to use it as an assumption of a way of existence, you know. So I quite fancy doing it; I quite fancy the types of irony I'll be working in; I fancy being able to make quite a lot of heavy statements, in a way. The thing that comes immediately to mind is Swift, getting into the type of heavy irony he would use in *A Modest Proposal*. I would like to get into that way of seeing the world.

(July 1985, Cumbernauld)

DMc: A Chancer *is very different from* Hines, *isn't it?*
JK: Aye aye. Well it's early work. Part of the problem in writing it is, that I'm writing it as the 38 year old Kelman, and I *was writing* it when I was your age, and it's very difficult because of what you know, and the sort of thing that you're aware of being able to do. So you can't get as excited in it and it becomes very very difficult to try and be wholehearted. You know, you're wanting to give him a kick all the time, the character, and you can't do it. You know, you can't even get really kind of intellectually involved with the character, it's not possible. So trying to retain faith with it as a work is very difficult, trying to capture the verve and the sparkle and the spirit of it, you know, occasionally managing to capture it again, in a slightly distanced way. Say at the end, certain things that would give me satisfaction now as individual chapters that I wrote, that I can handle now and I couldn't handle then. Such as the boy playing football, right, when he's actually having to *play* football, which is difficult to do because sport's always difficult to write. Where the boy plays football, and there's this big winger – now, that's difficult to write: when I was first writing the novel I couldn't handle that, I had to kind of get by it in some way which is slightly underhand but perfectly permissible as a writer. Well, if you've read *White Mule*, Carlos Williams leaves out all the hard parts. He would never do it as a poet, but as a prose writer's he's inferior, you know, he's a good short story writer, but he's not a good novelist. Like there's the battle of the union, the union's on the streets, and suddenly you have this sort of nice switch – well, not a switch – it's written from the wee girl right, the daughter. For instance the father goes away out and you get the next chapter beginning 'When he came back ...' and you think 'Fuck, what happened with all the amazing bit?' The sort of thing Dickens would never do, right, because Dickens would have to go and write the whole part, whereas Carlos Williams didn't, he went by it. If it was a poem Williams would never have done that, Williams was a very very honest and strong poet and he couldn't have cheated like that, he would have had to have done it. But in the prose, no; he's not a great novelist at all, and there was no

obligation on him to do it and he never done it. But that type of thing, for instance, like that, there's always bits you can skip over as an artist, you know. For instance in *Chancer*, I would have skipped over those bits earlier on – I did skip over them – and that was one of them.

DMc: Hines *I thought the best bits were all the internal workings in his head, in* A Chancer *it was the sort of set-pieces, like the confrontation with the bobies or else just at the exact middle when for one of the first times Kirsty and Vi and Tammas walk together down to the pond, trying to spot the rats, and also, maybe the best bit of all was the bit when Tammas goes in to visit Cathy when Vi isn't in, and there's the holding of hands bit, you know, the 'Is something going to happen here?' bit. I mean is that the kind of thing you were talking about.*

JK: I never write 'set pieces' and object to the use of the term in relation to my work. When you are involved in a novel, there are always problems to be solved in it, technical problems. In *Hines* you have different problems that I spoke of in the first part of this interview to do with transition and moving from nothing to a first person and back out again: things that are really difficult to do, and because of that it's exciting to do. Even apart from the story, say I've been interested to find out what your character does within the framework of the story: in early versions of *Hines* for instance, the confrontation in the union doesn't happen. I mean one of the early versions is about 300 pages and that confrontation doesn't happen: he chucks the job and goes on the broo. So to that extent, the story, while it's always really important, the technical problems are equally important. One of the things that draws me to the desk, for instance, is 'How the hell do you get by that? ... How do you get through this?' It can be really good. You see, that thing was missing in *Chancer* because those problems had been solved about ten or twelve years before. And the problems then in writing the *Chancer* were how to be absolutely concrete, you know, to do nothing that was abstract, nothing that was internal, there are some internal sections in *Chancer* but they are technically irrelevant, or redundant: they don't have to be there.

DMc: A few questions present themselves. For one thing, Hines *was obviously a very internal book, the technical problems were to do with internal things, whereas in this one the technical things were to do with keeping it all external. So why did you do two completely different things?*

JK: In where?

DMc: Well, why was one completely internal and one completely external? Or nearly.

JK: Fair enough. Well a lot that goes on with the character Hines is intellectual, it's even intellectual exploration, in a sense, it's to do with ideas: the character himself, Hines, is involved in ideas and normally those ideas are a function of conversation. They only come out in conversation. If he had pals that he spoke about, they would discuss philosophy and things. The sort of conversations that happen at uni., a lot, and can happen elsewhere, but not to the same extent. Or they're not taken for granted in the way they are, say, at university. If you are working an ordinary job – say as a busconductor – you can get these conversations, but they happen in a different way. You can't assume it, you can't take it for granted that this is part of life; there's always sort of wee games and rituals that go on, say, in an ordinary working class job, like Jeff Torrington would write about, for instance, in 'The Last Shift'. Now that type of thing, with the Walt Whitman book – Jeff and I have discussed this often – where you're a closet reader, you know. If you come out of the closet in a job like that, you're not gay, what you are is A Reader of Penguins – you smuggle in Penguin modern classics, and somebody might spot it and go 'Hey, what's that?' 'What do you mean?' 'Is that *The Lives of the* Saints I see sticking out of your pocket?' 'Aye.' 'Oh.' And you start to discuss Lindisfarne or something. (Laughter.) So usually that's a dialogue, a dialogue's necessary. In *Hines,* for instance, that is just about to come out on occasion; it never quite comes out. It's only a possibility with his driver, Reilly, and it never happens, although somehow it's always taken for granted that that has happened yesterday, but that's not part of the narrative. In *Chancer* that sort of thing is never a possibility – the character's only twenty, he's had an ordinary working class upbringing, there's been no structured intellectual carry on at all, there's been no further education, you know, he's left school at sixteen or whatever.

DMc: But he smuggles in his Readers Digests ...

JK: Well there are Readers Digests there, they're yellowing, it was intended that they weren't his, that they were there before. But it doesn't matter if they are or not, either's possible, but he wouldn't really bring them in, otherwise other books would have been mentioned.

DMc: Well I don't know, he does seem to read quite a lot.

JK: He reads all the time, he's always got a book on the go. But at that stage it's only something somebody does on their own, there's no dialogue; he's too young yet to have found out somebody because there would be nobody else at that stage who would know, unless it was one of his pals maybe the footballer is the likeliest one, possibly he would be reading. But at this stage you wouldn't really talk about it. There'd be no reason why you wouldn't, it just wouldn't come up. Maybe in two or three years time it might come up but at twenty I think, there would have been maybe one guy I could have spoken to about writing, you know, only one guy out of my whole circle, and it really wouldn't have been on, cause there would've been other things we were talking about, other things that were *central,* whereas when you're at university, *ideas* are central – ideas to do with philosophy and politics. I mean they would have been central when I was there ... amongst kids – kids! – amongst young people of twenty, you know, whereas at that time I was twenty-eight. It did occur to me too, you know, at that age I wouldn't have been involved with that; I would've been involved with ideas but it would have been in a different way: it would have been peripheral. It was really only ideas about making money, working, getting a job, hitting various places, you know, because at twenty I was doing the things my characters do in *An Old Pub Near The Angel,* like being away down in England and places, so the important ideas would have been Getting By. Ideas only happen when you have a degree of security – if you have a fixed abode you can sit around and chat, but if you're working in temporary jobs and living in temporary accommodation you don't really have time to do it, you know, and in a sense it's very difficult to write about that type of internal life. It really is, you can't do it within an ordinary narrative voice – I can't do it without an amazing irony – it can't be done. Because the type of things you're taking for granted are things to do with class.

The sort of problems that Jeff Torrington has had, for instance, in trying to write are the same problems that I have had in trying to write, exactly the same: other writers don't recognise them as problems, you know – I would regard those other writers as being quite naive: they've never realised the difficulties of talking about art if you're an ordinary member of the working class. Eh, they don't have to go through whole rigmaroles and rituals. Like coming out of the closet. You have to go through all that. I mean I would be able to say now, since I left school, which is twenty-four years ago, I could say there are about eight people I've met in all the jobs whom I could talk about literature with in that type of way. Like Jeff – you were talking about Jeff talking about Hegel – one guy I met had been writing, I remember talking to this guy, and he lived up the stair from Marie and me when we got married in Glasgow. It was just after we came back to Glasgow. Frank McGoohan, Frank and I used to get drunk quite a lot. Now Frank was a good bit older than me, but he was really involved with literature, you know, he used to make very good statements on Keats and things, really involved with literature; he used to sort of read it all the time and speak about it. And not many more like that. The type of guy, for instance like Owen in *The Ragged Trousered Philanthropists* who (as I said in the first part) just takes it for granted – just assumes the right of that kind of intellectual questioning. You see if you're trying to write that, you can't do it. You can't really do it from the outside at all. Now relating it to that thing there about external and internal, it cannot be done without a great deal of coyness or sort of sociological explanation of 'How it is possible for someone who left school at this age and worked as a labourer to be able to discuss Hegel.' Those kind of things aren't really possible within English Literature – it's a sort of logical absurdity of what English Literature is, you know, *it doesn't happen.* It happens in other cultures. For instance Yiddish or something, the teachings, everything about the religion, the teachings of the religion are part of literature; everything's a part of it: politics and philosophy are part of it, you know, and if you're a member of that religion then you're a member of that culture – that great sweep – you're privy to it. That just doesn't happen in our culture. For instance, servants within Yiddish – maybe this is sentimental or something or shows a lack of knowledge, but it seems to me that people – peasantry – within that culture are aware of all the great writers within the culture too and it's just assumed that they know, that they can talk about it in the same way as someone who is really wealthy. Learning and culture is not really a function of the wealth or the economic power of the top members within the society. I'm thinking of European Yiddish culture now, in comparison to Far Eastern or rather Russian Yiddish culture – the distinctions will probably be quite vast, you know.

But even just taking it as a general point, the idea that in our culture people who are low down the economic scale are always assumed just not to be involved in art and things, and to have no awareness of philosophy or the history of ideas; those things are supposed to be not a part of their culture, you know. Now, to try to write a novel within an ordinary working class framework means, and to do it as a whole person ie to do what all writers do, which is to discuss ideas, you have to try to give this whole explanation as to why it's possible for you to be interested and involved in such a thing, you know. So either you're going to have to use enormous, very deeply structured ironies, or else it's not really possible – I don't see how it's possible without that. You have to find some way round it. I felt that was always the problem for me anyway.

DMc: Do you mean if you're going to write a novel about the working class and you want to show that you're writing it from the

inside – you have to make the person you're writing about capable
of having these ideas and reading books and things to prove that
you are like him in that you are capable of writing a book?
JK: No. No, that comes afterwards. I think it's valid to think that,
but to me that's not a writer's question. Or rather, it can be a
writer's question, but it shouldn't be – that is a critic's question in a
sense because it is something that is asked after. No, it's not that, it's
to try and make a really authentic ordinary voice – an authentic
ordinary member of the working class. Take Jeff Torrington's short
story about that guy, 'The Last Shift', some stories of mine are
similar. When you read it you just naturally assume... I mean it's
taken for granted that this person is your ... You can talk to this
person on any subject under the sun – anything to do with the
history of ideas: if you want to go and talk to him about Hegel, if
the person doesn't know about Hegel, it doesn't mean that Hegel's
never been available, it just means that maybe a person hasn't read
Hegel but maybe they'll have read somebody else that is the equivalent or something. But that type of thing, that part of culture – of
high culture – is always available to them, it's always a part of their
own culture; it's not something that is cut off.

The best analogies would probably be black writers just to show
the type of jump that would have to be made for most people who
first come upon black writers and get a shock to realise that the
black writers are totally aware of what they're aware, and their
whole background is, say, Nietzsche; just what we would regard as
the ordinary intellectual tradition or something. And that shock, for
instance, to read black writers in Africa and go 'Christ, he knows
the same as me' with a wee shock, you know. That is the best
analogy, in the sense that that black writer is the same as this
working class writer in Britain.

DMc: *But you might read this black writer and see that the writer*
has read the same as you but the person he's writing about hasn't
necessarily read the same as you.
JK: No I'm not talking about that, I'm talking about the subject of
the writer, I'm talking about the characters, not the actual writer.
You see, one of the things that goes on in say English Literature is
the wee dialogue going on between author and reader about character. All the wee signals and codes. You were talking earlier about
the Aberdeen writer William Alexander, where you have a tran-
scription of dialect in the dialogue, and it's done in a phonetic style,
and the narrative is done in ordinary standard English, right? Now
that of course is a wee game going on between writer and reader
and the wee game is 'Reader and writer are the same' and they
speak in the same voice as the narrative, and they're unlike these

fucking natives who do the dialogue in phonetics. English Literature is based on that relationship between writer and reader and the person in the middle is the character. For instance, in the average novel written about a working class character, the assumption is that the character doesn't know as much as the writer and the reader, and often you'll get all those wee things such as dialect, for instance, in phonetics. In other words, the person who speaks is not as good, or rather not as intellectually aware as the writer or reader.

This is why so many working class writers seem to fail so often – apart from the fact that they're boring – you can't even ask 'Is there anything I can see here?' You just see someone who has sold out. There's not even any point in looking at their work, because the depth of the sell out is just so great. There's nothing.

*

DMc: Let's talk about the opening sentence of Hines *– in particular about its punctuation. You know what I'm talking about – the fact that it's two sentences separated by a comma.*

JK: I know that opening sentence of *Hines* quite well and I do not accept that at all. I spent a lot of time on it. You cannot make it a semi-colon; you can't make it a colon: it's got to be a comma, there's no question. The principle part of that sentence is the first one which is 'Hines jumps up'. There's no cause or effect: it's a picture of a fact; the fact is: somebody has jumped up. That begins the whole thing, the character jumps up, stands to attention – there is this movement going on. And then you start analysis, if you want to do that: Why did he jump up? It so happens he jumps up because his wife is about to lift over a pot of boiling water – an inadequate pot. That is the spark of life. In terms of drama that is all that is necessary, nothing else. It can't be a semi-colon, cause that puts too much emphasis onto it. It's got to begin in a really unemphatic way; even a semi-colon makes it emphatic, you know. It's got to be something that's so everyday.

I remember Alasdair Gray reading that for the first time and finding that horrendous and hair-raising, that first section, and saying it was really terrible for him to wonder whether this was all going to come to pass in a satisfactory way, if this girl was actually going to fill the bath without scalding herself. I don't even think I could read it like that. But that's exactly the kind of thing I was after, that drama, the drama of that moment, from something that was so mundane, so everyday. It's like a factory story, something that people do every day of the week, it's part of life, you know. But somebody who's not involved with that suddenly sees and 'christ, is this what this person does every week for £45?' Like say, a worker at the coal face, who risks the kind of death that most people would regard as an amazing nightmare. But that's what they do. Part of their job is to take the sort of risks that nobody would take for less than say fifty grand if they were middle class. Or like my one page story, 'Acid', I mean I used to do that, I nearly lost my hand. I've got the scar here to prove it, blah blah. But it's something you do every day of the week, it's part of the job: it's very very hard to get the drama of that, because the whole thing would seem to be a boring way of living, very boring indeed. Somebody who was watching from the outside might go 'Oh christ, how on earth can they manage that?'

DMc: Like in the copper rolling factory in A Chancer.

K: Aye, that kind of idea, although there's more leeway in that. The opening for instance of *Hines* is the same idea. Obviously there's no evaluation being made, it's just trying to set out a thing very basic. In setting out the fact, you have set out the danger, because the danger is inherent within the fact, you know. I mean the fact really itself is hair-raising; if you can put forward that fact, then you can put forward the hair-raising-ness of the experience, you know, which is why I go after all those wee effects, such as no abstractions – everything's concrete. It's only through the concrete that you actually get the terror, you know. Carlos Williams again. Just state the thing, don't think in terms of ideas; if you get the thing properly, then you've got it. If you state those terrible things that go on in a factory, if you just put them down, then you'll get the horror of it, you don't have to say 'This is horrible.' Just state it properly, and it's there. That's what Kafka does. Kafka's the first person to do that; nobody had done that before him. Or since. (Laughter.) I know, for instance, that what I do in *Hines* Joyce does not do in *Ulysses,* but I really do think he would have liked to have done that. (Laughter.) Honestly, I mean that. I'm talking about the transition, and I mean just in a technical way. That does not mean therefore I am better than Joyce or anything like that, I'm writing seventy years after him. I'm talking about the transition – transition and through, for instance Zola or something to Robbe-Grillet, the type of state-ment of something; that straight concreteness, you know, where every noun will be concrete: there's only facts being stated, there's no such thing as a value judgement. And going from there into an I-voice. James Joyce would have loved to do that. I'm not kidding you. I think the person who comes closest is Alasdair in *Lanark.* That's why Alasdair's starts off in the fourth book, because it's to do with the same problem. I could only say it with too much shorthand here and it would just sound rubbish. But it's to do with time. I think, for instance, that *Ulysses* is too long. I think it's too long, and it wouldn't have been as long if Joyce had had certain things at his disposal – certain technical movements, or certain ways of working narrative.

DMc: People like Anthony Burgess say that Joyce is the greatest master of English prose, or had the greatest technical control over English ever …

JK: You see, even saying that. The important thing is to have that mastery over the prose – it's nothing to do with English. Kafka was doing things that Joyce couldn't do, Kafka was doing things that Joyce was just not capable of doing. *The Castle* is far superior, just in terms of the sort of possibilities that are contained within any work.

I can give you an example, a straightforward concrete example of the problem: say you're writing a story in the I-voice. You see the problem is always to try and make the action happen to you as you're talking, to write a story where there is no space between the telling and the event: it's to be able to say 'Jack stuck the knife into Jill's head' in such a way that there's no past tense – you know how, say, in Muriel Spark where you get a slightly silly present tense: 'Jack is sticking the axe into Jill's head' you know, as though somehow that has the immediacy, and suddenly there is no story-teller, there is just the story, just the act. The problem for writers, writers of prose, is always to try and get it to the act without any distancing, with no narrator: a straightforward statement, or an enactment, a re-enactment of the actual scene. And one of the wee ways of getting that is through the I-voice, you know. I mean that's been happening now for about 200 years; that's so old in prose: that's what Goethe was doing in *Young Werther,* the I-voice. So you have someone saying 'He walked across the hill and BUMP Jill stuck the axe in the head, you know.' And you start to say 'Well how did you write it down, if there's an axe in your head? Was that your dying breath?' That type of problem, for instance, is a genuine problem in the sense that people have to tackle it – James Hogg has to tackle it. Wringhim – I mean what happens there? because that is the I-voice, right, and you find out the guy has written it all down and buried it at the cross roads, or whatever, and somebody discovers it. Lermontov uses it. That's a device that is as old as the first person narrative. Goethe does that in *Werther.* Goethe's the oldest guy I know that does that. He has a wee preface saying something like 'The following story was found by me. I am the editor. And here it is.' You know. So that allows his I-voice to die, commit suicide or whatever. So you still obtain that great immediacy of the I-voice. The I-voice can stop in mid-sentence and go 'So myself and

the Duke, we were fencing, and suddenly he thrust his sword ...'
And the story ends. Well, that's never happened to my knowledge,
but you get the point: that type of immediacy, that is what is
obtained, that is the goal, that is what has always been the goal.
That's what leads Joyce into *Finnegans Wake.* Honestly, there's
nothing else apart from that. To obliterate the narrator, get rid of
the artist, so all that's left is the story.

'The Only Real Phoenix' Notes on Utopia & Apocalypse

Richard Gunn

The time of apocalypse

IN 1807 HEGEL REPORTS to his readers his conviction that he and they inhabit a 'new world'. This world is the last, or final, world: Hegelian philosophy aspires to be 'wisdom', and wisdom (as distinct from mere love of wisdom) is possible only when 'spirit … has completed itself as world-spirit'. In 1830, in his lectures on the philosophy of history, Hegel repeats his conviction that his own time is an end-time: 'the time has come' in which God's providential scheme for history can be understood, but this time comes only when 'the ultimate end of the world … has been realised in a universally valid and conscious manner'. Historical wisdom is possible only when world history has run its course.[1]

The cast of thought displayed in these passages is so alien to us that we have difficulty, not merely in understanding Hegel, but in hearing what he says. Nothing is more common amongst commentators – including the writer of the introduction to one of the works from which the above quotations are taken – than to deny that Hegel believed in an 'end of history' at all. We refuse to believe that Hegel's words, which are sufficiently straightforward, really do mean what they appear to say.

Perhaps at any time before the present Hegel's readers would have been able to comprehend his meaning at once, and to welcome or condemn the scandal it represents. The so-called early modern period – the centuries spanning the emergence of capitalism – saw a many-sided affirmation of apocalyptic thought. Apocalypse, which etymologically signifies a revelation or uncovering, projects a denouement at which the sense of the plot of history's story may finally be known. The conviction common to apocalyptic writers was that 'the hour in which they were writing was witnessing the beginning of the end-time': 'what sets off apocalypticism from general eschatology is the sense of the proximity of the end'.[2] In its millenarian version, apocalypticism looks to the coming of the seventh, and final, thousand years of history: the thousand years corresponding to the sabbath of harmony, reconciliation and rest.

Apocalyptic thought is at least as old as Christianity. But already in the fifth century, Augustine was condemning the apocalyptic view that an era of blessedness might occur prior to the Last Judgement. For Augustine, 'the eternal felicity of the City of God in its perpetual sabbath' is to be envisaged only in otherworldly terms. Luther's 'two kingdoms' doctrine restates the Augustinian view against the millenarian followers of Thomas Muntzer at the time of the Peasant War. Apocalyptic thought, though frequently an acknowledged dimension of mainstream theology, no less frequently edged towards heresy and the endorsement of a radical social and political dream. Radicals held no monopoly on apocalypticism. Indeed, apocalypticism can be seen as giving birth to our sense of 'modernity' in general: Joachim of Fiore's (c. 1135-1202) third age, the age of the Spirit which succeeds the ages of the Father and the Son, can be seen as the 'modern' age insofar as (where Spirit prevails) the world is to be understood in immanent rather than transcendent or mythic terms. No appeals to a particularistic Father – or Son – figure can orient us in a world where Spirit is in us as much as we are in it. Modern natural science no less than modern ethics raises immanence above transcendence. David Strauss's *Life of Jesus* (1835) simply draws the conclusion: philosophical humanism is launched on its course when it is acknowledged that the unity of divine and human belongs, not in Christ as a unique and particular individual, but in the human species taken as such and as a whole.

Nonetheless, the filiation of apocalyptic with radicalism stands. Its signal exemplars were the Peasant Wars and the English Revolution of the seventeenth century. Winstanley believed that 'the old world is running up, like a parchment in a fire'. Abiezer Coppe gave the date of publication of his central Ranter tract (*A Fiery Flying Roll*, 1649) as 'the beginning of that notable day, wherein the secrets of all hearts are laid open'. The light of glory, which Luther had believed would shine only in the 'hereafter'[3], already illumines for Coppe the wickedness and at the same time the redemptive possibilities of the present world. For the radicals, the path to earthly blessedness lies through revolution. Hegel agrees, and construes the French Revolution – that 'glorious spiritual dawn' – in the same light. Better: it is the light of French Revolutionary practice which Hegel sees as shining in his own theoretical work. Only when this light fades does philosophy revert from the brightly-coloured phenomenological invocation of free practice to the *a priori* and conciliatory theorising of the later Hegel which paints 'grey on grey'.

The space of utopia

As well as witnessing a recrudescence of apocalyptic (linked to radicalism), the early modern period saw the discovery of utopia as the unique site – the no-place (*utopos*); or good place (*eutopos*) – where worldly dreams might be fulfilled. The 'classic' era of utopian thought opens with Thomas More (in 1516) and lasts up to, and beyond, the English civil war of the following century. More's Utopia, Campanella's City of the Sun, Andreae's Christianopolis and Bacon's New Atlantis all purport to be, in one way or another, ideal communities discovered by travellers in hitherto uncharted domains. Of course, not all utopias of the period conform to this pattern: for example Winstanley's *Law of Freedom* (1651), dispensing with a fictional format, simply records the laws of an ideal or desirable state. Nor is the idea of describing an ideal community in itself new. When Rabelais, in the first book of *Gargantua and Pantagruel*, describes an abbey in which traditional monastic discipline is inverted – its motto is 'Do as you will' – he is restating the medieval tradition of a land of Cokaygne:[4] interestingly, the same motif of monastic inversion figures in the 'Cokaygne' poem itself. The motif of inversion, with its satirical possibilities, reappears in works lying on the boundaries of the utopian tradition: in *Gulliver's Travels* and in Samuel Butler's *Erewhon* where – pointing up his contemporaries' inclination to regard social misfortune as blameworthy – disease is treated as a crime; and crime as a disease. One precursor of utopian thought deserves mention here, not least because of its unique solution to the problem of where – in reality or in dream? elsewhere in space or at a future time? – utopia is to be placed. Christine de Pizan's (1365-1429?) remarkable *Book of the City of Ladies* (1402) portrays her book *as* the utopia in which women are protected against misogynistic attack: the new Kingdom of Femininity is founded in 'the field of letters', so that to present arguments in defence of women is already to lay the city's foundations and to construct its walls. The motif of inversion appears in Christine's wholly reasonable contention that the minds of women are 'freer and sharper' than those of men.

Nonetheless, the pattern established by More remains a predominant one, and it is to works more or less closely derived from it (those of Campanella, Bacon and Andreae) that my discussion will refer.

We read such works with a mixture of hope, exasperation and delight. Exasperation and delight blend equally when we learn that Campanella's citizens 'wear white undergarments to which adheres a covering, which is at once coat and leggings, without wrinkles. The borders of the fastenings are furnished with globular buttons, extended round and caught up here and there with chains'. Delight outweighs exasperation when we are told that 'the only real phoenix is possessed by the inhabitants of this city.'[5] Hope is aroused but the threat of pedantry and tedium looms when Andreae informs us, early in his work, that we shall meet each one of Christianopolis's four hundred inhabitants in turn.[6] If 'life as a whole is full of utopian projections, mirrored ideals, dream-manufactories and travel pictures', and if 'every great work of art' includes a 'utopian perspective', why should dismay and disquiet colour our response to just those works where a utopian perspective is brought into explicit view? Must all utopia be tinged with the bathos which is evident when – to take a later example – Edward Bellamy (1850-1898) specifies that credit cards in Boston in the year 2000 are made of 'pasteboard' and when he warms to the praise of a society which achieves the distribution of consumer goods by means of a network of hydraulic tubes?

Bellamy's *Looking Backward* (1888) can be dismissed, as it was by Morris, as decidedly unimaginative and second-rate. No such dismissal can answer to the challenge of the classic utopian works whose pungency and fascination is clear. The matter is the more complex since their challenge stems, in the last instance, from the circumstance that it is in just those features which arouse disquiet that their fascination lies. Utopia has been characterised as displaying a 'rage of order',[8] and from one angle its least attractive feature is its exclusion of both what Hegel calls 'subjective freedom' and the notion of civic participation (or 'politics') which, in the early modern period, the republican tradition regarded as intrinsic to the dignity of man. In Hannah Arendt's terms, utopian thought assimilates 'action', or interaction, to the apolitical structure of blueprint-oriented 'work'.[9]

And yet it is the 'order' of utopias which bathes them in a serene and radiant light. Only secondarily is this order political or social. In Bacon, it is the order of knowledge itself, organised on a system of the division of intellectual labour. The heart of New Atlantis is Salomon's House, half museum and half research-institute, and the euphoric force of Campanella's 'only real phoenix' is evident when Bacon's visitors are told: 'We have diverse curious clocks, and other like motions of return, and some perpetual motions'.

In Campanella (1568-1639), the order of knowledge is presented as the organisation of physical space: on the City of the Sun's concentric walls are depicted mathematical figures, geological samples, flora, fauna and 'all the mechanical arts'. Andreae's (1586-1654) citizens mingle work with the practice of research. For both Campanella and Andreae, physical space is also social space which is also cognitive space: utopian society is transparent because, since everything has its place, everything can be seen. The City of the Sun 'is divided into seven rings or huge circles named from the seven planets, and the way from one to the other of these is by four streets and through four gates, that look towards the four points of the compass.'[10] At the centre of the city is a temple which should be the temple of the sun (implying heliocentrism) but which Campanella, writing in prison, allows to include (geocentrically) a model of the earth. The background to this sort of description is the radially planned ideal cities of the Renaissance architects, of which Filarete's 'Sforzinda' (dating from the 1460's) is the best-known example.[11] The prototype is Plato's description, in the *Critias,* of the capital city of an idealised Atlantis: Plato's city is radially planned, with concentric circles of alternating strips of land and canals.

Christianopolis is designed as a square fortress with four gates again facing towards the compass-points; within its walls are four parallel lines of houses, stores and workshops with symmetrical towers where those responsible for the maintenance of order reside. Each of the four sides of the city is devoted to economic production of a different kind. At the centre of Christianopolis is a 'college' – the 'innermost shrine of the city' – devoted to research, education and worship; it includes a pharmacy whose completeness and principles of classification make it 'a veritable miniature of all nature'. Like a modern detective story – which represents yet another image of rational transparency – Christianopolis comes complete with an architectural drawing and a plan.

Campanella's phoenix and Bacon's moderately-numbered 'perpetual motions' bring home to us how remote, not only from our own time and place but from all worldly times and places, these utopias are. Whether or not Campanella believed in phoenixes or Bacon in perpetual motion, this sense of remoteness stands. We are at the utter ends of the earth, and the route to utopia involves long journeying, the trial of shipwreck or (for Bacon) 'a kind of miracle' that comes in answer to a prayer.[12] Andreae adds that his traveller undergoes a threefold examination as to his character, knowledge and views of life before being admitted to Christianopolis; similarly, 'tests and restrictions' (Davis, loc, cit.) provide a *rite de passage* which Bacon's seafarers must undergo. All this establishes the difference of utopia from the world we know. The same difference is underlined in More's melancholy remark that there are many things in Utopia 'which in our cities I may rather wish for, than hope after'. Utopia is the outcome of a free dreaming, cut loose from its ties to the hopes or expectations of any present age. If, as is sometimes argued, Campanella's City of the Sun has more activist overtones, this is to be explained by his involvement not only in the utopian but in the apocalyptic tradition. (See note 16, below.)

That which we cannot hope for we cannot, ultimately, desire or want: desire evaporates, not because the object of desire is impractical but because to desire is to hope, even against hope, that the means of satisfaction lie to hand. Whether we might want to live in the City of the Sun or Christianopolis is irrelevant. Utopias are calm images of eternity, disconnected from the storm and stress of a world where desiring prevails. Only the uncoupling of utopia from desiring allows their fascinating aspects to emerge in their true and untroubled light.

Utopia as a police action

I suggest that the apocalyptic tradition is the context within which the rise of utopian thought can most usefully be seen. Utopias are not millenniums, and two contrasts serve to establish the distinction. The first is obvious enough: the transparency of utopia is linked to *spatial* considerations, while the intelligibility of apocalypse depends on a particular interpretation of historical *time*. Apocalypse is history's last, or second last, act: it retrospectively illumines the plot which has unfolded over previous millennia while at the same time deriving its own sense from the drama which it brings to a close. The conception of time implied by apocalypse is 'linear', although not in the sense of an indefinite quantitative extension because (a) time is characterised by 'closure' in the sense that the plot has a beginning and an end,[13] and (b) the time elapsing between these two points in not homogeneous but, rather, structured in terms of a continuously resumed project which can be viewed either as God's or man's. In utopia, time disappears and a *plan* of Christianopolis can provide intelligibility because – and this merely says the same thing in different ways – either nothing changes, or the author/reader occupies the standpoint of an eternal present or *nunc stans*. The question of time will be pursued further in my comments below.

The second, less obvious, difference between utopian and millenarian thought is that identified by J. C. Davis in his discussion of the relation of utopias to 'ideal society' literature taken as a whole (Davis, op. cit., ch 1). The *differentia specifica* of utopian societies is that they are characterised by rules, regulations and constraint. The scenario of apocalypse is regenerative and redemptive; in utopias, despite their otherworldly location, human nature undergoes no basic change. Just for this reason, rules and discipline are needful, and Rousseau's declaration that he will take 'men as they are and laws as they might be' may stand as an indication of the characteristic outlook of utopian thought. (This appears partially contradicted by Andreae's emphasis on religious conversion. But the atmosphere of Christianopolis remains heavily disciplinarian, and complete regeneration via religious conversion would run counter to Andreae's Lutheran cast of mind.) Millenarian thought, on the other hand, is only a step or two behind the anarchism of the Ranters: in the age of the Spirit, where 'everything that lives is holy', laws are superfluous since desire – as a divine creation – is *per se* good. 'He who desires but acts not, breeds pestilence' (Blake): the redemptive and antinomian dimensions of apocalyptic can always be summoned in defence of the Blakeian view.

Just these antinomian principles are what utopia excludes. Setting aside questions of influence and historical causation, one is tempted to say: they are what utopia is designed to exclude. If apocalyptic is the context for the rise of utopia, utopia might almost be described as a police-action against the radical challenge which – either tacitly or explicitly – apocalyptic contains.

Davis sees the early modern utopias as prefiguring 'the growth of the centralised, bureaucratic, sovereign state with its impersonal, institutional apparatus' and its 'assumption of obligation in every area of human life'; the utopian 'provides the imagery for the process which ... has dominated social evolution for the last four centuries and shows no sign of losing its dominance now' (op. cit. pp 8-9). The force of this point is to be distinguished from the banal and once fashionable view according to which 'we' (the 'liberals') are non-utopian whereas 'they' (the 'totalitarians') are. Precisely bourgeois-liberal society is heir to the utopian dream. The 'Platonism' of utopia – its articulation of social and physical space as a transparent map of knowledge – is of a piece with its, also Platonic, exclusion of civic participation and 'subjective freedom'. This Platonism finds its concrete social expression in the institutions of 'discipline' of which Foucault is the main indictor and the chief connoisseur. Every utopia is a 'panopticon' from the standpoint of the reader who gazes upon its map; a utopian text just is such a map – a map of knowledge/power – whether it is presented as a diagram or in words. The more or less Platonic fertility regulations favoured by utopians are the politics of life charted by Foucault in *The History of Sexuality*. Foucaultian individuation and 'normalisation' – the knowledge of the individual, not abstractly but in his or her particularity, by bureaucratic criteria – finds its paradigmatic example in the examination which the entrant to Andreae's Christianopolis undergoes. The entrant notices that, while addressing him, the second examiner 'was studying the calmness of my being, the modesty of my countenance, the closeness of my speech, the quiet of my eyes, my personal bearing, with such thoroughness that it seemed to me he should scrutinize my very thought, with such affability that I could conceal nothing from him, with such respect that I felt I owed everything to him'.[14]

Foucault's discussion of 'discipline' generalises Marx's analysis of work in *Capital*, and it is Marx who points up the irony that capitalist society, whose premise is the discipline of the multitude, presents itself as that social formation under which 'subjective freedom' comes into its own.[15]

This said, the contrast between utopia and apocalyptic should not be overdrawn. In the first place, utopia and apocalyptic may coexist within the output of a single writer. This is most strikingly so in the case of Campanella, who dissolves the crystalline fixity of the City of the Sun when he remarks that its inhabitants 'wait for the renewing of the age, and perchance for its end.'[16] Winstanley moves from apocalypse to the utopia of *The Law of Freedom* just as the Digger revolution meets with defeat. Joachim of Fiore, whose importance for the apocalyptic tradition has been noted, is also an inventor of utopia: the Joachite age of the spirit opens with St Benedict, whose Rule became 'the monastic code of Western Europe',[17] and the Twelfth Table of Joachim's *Figurae* presents, complete with plan, a description of an ideal monastery which Joachim describes as 'the arrangement of the new order (*novus ordo*) pertaining to the third state (the age of the spirit) after the model of the Heavenly Jerusalem' (McGinn op cit. p 142 and Plate VIII). The indebtedness of utopias to the image of monastic order is frequently noted,[18] and it is plain enough from St Benedict's *Rule* that monastic discipline was supposed to construct order within a community of individuals whose holiness and level of culture might always leave a good deal to be desired. As Davis stresses, utopia too is premised not on redemptive change but on a social order wherein individuals find it rational to behave in a virtuous way.

In the second place, the nature of utopia's police-action has to be understood. Utopia sets out, not to annul the millenarian impulse, but to redirect it (a) from anarchy towards order and (b) from the scenario of a this-worldly realisation towards the contemplation of a 'beyond' cut loose from all relation to historical time and place. The police-action proceeds by incorporation rather than by direct attack. And, for this reason, utopia remains 'transcendent' – which is not at all the same as other-worldly – with respect to the social arrangements which prevail in the here and now. Hence utopia can be a mode of revolutionary theorising, albeit a mode which (through its links with order and discipline) supplies grounds for disquiet and is always double-edged. In effect, the 'utopian socialists' attempt to turn the weapons of capitalism against capitalism itself. Only Fourier, their supreme genius, manages to construct a genuinely libertarian society by linking the utopian impulse with the impulse to play. Strikingly, it is Fourier who provides the point of reference when Morris sets out to demolish Bellamy's *Looking Backward* – the work which represents the nadir of utopian socialist thought.

The world turned upside down

Can the victory of utopia over apocalyptic be reversed? In an age where utopia is 'the one country at which Humanity is always landing' (Oscar Wilde), can we – returning to our starting point – hear what it is that Hegel has to say?

Marx sets out to reverse this victory in his heroic silence concerning communism, which he regards, proleptically, not as '*a state of affairs* which is to be established' but as 'the *real* movement which abolishes the present state of things'.[20] Marx's silence as to a communist 'state of affairs' is the sonorous and resonant theme which is sounded by every word of analysis and indictment which he writes. Marx's scrupulous discourse on the city of this world (capitalism) entails a silent, and therefore no less scrupulous, discourse on the city whose appearance is possible only after human 'prehistory' has reached its end. This silence is generally misunderstood as no more than a personal, and an evasive, quirk. In fact it clears the ground for a perspective on historical time which extends back to Hegel and beyond, and which – since to *describe* a condition of freedom would be to *constrain* and thereby contradict it – allows the libertarian aspect of apocalypticism to come into its own. Similarly, Marx's critique of utopian socialism is usually misunderstood as targeted only against the arbitrary and fanciful aspects of utopian thought. I suggest that his critique of utopia should be seen as a parallel to his attack on the Young Hegelians, who 'in spite of their allegedly "world-shattering" phrases' are in reality 'the staunchest conservatives': behind Stirner's Association of Egoists, for example, Marx discerns the outlines of the existing, bourgeois, *status quo*.[21] Utopia is objectionable not because society denies, but because all to easily it incorporates, the utopian dream.

Can we break the silence which Marx, for good reason, imposes upon himself? I suggest that we can do so only by taking up the issue of *time* which, as already suggested, demarcates utopian from apocalyptic thought. Here, only a few indications can be given to show what such a discussion of time might involve.

According to Lenin, Marx's *Capital* can be understood only by means of Hegel's *Logic*. I would suggest, similarly, that both Marx and Hegel can be understood only by means of a reading of Boethius's (c. 480-524) *Consolation of Philosophy*. Book Five of Boethius contains the account of 'eternity' which supplied philosophy with its signal point of reference for the subsequent thousand years: eternity is seen as the *nunc stans* or 'eternal present' within which all moments of history are laid out co-temporally before God's view. And it is over the status of 'eternity' that the battle between utopia and apocalypse must needs be joined.

Boethian eternity is the prototype for utopian thought. Utopian social and architectural designing fixes time as space: whoever looks at utopia's map sees not only what is, but what has been and will be, the case. Only spatial differentiation is admitted since society, being ideal, will continue forever in its present course. Utopia is eternity actualised at no-place on the surface of the earth.

For Boethius, the standpoint of eternity – the standpoint from which all time lies presently before us – is located outside of history in an other-worldly 'beyond'. The whole *line* of history is visible from eternity's *point* only on condition that this point does not lie on that line. The standpoint of eternity is atemporal, so that 'eternity' is precisely the opposite of 'immortality' if the latter is understood to mean indefinite continuation in and through time.[22]

Hegel, renewing the tradition of apocalyptic, *relocates* the Boethian eternity, transposing it from a point above and beyond the line of historical time to a point on that line: specifically, he situates it at or beyond that line's end. (The 'closure' of apocalyptic time has already been noted). There can be no doubt that *what* Hegel situates at the end of history is 'eternity' – in the *Phenomenology*, it is precisely Boethian eternity which he is concerned to gather out of religious thought[23] – nor that this is *where* he situates it; spirit, which can be comprehended only once history is complete, is that which 'is eternally present to itself and for which there is no past'.[24] 'Those moments which spirit appears to have outgrown still belong to it in the depths of its present'.[25] All moments of past history are thus co-present in the post-historical moment which follows history's end, just as all moments of historical time can be viewed simultaneously by Boethius's God. For Hegel, Boethius is the paradigmatic philosopher of the 'unhappy consciousness', ie, of the consciousness of a Christianity which yearns for changelessness and eternity beyond, and outwith, the flux and chaos of historical time.[26] The dramatic shape of Boethius's book confirms this view: the figure of Philosophy consoles Boethius, who languishes in prison, by reporting to him the character of an eternity which lies, unattainably, beyond the confines of time and space. For his part, Hegel construes Christianity's separation of the world of 'pure consciousness'; (the 'beyond' wherein lies eternity) from the world of 'actual consciousness' (or history) as arising from alienation which obtains in real social and historical life: the contradiction between 'pure' and 'actual' consciousness has its roots in a contradiction lying within 'actual' consciousness itself.[27] His own philosophy sets out to overcome the standpoint of the unhappy consciousness by transposing eternity from the 'beyond' of pure consciousness to the dimension of actual history. This transposition is possible only at the end of history, since only then are the alienations within 'actual' consciousness overcome.

Thus Hegel renews apocalypticism by reclaiming, for it, the standpoint of the eternal present which was central to utopia's design. This is the core of truth in Croce's remark that Hegelian philosophy 'resolves religion into itself and substitutes itself for it',[28] Here, our concern is with the implications of Hegel's transposition for utopia. And the central point is that the Hegelian *relocation* of eternity changes the significance and *structure* of eternity itself.

Boethius had intended his notion of eternal presence to reconcile God's 'universal foreknowledge' of events with human 'freedom of the will': a predestined future implies determinism, but 'the knowledge of present things imposes no necessity on what is happening'.[29] And yet, of course, this argument defeats itself because the fixity of all past and future events *as present* leaves no room for either God or man to accomplish anything other than what this eternal present already contains. As in utopia, so in eternity, all space is filled – only thus can its contents be known – in such a way as to admit of no gaps or lacunae through which a freely chosen, and hence novel, future might arrive.

Hegel's transposition of eternity from the 'beyond' of the unhappy consciousness to the immanent plane of history allows the claims of freedom to be made good. To see how this is so, we can reflect on the *difference* which distinguishes eternity, or post-history, from previous (ie historical) time. And we can reflect also on the *continuity* by which, on the Hegelian scheme, eternity and previous time are linked.

Eternity, or post-history, remains *distinct* from previous time since action *sub specie aeternitas* is no longer the deterministic outcome of past events. In post-history, there is no 'time', in the sense of an abstract and homogeneous progression leading from past to present to future, but only the 'time' or temporality of freely chosen actions and projects themselves. So to say, posthistorical individuals live not *in* time – as they did prior to history's end – but *as* time:[30] time exists only as the rhythm and the structure of what it is they choose to do. The past cannot determine the present since, now, the past exists only relative to the present occurrence of free choice. The past is solely the 'ground' which is constituted as such by the appearance of the 'figure' of freedom, and hence its deterministic spell is broken. In Hegel's succinct expression, 'there is no past'. The past lives on 'in the depths of the present' not in the sense that it determines this present, but in the sense that it is always some specific free and present action which, as its context or background, makes a particular interpretation of the past appear.

Eternity is also *continuous* with previous time insofar as it is situated within (or, rather, beyond the limits of) history's plane. Just for this reason, although the past is annulled, the openness of time towards the future remains in play. History is the domain of action and, more specifically, of action conditioned by its past; as continuous with history, eternity is no less a domain of action – but of action which the past no longer constrains. Action *in* time is past-determined, whereas action which *is* time knows nothing of a past which determines it but only of a future towards which it aims. The future remains in play since openness towards the future just is the structure of an action or project which intends the achievement of a not-yet-obtaining result. Accordingly, post-historical time (or secularised eternity) is time characterised solely by 'the primacy of the future'.[31] Under the sign of a future emancipated from the past, a present freedom is able finally to obtain.

Thus Hegel's apocalypticism redeems Boethius's defence of freedom. Utopia renders this defence impossible, since it builds precisely on the fixity – the crystalline order and perfection of an unchanging and unchangeable present – which denied success to the argument for freedom presented by Boethius himself. Hence nothing is to be gained by calling Hegel's 'new world' or Marx's communist society a utopia. Utopia is the contemplative dream of an unhappy consciousness which is no longer unhappy only because, with More, it has uncoupled its 'wishes' from any object of serious and practical 'hope'. Whoever lives in utopia lives *in* a time which, just because it is fixed *as space* and thus rendered entirely present, excludes even the minimal freedom that goes along with actual history. History allows for freedom insofar as *fortuna* makes continual incursions into all ordered and regularized social domains. According to Boccaccio, *fortuna* 'arranges and rearranges' human affairs 'after her own inscrutable fashion' and does so 'without following any discernible plan':[32] it is the dreadful accident of the plague which clears the free space in which his own storytelling takes place. The 'plan' of utopia forecloses on the freedom which disorder brings. Utopia's instantiation as disciplined capitalist society represents an attempt to harness the most powerful productive forces ever created to destroy the play of fortune once and for all. Capitalism has taken seriously, and acted upon, the prescription which in Machiavelli appears only as a dubious joke: 'because Fortune is a woman', avers Machiavelli, 'it is necessary, in order to keep her under, to batter and maul her'.[33] Hegelian post-historical freedom amounts to a reversal of this utopian enterprise. In post-historical eternity, the opportunity and freedom which were *fortuna*'s bright gifts come once again into their own. No longer, however, is *fortuna* a power over and against individuals. In a non-utopian eternity, her free play is that of the free because 'undeducible'[34] actions carried out by the human individuals themselves.

The gay science of Boccaccio's storytellers, with their ready intelligence and their sense of how precarious is the situation under which their free interaction unfolds, prefigures the 'new world' at which radical apocalypticism also aims. In such a world, utopian order is needless since individuals then '*recognize* themselves as mutually recognizing one another'.[35] Moreover, order is necessarily excluded since what is recognized is precisely each individual, in his or her freedom, rather than the role-definitions which (in history as opposed to post-history) each individual bears. For Hegel, mutual recognition, which prevails only after history has ended, brings with it the possibility of theory which can attain truth. Truth-claims – that of his own theory included – can be redeemed only where a free and mutually recognitive audience is to be found. So too for Rabelais: the wine consumed in the anti-monastic (and hence anti-utopian) Abbey of Thélème is the wine, not of pleasure solely, but of learning.

Two images – Bacon's perpetual motion machines and Campanella's 'only real phoenix' – stand as representative of utopian thought. Utopia just is such a machine with the regularity and order which the notion of perpetuity implies. This order fascinates us because we know that, whatever the scale of the productive forces harnessed to actualise it, no such order can ever finally be attained. In the last instance, utopia is not merely counterfactual but counterpossible as well: in this lies its challenge. Utopia escapes from the world of discipline which it itself conjures and which it helps to bring into effect. Campanella's phoenix arises from the ashes of order, and the flames which consume it consume, at the same time, the utopian dream whose immortality was to be thereby assured. Like Hegel's Owl of Minerva, Campanella's phoenix takes flight towards 'the renewing of the age' and, in doing so, casts the shadow of dusk upon the actual no less than the imaginary utopian world.

Notes

1. G. W. F. Hegel, *Phenomenology of Spirit* (Oxford 1977), pp 3, 7, 488; *Lectures on the Philosophy of World History: Introduction* (Cambridge, 1975), pp 40-2.

2. Bernard McGinn (ed), *Apocalyptic Spirituality* (SPCK 1979), pp 5, 14.

3. Luther, 'On the Bondage of the Will' in E. Gordon Rupp and Philip S. Watson (eds), *Luther and Erasmus: Free Will and Salvation* (The Westminster Press 1969), pp 331-2.

4. The 'Cokaygne' poem, dating from the 14th century, is given in A. L. Morton, *The English Utopia* (Lawrence and Wishart 1978), pp 279-85.

5. Tommaso Campanella, 'The City of the Sun' in Henry Morley (ed) *Ideal Commonwealths* (George Routledge and Sons 1885), p 223. Alternative translations of the 'phoenix' passage, drawn from different editions, can be found in Marie-Louise Berneri, *Journey through Utopia* (Freedom Press 1982), p 97, and in the recent translation of *The City of the Sun* by A. M. Elliott and R. Millner (Journeyman Press 1981), p 19. Do the Solarians possess a real phoenix, or a picture of a phoenix they know to be real? (On phoenixes, see Ovid's *Metamorphoses* Penguin Edn., p 345.)

6. Johann Valentin Andreae, *Christianopolis* ed F. Held (New York 1916), p 150. Fortunately this promise is not kept.

7. Ernst Bloch, *A Philosophy of the Future* (Herder and Herder 1970), pp 88, 95.

8. George Kateb (ed), *Utopia* (Atherton Press 1971), p 8.

9. Hannah Arendt, *The Human Condition* (University of Chicago Press 1958), chs IV and V. See also Judith Shklar's reference to Arendt in F. E. Manuel (ed) *Utopias and Utopian Thought* (Souvenir Press 1973), p 105.

10. 'The City of the Sun', Morley edn., p 218.

11. See F. E. Manuel and F. P. Manuel *Utopian Thought in the Western World* (Blackwell 1979) ch 5: S. Lang, 'The Ideal City: From Plato to Howard', *Architectural Review* Vol. 112 (1952); and Helen Rosenau *The Ideal City: Its Architectural Evolution in Europe* (Methuen 1983).

12. Cf J. C. Davis, *Utopia and the Ideal Society* (Cambridge 1981), pp 107-8.

13. J. L. Russell, 'Time in Christian Thought' in J. T. Fraser (ed), *The Voices of Time* (Allen Lane 1968), p 63. Russell's point concerning 'closure' applies to Christian thought *per se* rather than to apocalyptic thought specifically. Cf Mircea Eliade, *The Myth of the Eter-*

nal Return (Princeton 1971), p 143.

14. *Christianopolis* p 147

15. Marx, *Grundrisse* (Penguin Books 1973), pp 239-50; *Capital* Vol. I (Penguin Books 1976), pp 279-80.

16. The City of the Sun', p 261. For the apocalyptic theme in Campanella's theory and practice, see Manuel and Manuel, op. cit., ch. 10.

17. Justin McCann, Preface to *The Rule of St Benedict* (Sheed and Ward, 1976), p vii.

18. Eg Berneri, op. cit., p 55; Manuel and Manuel, op. cit., pp 18, 48-51; Davis, op. cit., pp 58-9, 72, 79-80, 371. Hence the signficance of the 'inverted' monasteries in the 'Cockaygne' poem and in the 'Abbey of Thélème' section of Rabelais' *Gargantua and Pantagruel* Book 1.

19. William Morris, *News from Nowhere* (Routledge and Kegan Paul 1970), p 55. For Morris's opposition to Bellamy, see Morton, op. cit., ch VI.

20. Marx/Engels, *Collected Works* Vol 5 (Lawrence and Wishart 1976), p 49.

21. Ibid, pp 30, 411. (Evidently, Stirner is an anarchist rather than a utopian. My suggestion is that Marx's critique of utopianism might be understood by analogy with his critique of Stirner).

22. Cf Arendt, op. cit., pp 17-21.

23. Hegel, *Phenomenology*, pp 414-5.

24. Hegel, *Lectures* p 24.

25. Ibid, p 151.

26. Cf the reference to 'consolation' to Hegel, *Encyclopaedia*, para 147. As usual, Hegel mentions no names but the allusion to Boethius is clear.

27. *Phenomenology*, p 295.

28. Benedetto Croce, *What is Living and What is Dead in the Philosophy of Hegel* (Macmillan 1915), p 71.

29. Boethius, *The Consolation of Philosophy* (Penguin Books 1969), pp 150, 156.

30. Cf *Phenomenology*, pp 27 ('time … is the existent concept itself'), 487.

31. Alexandre Kojève, *Introduction to the Reading of Hegel* (Basic Books 1969), p 134; cf Martin Heidegger, *Being and Time* (Blackwell 1967), p 378. Kojeve misunderstands p 487 of the *Phenomenology* and therefore concludes that the time which is 'annulled' at the end of history is the time *as* which, rather than *in* which, self-consciousness exists. This leads him (op. cit., pp 185ff) to the view that, following the Hegelian end of history, only time 'in which' – spatialised, homogenous time – and not time 'as which' exists: accordingly, the end of history means for Kojève an end to all human projects and hence the 're-animalisation' of man. Within the terms of the present argument: Kojève reads Hegel as a utopian, and sees the end of history as that utopia wherein all human desire meets with definitive satisfaction and nothing further remains to be done. Against Kojève, I wish to maintain that the whole point of Hegel is to challenge, through a renewal of apocalyptic, the hegemony of utopian thought.

32. Boccaccio, *The Decameron*, II, 3 (p 127 of the Penguin Books edn.).

33. *The Prince,* ch 25. Ch 15 contains Machiavelli's protest against utopian thought .

34. Kojève, op. cit., p 46.

35. *Phenomenology*, p 112.

Notes on a Poetry of Release

W. S. Graham

1

THE ORIGINAL DISEASES and cures of those fictional problems of Morality (involving Politics and our each illusion of a Liberty) live in each of us and express through how we lift a cup, walk, or blow the dandelion seeds into the air to tell the time. Let me be the poet writing in a disguise of the 1st person about the intricate marriage between those problems and the poem and the searching reader. Though those problems move me as a man to varied action I try to put them out (at least as a conscious direction) when I begin to make my poem. Those problems move me and work to successfully direct the outside accidents and me through accident. With words my material and immediate environment I am at once halfway the victim and halfway the successful traveller. There is the involuntary war between me and that environment flowing in on me from all sides and there is the poetic outcome. I am not the victim of my environment. History does not repeat itself. I am the bearer of that poetic outcome. History continually arrives as differently as our most recent minute on earth. The labourer going home in the dusk shouts his goodnight across the road and History has a new score on its track. The shape is changed a little. History as a crowd divides and divides into its population where I am a member and at last I am left to say my history has my eyes and mouth and a little likeness of my father. Time and time again I am scored by the others and their words and the diseases and cures war and change in their part of me. First I'll put them aside for my poem is to be a successful construction of words, a construction in which anyhow those cures will act whether the poem is about a pinhead or Lanarkshire.

The most difficult thing for me to remember is that a poem is made of words and not of the expanding heart, the overflowing soul, or the sensitive observer. A poem is made of words. It is words in a certain order, good or bad by the significance of its addition to life and not to be judged by any other value put upon it by imagining how or why or by what kind of man it was made. It is easy to strive to make a poem out of the wrong material like a table out of water. It is easy to mistake a poem for a different thing with a different function and to be sad when it does not put out what it is not. In the end then are those still words on the paper and arranged half-victim to the physical outside, half-victim to my Morality's origins, out of this dying and bearing language. All the poet's knowledge and experience (as far as the people who wait outside his gates are concerned) is contained in the language which is obstacle and vehicle at the same time. The shape of all of us is in this language. Our riches and poverties have affected every word. For the language is a changing creature continually being killed-off, added-to and changed like a river over its changing speakers. The language changes along with all of us and is headline litmus record wreckage pyramid shame and accomplishment of all we do and have done and (through Poetry) might do. Each word is touched by and filled with the activity of every speaker. Each word changes every time it is brought to life. Each single word uttered twice becomes a new word each time. You cannot twice bring the same word into sound.

It is a good direction to believe that this language which is so scored and impressed by the commotion of all us since its birth can be arranged to in its turn impress significantly for the good of each individual. Let us endure the sudden affection of the language.

2

I must first begin with first the illusion of an intention. The poem begins to form from the first intention. But the intention is already breaking into another. The first intention begins me but of course continually shatters itself and is replaced by the child of the new collision. I try to have the courage to let the last intention be now a dead step and to allow myself to be taken in hand. Yet I must not lose my responsibility, being that explorer who shoots the sun, carries samples of air back to civilisation, and looks his forward. The poem is more than the poet's intention. The poet does not write what he knows but what he does not know. A man's imagining suddenly may inherit the handclapping centuries of his one minute on earth. He has to explore the imagination by using the language as his pitch. On it he must construct (intuitively to an organic as true as a tree) an apparatus which will work and to a special purpose. It is no help to think of the purpose as being to 'transfuse recollected emotion' or to 'report significantly' or indeed to think of it as a putting-across of anything. The poem itself is dumb but has the power of release. Its purpose is that it can be used by the reader to find out something about himself. Words are ambiguous. He must face it that words are ambiguous, but realise that this has to do with the fundamental force of poetry and is to be used to a positive end. The poem is not a handing out of the same packet to everyone, as it is not a thrown-down heap of words for us to choose the bonniest. The poem is the replying chord to the reader. It is the reader's involuntary reply.

What is to be done? To bisect the angle between God and Man and find the earliest distance between heart and head. To join Man and Word and project his consciousness of the prophetic in the language into the world. To be the labourer carrying the bricks of his time and on the scaffolding of an unknown construction. To bring about the reader's Involuntary Belief. To present before him an addition to the world like this which Blake made where the reader is left not to agree or disagree as to its rightness but to answer from a new cave flooded to light,

> For every thing that lives is holy, life delights in life;
> Because the soul of sweet delight can never be defil'd.
> Fires inwrap the earthly globe, yet man is not consum'd;
> Amidst the lustful fires he walks: his feet become like brass,
> His knees and thighs like silver, & his breast and head like
>   gold.

I go my way. Then I find the muse laughing her fill in the Atholl Arms, fixing her face genteel not to be thought the whore she is. She's drunk and says, 'give us Kevin Barry,' but singing's stopped this long time, and the bar is thumped like a drum at the least hint of a note. Glasses go over and we are all at words. Shapes of language (right out of the gasp and gesture of speech) spill round our ears and I am at once the man of technique who books the phrases of drinking and affection so that later I might explore the mechanics of the memorableness and vitality. Down the page I've written, 'fairly his mile' 'anyhow here's Mary will tell you right,' 'have you lately heard tell,' and like the unrehearsed possibilities of a dream beginnings, endings, and those swift metaphors of the moment break into sound in the ear. An organic rhetoric is built up which charges and maintains the formal mechanics of poetry. The syntax holds a poem's infinite number of overtones which are magnified to a greater memorableness. A poem is charged to that power of release that even to one man it goes on speaking again and again beyond behind its speaking words, a space of continual messages behind the words like behind Joyce's words like this:

It's something fails us. First we feel. Then we fall. And let her
rain now if she likes. Gently or strongly as she likes. Anyway,
let her rain for my time is come. I done me best when I was let.
Thinking always if I go all goes. A hundred cares, a tithe of
troubles and is there one who understands me? One in a
thousand of years of the nights?

I try to remember those adventures along those lines of words.
Though do I move along words in a poem when, after all, as I am at
the last word and look back I find the first word changed and a new
word there, for it is part of the whole poem and its particular life
depends on the rest of the poem. The meaning of a word in a poem
is never more than its position. The meaning of a poem is itself, not
less a comma. But then to each man it comes into new life. It is
brought to life by the reader and takes part in the reader's change.
Even the poet as a man who searches continually is a new searcher
with his direction changing at every step.

> For ever as the seeker turns
> His worshipping eyes on prophetic patterns
> Of shape arising from all men
> He changes through, he shall remain
> Continually stripped and clothed again.

Let the poem be a still thing, a mountain constructed, an addition
to the world. It will have its own special function and purpose, to be
that certain mountain. And there is the reader going on to it with his
never-before exploration after his perfect hunger's daily changing
bread. A poem is a mountain made out of the containing, almost
physical language, and with the power to release a man into his own
completely responsible world larger than that outward solid geography.

> Man setteth an end to darkness,
> And searcheth out to the furthest bound
> The stones of thick darkness and of the shadow of death.
> He breaketh open a shaft away from where men sojourn:
> They are forgotten of the foot that passeth by:
> They hang afar from men, they swing to and fro.
>   (The Book of Job)

It is a good direction to believe that this language which is so
scored and impressed by the commotion of all of us since its birth
can be arranged to in its turn impress significantly for the benefit of
each individual. Let us endure the sudden affection of the language.

This was written for Poetry Scotland forty years ago. If you've never read his work, go and get his Collected Poems *from the library or a bookshop. Later this year [1986] we will be devoting a section of the Review to reminiscences of Graham and critical appreciations of his work. Would anyone interested in contributing a piece please contact us as soon as possible.* *

---

* This notice led to a major feature on W.S. Graham's work in issue 75, published in 1987.

New Glasgow painting in context*

Ken Currie

IN THE LAST EIGHTEEN MONTHS or so there has been an unprecedented amount of attention given to the City of Glasgow. This has occurred primarily through the District Council's promotional campaigns and its work in revitalising areas of the city suffering years of neglect and deterioration. Remarkable changes are taking place – from the stone-cleaning of almost all Glasgow's remaining tenements, to the opening of the new Scottish Exhibition and Conference Centre at the once thriving Queens Dock. After six grinding years of Thatcherism; although not in itself immune from the effects, Glasgow is a city buoyant with confidence and optimism. These changes are not only physical, and less happily economical, but cultural as well.

There has also been a large amount of attention focused on the visual arts in Glasgow which, in sharing this same pervading sense of confidence and optimism, have seen the emergence of a number of young artists currently achieving remarkable success at home and abroad. The main protagonists in this 'success story' so far have been Adrian Wiszniewski and Steven Campbell, who have now safely embarked on international careers, and enjoying all that goes with them. The recent *New Image Glasgow* exhibition (which included some of my own work) made a huge impact in both Glasgow and London, receiving a great deal of criticism both hostile and favourable, but never indifferent. As one of the artists resentful of being lumped in with this 'New Glasgow School' I feel that the whole phenomenon has to be put in perspective. To do this we must look at the context out of which the 'New Glasgow School' emerged, as a way of gauging its significance.

Scottish Art, particularly in the West, is noted for two main characteristics – a boldness of colour and paint handling and a subject matter deriving primarily from landscape. This tradition can be

* First published 1986

traced back to the French, and in particular, Fauvist, influence on Scottish painting, exemplified by the work of such artists as J. D. Fergusson and Peploe. It was a tradition rigorously maintained for decades by the Painting Department of Glasgow School of Art, resulting in the weakness of much Scottish Painting when compared to, say, art in Germany over the same period. It is an immensely flawed tradition in that it seems unable to deal with more challenging subject matter or explore ideas, in the philosophical or literary sense. It therefore has a kind of built-in obsolescence – a numbing vacuity in the face of the reality of Scotland both today and in the past.

There has been a continuing crisis of subject-matter in Scottish Painting born out of, amongst other things, an intellectual and cultural parochialism – a kind of insular, northern ignorance which many influential Scottish painters, in their arrogance, saw as strength, not weakness. In actively pursuing this, many painters remained unconcerned with a lot of European painting. More importantly, through a sort of infuriating anti-intellectualism, they ignored a great deal of modern European thought, vital to the work of their contemporaries on the Continent. All this, however, is really giving them the benefit of the doubt – the real problem is the sheer amateurism of much of Scottish Painting, coupled with feeble ambition and a raging paranoia about being influenced by political, philosophic or literary ideas.

In Glasgow, this has manifested itself in a continuing and historic failure of painters to face up to the reality of their native city. It is a city with many qualities worthy of serious consideration by artists, but consistently ignored – a working-class city with a proud record of struggle; a breathtakingly visual city; a city with a deep and often moving history; a heroic and pioneering industrial city world famous for shipbuilding and engineering with a workforce unique in Britain for resilience, warmth, humour and commitment. A city also of unemployment, of bleak peripheral housing schemes and derelict factories, of drug abuse and alcoholism. Where this kind of subject matter has emerged in painting, as in the work of Joan Eardley, it has always been tainted with a sort of liberal sentimentality, showing the 'character' of the slums, the 'quaintness' of poverty and at the same time neutralising the potential impact of bringing these images onto canvas. The tendency for Glasgow artists to be predominantly middle-class may account for their lack of sympathy with this kind of subject-matter, reacting against the sheer drabness of Glasgow by painting colourful, but resolutely boring, landscapes 'tending toward abstraction'. In this sense the work of many Scottish painters is pitiful in comparison with our writers, poets, dramatists, theatre groups, film-makers and musicians who, in recent years, have made an outstanding contribution to the emergence of an indigenous and committed national culture.

Aside from these comparatively lofty problems there is also the crucial problem of being an artist in Glasgow – of solely supporting oneself on the sale of work. Historically, teaching was always the safety net, something to 'fall back' on. Over the years this has amounted to part-time artists producing part-time art and the often merciless wearing down of many artists' talent. Coupled with this is the dearth of exhibition space in Glasgow and the accompanying array of dealers to handle the sale of work and run the galleries. The problem is that there is no real demand for art in Scotland; it has never really been seen as a viable investment for Scotland's wealthy, perhaps because of a kind of residual anti-culturalism left by Scottish Calvinism on the conscience of the rich. There is no 'art world' on the scale of say, New York, London or Dusseldorf, with a rapid and dynamic flow of art and money (although we all despise how capitalism has enmeshed art with money, it boils down to simple economics; paint and sell or starve – principles will never pay the rent and this is called pragmatism, not an excuse).

There is another, more subtle, obstacle for artists working in Glasgow. That is the popular mistrust of art as a career. Many people, who do significantly more important things than painting for a living, see artists as bohemian, as drop-outs and outsiders living on the fringes of society and solely self-interested. Although this in many ways is not far from the truth, it is a fact that art is not given the same respect as a profession as in, say, New York, Germany or France, particularly if you come from a working-class background. It is the heritage of *workerism* in Glasgow that has constantly marginalised writers and artists.

This crisis of subject-matter, the stifling burdens of an outmoded tradition, the intellectual and artistic parochialism coupled with the difficulties of pursuing a professional career in painting all constitute a mountain of a problem that each Scottish artist had to climb before even putting brush to canvas. It is in this context that the emergence of a new dynamic in Glasgow Painting must be seen.

The late seventies and early eighties saw the emergence in Glasgow of a number of different artists who wanted, in varying degrees of awareness, to tackle these problems head on. All were united in condemnation of the traditions of Scottish art as well as in a kind of burning ambition to achieve something new. They were also united in a predilection for figurative imagery as a reaction against the semi-abstract painting that flourished in Glasgow School of Art for years. They differed in the nature of that figurative imagery and its aims, ranging from the poetic to the political. They had no common programme, rarely exchanged ideas, at times were diametrically opposed in terms of subject matter and content and were fuelled by a passionate, often violent, rivalry. On the one side were those, like Campbell and Wiszniewski, who latched onto the more international dimension of the trend toward figuration. Their work appeared unique in that it linked this international influence with enough indigenous elements to appeal to an ever-hungry art market. They seized, not without a hint of opportunism, on the avenues now opened up as a result of the world attention given to figurative painting.

This international focus on figuration also opened up opportunities for a loose grouping, who were concerned in dealing with social and political issues in their work, facing up to some of the realities of modern Glasgow. This more committed and hard-hitting kind of painting which won few friends in the establishment, manifested itself in a number of different ways. For example, in the work of Pete Howson, whose concern was to explore Glasgow low-life, taking us on a nightmarish but utterly plausible journey through a world of gangs, street fights, seedy pubs, strippers and boxers. He shows us the victims of capitalism in despairing but vital images. In contrast, other committed artists saw the need to apply a socialist analysis to the problems confronted by Howson. For example, Central Designs, formerly COG, abandoned gallery-based art in favour of working directly with the labour movement, offering their skills as designers in the production of visual material such as banners, posters and exhibitions.

All of them, however, have radically altered the contemporary face of the visual arts in Glasgow. We are now in a situation where Glasgow artists are achieving success not seen for decades and have been described as '... the most dynamic and coherent group of painters working in Britain today.' The repercussions of these developments will go towards solving – at least partially – some of the problems outlined above. The possibility now exists, as John Maclean said way back in 1919, to 'make Glasgow a revolutionary centre second to none.' The road is now clear for the emergence of Glasgow as a major European centre for art by the end of this century.

On the surface I find little to complain about in these developments and intend to avoid knee-jerk reactions which cynically condemn it all with a sort of holier-than-thou purity – the curse of the dogmatic left. To condemn or dismiss things out of hand without proper analysis is not, I believe, in the spirit of Marxism. Everyone must at least broadly agree that the situation we have now is a vast improvement on what we had before. Yet there are dangers, particularly that these developments are not followed through, backed-up and reinforced. Glasgow could simply be 'flavour of the month' – something new for bored journalists and art critics to write about. There is also the disturbing fact that many reputations are perilously staked on the success of particular artists and we must ask how much of this phenomenon is the result of hype. Aside from this there is the acute danger that many art students and established artists, eager to emulate the commercial success of the likes of Campbell and Wiszniewski, may, at the expense of artistic quality and integrity, jump on the bandwagon. The opportunitism of inferior no-hope artists could ruin the whole thing and there's not much that can be done to stop it.

Yet there are now new opportunities to put into effect a number of ideas formulated by Left artists in the city, who are now in a position to work out a set of demands about how things should develop. Unlike London, where art is bogged down in an incestuous world of galleries, dealers, critics and their pals, we want to see the democratization of art in Glasgow with resources directed not only to the development of better facilities for art and artists but also to arts projects based in local communities. There, the visual arts could be thoroughly demystified, popularised and socialised, giving artists the chance to fulfil a useful social function within the city. Opportunities also exist for the involvement of the labour movement in these initiatives, not unlike their involvement with Glasgow's Mayfest, supporting or sponsoring artists in return for their services.

Painters today have a crucial responsibility to contribute to the revitalisation of Scottish culture in the same way that our writers, poets, dramatists, etc. are doing. The problems of an emerging, challenging indigenous Scottish culture are well-known as we struggle against the many forms of cultural imperialism that have stunted its growth. This is not simply cultural nationalism, but a desire to assert the hegemony of an authentic culture against the damaging and divisive dominant representations of Scotland. It will be a culture inseparable from politics and ideas – a culture of ideas – a popular and ultimately political culture. Painters must be at the heart of this struggle. The prospects are exciting, but also hugely challenging.

Polemics:
Glasgow Painting Now*

Malcolm Dickson

'There is no doubt that this art is a sign. For me it is a sign of
disaster, for Bonito Oliva it is a sign of hope.'
Giulio Carlo Argan in *Trans Avantgarde International*

THE 'PHENOMENON' OF NEW PAINTING in Scotland has
been represented and monopolised by a group of six men who
exhibited together in a show calling itself *New Image Glasgow,* and
initiated, selected and written about by Alexander Moffat. These
painters (Stephen Barclay, Steven Campbell, Ken Currie, Pete
Howson, Mario Rossi and Adrian Wiszniewski) trained at Glasgow
School of Art, where Moffat is a tutor, and all of them arrived at
their present mode of expression – some more independently than
others – by assimilating an internationally approved style which has
been interpreted as operating in a specifically Scottish context. The
'momentum' running through Scottish painting according to those
establishment figures who appeared with Richard Cork in *Scottish
Canvas* during Radio Three's 'Scottish Season' in 1984. This style
of a robust dynamic characterised by an extravagant use of colour
and an excessive use of paint has been clarified, or brought to a
head with the new impetus currently spreading like wildfire through
the art schools and garrets of Scotland.

'New Image' as a category for an identifiable group of artists
working within the same moment of time and making a commercial
impact outside their native city is a novel situation, though as a
'coherent group', their forms of representation, their models, the
references and associations of their art are of the past. Richard
Chapman, who was exhibitions organiser at the Third Eye Centre
where *New Image Glasgow* was first shown before going on tour,
identified this succinctly in the introduction to the show's catalogue, the unifying characteristics being:

* First published 1986

... adoption of a manner of delineating the figure and applying paint that can be traced quite specifically to moments in the history of art ...

These artists seem to have aligned themselves with modes of expression which are already known to give a ready made context of their work ...

Works that draw upon the resources of familiar styles and genres have a certain outmoded quality, a nostalgia for times beyond the personal experiences of these young men ...

In the same catalogue Sandy Moffat, impresario and patriarch of *New Image Glasgow,* displays a certain amount of wit and nerve by asking the rhetorical question 'Why should such a concentration of vital young painters suddenly burst forth in Glasgow, a city where for the past quarter of a century the visual arts have appeared backward looking and parochial?' Moffat has, for a certain number of years, been a crusader for the return of History Painting. His studio in the art school was for a long time, and still is, distinctive from all the others in playing host to figurative painters who were eager to combine political, philosophical, historical and religious themes in their art. *The British Art Show,* in which Campbell and Wiszniewski were represented and of which Moffat was co-selector, gave platform to the call for a return of figurative painting on a grand scale. Seeing Bellany, Kitaj, Burra, Spencer and Bacon (amongst others) as representing narrative figuration's post-war battle with abstraction, Moffat saw in these 'New Image' artists a vague lineage and something that represented a victory for dynamic figuration. The moral and aesthetic, according to the lip motions of the Academy, have been blended. Where do we go from here? 'New Image' rediscovers the use of the figure in humanist and literary themes and its potential marketability. Without exception, writers of this new 'phenomenon' have looked through their tinted prisms and seen that this heralds a new day for Scottish art. It offers a lot of challenge to the drab monotony of Scottish painting: bold, distinctive approaches to the figure, great skill in the execution of colour and marks, its embrace of Romantic and grandiose themes. 'New Image' presents the opportunity of catching up with the fashions in contemporary art whilst missing out completely late-modernist tendencies such as performance. It also offers international prestige, the artist as Romantic hero, accumulation of wealth, social and cultural power and a reassertion of the Marketplace.

Ken Currie, a constant thorn in the side of the art school establishment whilst a student, was justified in pointing out the conservatism and opportunism of previous painters in Scotland. Reviewing (in Stigma 2, Glasgow School of Art, 1983) the appalling *Contemporary Art From Scotland* shown at the Kelvingrove Museum a few years ago, he had this to say:

> ... many of these artists in this exhibition seem to have an overt and blatant concern with money and, inevitably, status. They have dramatically reduced the scope and vision of their art in order that it may become a saleable commodity, a potential piece of private property and a casual investment for Scotland's doomed and essentially philistine bourgeoisie

He then goes on to condemn the price of these works, none of them selling for less than £500, which 'would take a welder from Govan shipbuilders one month and more to save up and buy the cheapest of these paintings. Who said they were for the people anyway; are they not simply for a wealthy elite in our society?' Currie's arguments still stand though this time against himself. The ghost of his former self has come back to haunt him. At the 'New Image' show, four of his works were sold, three to private collectors and one to the Scottish Arts Council. The prices ranged from about £350 to £450. As I write, he may be clinching a new sale from his April/May 1986 show in Bristol's Arnolfini. His previous intransigence and hard-line stance was vulnerable and has subsequently been dropped, which probably does not conflict with his role as a devoted disciple of the Party, unable to believe that a socialist consciousness can develop without the aid of a party. Every man has his price. Currie's concessions to the ruling order and his apologetics confirm this. It has been pointed out that 'New Image' also represents a class shift; from middle to working-class backgrounds. This seems only worth mentioning to stress that the ruling class are always willing to accept a few initiates and that, basically, the working class can be talented. Currie is the only artist who brings to bear a wealth of images from working-class history and its implications for socialism. He represents his socialism by a cold mechanical world of depersonalised proletarians, in harmony with industry: all cloth-capped and stupidly expressionless. Currie's paintings and drawings are moving, however, flickering images of the dead class struggle in the darkness of Modernity. Because his work represents a class position, it is unlikely that his work would have been accommodated and bought a year ago at the height of the miners' struggle. As that represented, perhaps, something that is now fading, Currie's work is more consumable and the man himself is no longer a threat. The 'use-value' of his work has been neutralised. In 1983, as a critic of art-as-commodity, he had this to say in *Stigma 3*:

most works of art have to become pieces of private property, the fact that they can be bought and owned as commodities. This is because capitalism seeks to reduce everything in society to its material value alone, including art.... Capitalism demands a commercial art that does not challenge the existing order.

This was one reason for the creation of the term 'Community Art', a tactical move by the establishment to siphon off radical art and to divert the working-class intelligentsia from causing trouble in the realms of high art. As a community art activist, Currie wants his bread buttered on both sides. In *ER 72* the viewpoint on New Scottish Painting was represented by Ken Currie and Sandy Moffat (nothing to do with monopoly but lack of other decent contributions after an open invitation by poster). Here Currie's apology for his complete turnaround in principle verges on the pathetic:

There is no 'art world' on the scale of, say, New York, London or Dusseldorf, with a rapid and dynamic flow of art and money (although we all despise how capitalism has enmeshed art with money, it boils down to simple economics; paint and sell or starve – principles don't pay the rent and this is called pragmatism, not an excuse).

Despite what Currie says, this is an excuse, and his self-appointed position on other people's judgements verges on the offensive (my italics):

we all despise how, ... everyone *must* broadly agree that the situation we have now is a vast improvement on what we had before.

It wouldn't have taken much to improve the situation. Double standards misproportion of facts leads to exaggeration which would be hysterical if we hadn't heard it one hundred times before:

The possibility now exists, as John MacLean said way back in 1919, to make Glasgow a revolutionary centre second to none.

Seen from afar the situation may look lively, but seen from the inside it seems that if enough people believe the city is 'buoyant with confidence and optimism' then it must be true. The criticism of Currie is endless; he talked of the dearth of exhibition space in Glasgow without mentioning the artist-run Transmission, the only gallery in the city that puts art before self-interest and that doesn't ask you to be a potential money-spinner to get a show. Ken Currie requested to have his membership frozen from that same gallery one and a half years ago (in effect he resigned) with the reason that his art operates outside and rejects the gallery system, though his verbal reasons were that the committee of that gallery were 'bourgeois' which had more to do with his inability to collaborate with other artists on *an equal basis* in a broad-based creative venture. Currie, 'the most politically committed of the new painters', exposes his newfound privilege in his very defence of it:

> Many artists ... eager to emulate the commercial success of the likes of Campbell and Wiszniewski, may, at the expense of artistic quality and integrity, jump on the bandwagon. The opportunism of inferior, no-hope artists could ruin the whole thing....

That there is a bandwagon at all to jump onto suggests the inauthentic nature of a fashion, and his offensive remark about inferior no-hope artists whatever they may be, confirms this Marxist's role in the division of labour and the new class power this cadre now commands. There is more to being a political artist than painting pictures of the masses being oppressed or being liberated. For Currie, politics is a 9 to 5 job which is about as radical as wearing white socks and Doc Marten shoes. (See the interview with him in the 11th January 1986 issue of *7 Days,* where Graham Ogilvy claimed that Currie was 'working class right down to his white socks and Doc Marten shoes' (no irony intended). This is a testament to the poverty of moribund politicos.

That economic forces determine the form, content and direction of art has been completely overlooked by those critics praising *New Image Glasgow*. The market's demand for 'easel painting' corresponds with the shift to the Right in the social fabric of our times, to safe and unoffensive options. Creating a few stars in the art world is not threatened by the Conservative government's philistine attacks on Fine Art and at the same time these success stories validate capitalist self-interest. The distribution of privilege to a few does not further the interests of the majority of artists in broadening the creative space (mental and physical) or in developing financial opportunity for the realisation of artistic projects. The continued emphasis on the fame and art of a few does not invite a better understanding and appreciation of art, or help to dispel the stigma in the minds of a non-art public towards fine art. The qualification of the New Image painters has come from their economic success (Campbell in New York, Rossi in London), their potential economic success by emulation (Barclay) and by their recuperation by success (Howson and in particular Currie), the latter while criticising capitalism's control of art, benefiting from the commercial interest in narrative figuration. The flagging market, hungover from Minimalist and Conceptualist tendencies in the seventies, has been bolstered by increased investment value, increased velocity in the exchange of art commodities. The publicity that has followed the 'New Image' painters has given these artists an enormous amount of promotion, which could have easily gone to any one of a number of artists in Glasgow (though this is not the case with Campbell, 'New Image' would not have been possible without him). The demand has gone up, prices increase, the artist is in a position he can maintain for as long as he has the panache to move with the whims of the moment. During an interview in the Mayfest issue of *Artwork,* Alasdair Gray said, 'Resentment is a great waste of energy'. However, any artist in the city cannot be blamed for feeling envious and bitter at this spectacle. By denying that these painters are a group, and then categorising them under the title *New Image Glasgow,* they become a group. In the editorial to *ER 72,* Peter Kravitz mentions that one of the benefits of *New Image Glasgow* was that students are unwilling to vacate their studios when the art school closes in the evening. I suspect that this is more to do with a massive surge of careerism than with a generative cultural atmosphere.

The trouble with success is that the work in question encourages copying, it becomes a formula for success. Fuelled and envious of the commercial success of Campbell, students are falling over themselves to be big, novel, brash, banal and meaningless. Devotion engenders authority.

Calum MacIntyre reviewing Campbell's Fruitmarket show in *Variant*
(no. 2 1985)

The talk surrounding 'New Image' takes something in the guise of the political; Moffat talks of the 'revolutionary potential'* in Glasgow of this art, though political struggle and social change is not what he is referring to. No polemical stance has accompanied the exhibition, no historical or political critique, which is precarious in a city where no magazine or forum for discussion of ideas exist. What critical discussion the appearance of the new art magazine *Alba* (edited by Peter Hill and financially backed by the SAC) will invite remains to be seen. The first issue is due out soon. The Scottish Art world is still controlled by a close-knit group of people, Arts Council officials, art school teachers, one or two critics, a couple of gallery owners or directors and a few businessmen with an eye for the aesthetic. Criticism and open discussion are important if the situation of false consciousness and fake dialogue is to be avoided.

The growth and development of any art form not only depends on the quality of its practitioners, but also on the quality and range of those who write and comment on it .... Too often public opinion is shaped by misinformed and disinterested writing on art and artists....

From *Circa* Belfast, Nov./Dec. 1985, No. 25)

Whether the situation in Scotland is relevant to the broader international arena remains to be seen. That structures remain unchanged, that things are still controlled by the same people, that the situation is all the more competitive, leads me to be sceptical. The artistic/political subculture, the development of cross-community contacts has yet to be discussed in its implications. In time-honoured tradition artists are once again turning their backs on the world. The flatulence of *New Image Glasgow* leads me to conclude that what we are witnessing is less the new day for Scottish art than a false dawn in which expectations will perish with the dew.

* From *The Visual Arts in Glasgow* (Arts Review/Third Eye Centre, Glasgow, 1985.)

Alex La Guma (1925-1985)

James Kelman

(Said Chinaboy):

> 'I'd like to sit down in a smart caffy one day and eat my way right out of a load of turkey, roast potatoes, beet-salad and angel's food trifle. With port and cigars at the end.'
>
> 'Hell,' said Whitey, 'it's all a matter of taste. Some people like chicken and others eat sheep's head and beans.'
>
> 'A matter of taste,' Chinaboy scowled. 'Bull, it's a matter of money, pal. I worked six months in that caffy and I never heard anybody order sheep's head and beans!'
>
> 'You heard of the fellow who went into one of these big caffies?' Whitey asked, whirling the last of this coffee around in the tin cup. 'He sits down at a table and takes out a packet of sandwiches and puts it down. Then he calls the waiter and orders a glass of water. When the waiter brings the water, this fellow says: "Why ain't the band playing?"'
>
> We chuckled over that and Chinaboy almost choked. He coughed and spluttered a little and then said, 'Another John goes into a caffy and orders sausage and mash. When the waiter brings him the stuff he takes a look and say: "My dear man, you've brought me a cracked plate." "Hell," says the waiter. "That's no crack. That's the sausage".'
>
> After we have a laugh over that one Chinaboy looked westward at the sky. The sun was almost down and the clouds hung like bloodstained rags along the horizon. There was a breeze stirring the wattle and portjackson, and far beyond the railway line, a dog barked with high yapping sounds.

– an extract from a short story by Alex La Guma, a South African writer who died of a heart attack in October last year; he was sixty years of age and living in Havana, the ANC's representative in Cuba. I first came upon his work a few years ago, the early collection entitled *A Walk in the Night.*[1] One story in particular really stuck with me, *A Matter of Taste,* from which the above is taken. It is a marvellous bit of writing, telling of three men who meet over a pot of coffee in the middle of nowhere. They have a meandering conversation centred on food, then the two help the third hop a freight train heading for Cape Town where lies the possibility of working a passage to the USA. In the racial parlance of white South African authority the two are coloured and the third is white. La Guma himself was coloured. If the reader forgets such distinctions it won't be for long for it is always there, the backdrop to his work, inextricably bound in with the culture he worked from within. Even in that brief extract above the divisions are evident, where Whitey sees choice and Chinaboy knows differently.

The title story of the collection is a novella, *A Walk in the Night*, a very fine piece of writing which I did not appreciate at the first time of reading. There was something missing for me which I see now as structural. In *A Matter of Taste* that element existed and in consequence my appreciation of the story was much more immediate. *A Walk in the Night* is a bleak tale, set in the coloured District 6 which used to be one of the worst slums in Cape Town until it was done away with altogether, to create space for white development. A young man by the name of Michael Adonis gets the sack after a verbal disagreement with a white man. For the rest of the evening he wanders about in a semi-daze, going for a meal, periodically meeting with acquaintances, would-be gangsters. Eventually, in a moment of stupidity he vents his anger on an elderly white Irish alcoholic who lives in the same rooming house. The old man dies. Then the white policemen arrive and one of Michael's acquaintances winds up being mistaken for him, the killer. It is a memorable story, just like the others in the collection. The structural element I spoke of as missing for me in my initial reading is to do with empathy; I found it very difficult to be with Michael Adonis, the world he moved in, it was alien to me. It was less alien on the second reading. The last time I read it I knew the world he moved in even better.

Speaking purely as a writer it is good to feel anything and everything is possible in experiential terms. The existence of apartheid makes such a thing less easy to assume. In a good interview by Ian Fullerton and Glen Murray[2] the South African writer Nadine Gordimer – who regards La Guma as 'the most talented black (sic) novelist since Peter Abrahams'[3] – believes it is not possible for a white writer in South Africa to write from within 'particular areas of black experience' and because of this

> cannot create black characters. The same thing applies the other way about. But there is that vast area of our lives where

> we have so many areas of life where we know each other only
> too well, and there I see no reason why a black writer can't
> create a white character or a white a black.

There is a fine point being attempted here although at first sight it might appear contradictory. In fact she doesn't quite bring it off and a question later she backs away, saying there 'is something beyond the imaginative leap'. It has to be remembered that Gordimer was replying in an interview and to the best of my knowledge did not have the benefit of being able to work out her comments on the page. I think though that if she had, to risk being presumptuous, she may have brought in the use of basic structural techniques like the first and third party narratives, and developed her argument from there. In a straightforward manner, third party narrative allows the writer to create characters from the outside where 'skins rub against each other', but allows the writer to draw back from certain areas of experience, the sort which are to the fore psychologically and seem to demand the creation of character from the inside, commonly wrought by the writer in first party narrative, although other methods are always possible.

Alex La Guma has written at least four novels; they are available in Heinemann's African Writers Series, a good series but difficult to get a hold of and at the time of writing not a solitary thing by La Guma is available in Europe's largest public library, Glasgow's Mitchell. I managed to read two of the novels; on that basis I have to agree with Lewis Nkosi, that La Guma is only 'a competent novelist who after the flashing promise of that first collection of stories seems to have settled for nothing more than honourable, if dull proficiency'.[5] *The Stone Country* is an extended and developed version of the short story *Tattoo Marks and Ials;* it is written in the third party and is based on the writer's direct experience of prison. There are many good things about the novel and too there are its defects, including a bit of a rushed, fairly predictable ending. But Yusef the Turk is a fine character and the Casbah Kid also, though occasionally La Guma glamourises a little too much. And the converse of that is the deadened Butcherboy, a creation that only manages to get beyond the stereotype of hulking bully. The central character is George Adams, in prison for belonging to an illegal organisation which in the case of La Guma could simply have been the Communist Party since it has been banned for some forty years in that country. The novel is certainly 'competent' and La Guma's dialogue and working of the relationships between the prisoners often rises to the standard of the early stories. He uses the 3rd party narrative in a restricted fashion, only rarely attempting to get within characters other than George Adams; thus we are seeing how folk act rather than how they think – which lies at the root of Gordimer's point as far as I understand it. This also provides a structural base for the reader unfamiliar with prison life in South Africa. I mean that to some slight extent we can be with George Adams in his dealings with an environment alien to him.

As far as I am aware La Guma's last published novel is *Time of the Butcherbird* which appeared in 1979; this ended a silent period of seven years. According to the publisher's blurb the author gives 'a rounded picture of all the people in a small community inexorably moving towards tragedy'. I think this is what La Guma intended but I also think he fails and that he fails in a predictable way. He uses the third party narrative voice but does not restrict it. Instead he sets out to give the psychological workings of assorted individuals, both blacks and whites, and falls into the trap of stereotyping; the poor white woman, Maisie Stopes, and the militant black woman, Mma-Tau, are both obvious examples of it, the former being a sleazy semi-slut while Mma-Tau, is a vast 'Mother Earth'. It has to be said that the writing is hurried, often clumsy, and requires a straightforward editing. The person for that would have been La Guma himself. Failing that, maybe someone at the publisher's office could have attempted it. I'm not sure what the Heinemann policy is. The African Writers Series is good but generally speaking the productions themselves are inferior, the actual paper cheap, the proofing not of the best – and did La Guma censor himself in *The Stone Country* or was it done by another hand?

La Guma's great skill lay in his dealing with day-to-day existence, his precise and 'concrete observation which is the correct starting point for all materialists'.[6] The highpoint in *Time of the Butcherbird* is the introduction of Shilling Murile from the time that he is 'sitting in the ditch' straight through until the end of the period he is with the shepherd Madonele, some 4,000 words later, as they move off together 'through the crumbling dunes, smelling the smoke'. It is a brilliant piece of writing. It shows the true mark of the artist. Perhaps it also shows why La Guma could have felt capable of trying a novel like this. It was a risk and he failed. In that short story *A Matter of Taste* the risk was an easy sentimentality but he succeeded. The best artists always take risks.

Realism is the term used to describe the 'detailing of day-to-day existence' and most writers who advocate social change are realists. Incidentally, one of the areas of exclusion under the South African Censorship Act is the 'advocation of social change'[7] and, of course, La Guma's writing has always been banned there. There is nothing more crucial, and potentially subversive, than gaining a full understanding of how the lives of ordinary people are lived from moment to moment.

Ordinary people. In the African Horn the children of ordinary people are eating insects. It is a fact of existence so alien to other ordinary people that it cannot be admitted; there is an element lacking, a sort of structural base that does not allow us to be with people for whom starvation is death and not simply a concept. To face such a fact in literary terms seems to me to be, by definition, only possible via the work of a writer prepared to encounter the minutiae of day-to-day existence. And as far as I can see, any formal advances in prose have occurred directly because of that conflict; formal advances and 'imaginative leaps' may not be the same thing but at the very least they are inextricably linked.

As long as art exists there are no areas of experience that have to remain inaccessible. In my opinion those who think otherwise are labouring under a misapprehension which will lead to a belief that it is not possible to understand someone else's suffering, that we cannot know when someone else is in pain, that whenever I close my eyes the world disappears. It is an old problem. It has been kicking about in philosophy for several centuries. Just when it seems to have gone it reappears under a different guise and leads to the sorts of confusion we get in discussions to do with art and realism – naturalism – relativism – modernism – existentialism, and so on. One good example of this concerns the work of Franz Kafka. He is probably the greatest realist in literary art of the twentieth century. His work is a continual struggle with the daily facts of existence for ordinary people. Kafka's stories concern the deprivation suffered by ordinary people, ordinary people whose daily existence is so horrific other ordinary people simply will not admit it as fact, as something real, as something verifiable if they want to go and take a look. He seems to bend our line of vision so that we see round corners and perceive different realities. A few other artists also do this or attempt to; they work in the minutiae of existence trying to gain access to and make manifest those dark areas of human experience, and suffering.

Most writers from oppressed groups are under pressure of one kind or another. Time becomes the greatest luxury. Without time the work cannot be done properly. To read *Time of the Butcherbird* is to see a writer of enormous potential labouring to perform a workaday chore. But to criticise the lack of development in La Guma's prose[9] is to assume certain things concerning the role of the writer in society. La Guma could not be divorced from his society, no matter how hard the white South African authority attempts it. His whole background was one of radical commitment. His father was James La Guma, a former president of the Coloured People's Congress. Both he and Alex were members of the Communist Party throughout their lives and in 1955 they were involved in the formation of the Congress Alliance. This comprised the Indian Congress, the African National Congress, the Coloured People's Congress and the white Congress of Democrats. When the treason trials took place in 1955-61 Alex was one of the 156 leaders of the Alliance to be charged by the state. Then began the series of imprisonments and house-arrest, which only ended with his departure from South Africa in 1966. He lived in London from then until 1979, although the literary people in control down there seem never to have noticed. For several years he was secretary of the Afro-Asian Writers Organisation (in 1969 he had won their Lotus Prize for literature).

Exactly one week after La Guma's death the poet Benjamin Moloise was murdered on the gallows by South Africa's white authority. Less than ten years before another good young poet, Arthur Nortje,[10] committed suicide in Oxford days before he was due to be deported back to South Africa.

In Roque Dalton's 'Declaration of Principles'[11] the poet can only be, as far as the bourgeoisie is concerned, a clown, a servant or an enemy. La Guma was always an enemy. In South African society at present there is no other role available, whether for ordinary people or ordinary poets.

Other work available by Alex La Guma: *And a Threefold Cord* and *In the Fog of the Seasons End* (both Heinemann A.W.S.) An anthology *Apartheid* and an account of his travels in the USSR, *A Soviet Journey* do not seem to be available as far as I know though both are mentioned by his publishers.

Notes

1 *A Walk in the Night* (Heinemann African Writers Series 1968).
2 *Cencrastus* magazine (Autumn 1981).
3 In her essay to be found in *Aspects of South African Literature* ed. C. Heywood (Heinemann 1976).
4 *Cencrastus* (Autumn 1981).
5 *Tasks and Masks* (Longman, 1981).
6 *Ibid.*
7 See Ian Fullerton's article in *Cencrastus* of summer 1980.
8 Probably the Hungarian critic Georg Lukacs has written the seminal work on Kafka and modernism.
9 In his *Twelve African Writers* Gerald Moore says differently. He believes La Guma's short stories are inferior to his novels. I find this extraordinary.
10 Two of his poems can be read in *The Race Today Review* February 1986.
11 *Edinburgh Review* number 69 (1985).

It Was

Janice Galloway

she knelt to pick it up

it was

It was toward evening and the colour was seeping from the grass verge under her feet. Twostorey council terraces with frames of paint borders round the windows, flaking like late-in-the-day eye-liner, lined the opposite side of the road; behind her, a straggling T-junction split the erratic paths of children and women following the ground home with headscarves and late shopping. Both sides of the road had verges with lamp-posts, furred in their own bleachy light, and small close-stacked houses. None of the buildings was new.

Older couples would be sitting on the scratchy roses of their ancient settees inside watching slot telly – its blue-flickering familiarity was throbbing against dark sideboards: flame buds would be growing on coals still smoking with newness in the grates. She could hear Eamonn Andrews telling them that that *This Was Their Life*. Seven o'clock?

She wasn't sure if she knew this place or not. Something was homely about it, something that though not kent was not strange. With effort, she turned her gaze down to her feet and the sepia grass; her verge neighboured the dull macadam of the road to the edge of her vision at what must be the crest of a hill. Then, it would roll down out of sight and tumble on till it reached the sea. Overwhelmed, she knelt to feel the cling of the cool blades wrap the bare skin of her knees, exposed between long socks and dark grey skirt. Her eyes closed, near to weeping with the pleasure of it. Suddenly she was afraid, in panic at the foolishness of her joy and that someone might witness it. Surely she was too old for this kind of thing (her eyes felt wrinkled with strain) she opened them quickly

and found herself

standing at the now-grey privet hedge of one of the smarter pebble-dashes on the corner, her hands resting on the stubby hardness of cropped branches. It smelled of twilight and being outside. Scented stock wafted up sickly from underneath it. Gradually aware of their dull ache, she·lifted her palms, pitted from the striving of the blunt-edged bush, and slid them into jacket pockets. Inside, her nails trapped crumbs, vying with them for the corners, for it was now blue-dark and getting noticeably chillier.

then the glitter of it caught her eye

then the glitter of it caught her eye

There was
something shiny in the earth at the foot of the wall, just under the drainpipe and less than halfhidden. It was at the foot of the facing roughcast of the across the patch of stock. The hedge pushed at her blazer. Her hand was on the drainpipe, a clod of thick rust trapped her shoe: to stoop to look she knelt

she knelt to pick it up

it was

Dusty, trailing crumbs from her pockets, her fingers – now quite dull with warmth – found its edges and curled under. The smell of the earth lifted as it parted to free one corner

She knelt to pick it up
It was a face. A little crusted and with eyes shut tight against encroaching dirt: a little flattened from having lain there its indeter-minate time and being pressed against the concrete slabs. Her body and her breathing were smooth and calm though her eyes ticked seconds round the rim of it.

Pushing her lips apart and outward, she puffed feeble breath at the closed lids. Then more boldly she began to pick at the halfhard veil of mud with the unclean nail of her right index finger, clasping the whole face in her left hand with its cheek nestled in the flesh cup of her palm. As the flakes fell away, the skin showed pink and surpris-ingly clean beneath and she became more intent on the task. Most concentration and skill would be needed where the dirt crowded thickest in invert furrows at the creases of its eyes. She had to change tactic, retracting the nail and brushing with a plump pad of fingertip instead. This seemed better: the silt crumbled and parted fairly dryly to slide out of the cracks it had claimed as right over who knew how long. She blew gently again to help its progress. There was a sucking sound and an intake of air   Her eyes snapped wide and lips drew back their kiss   It was

The little man smiled as he took her elbow. There was no need to acknowledge anything unusual in the situation for nothing was.

Come on and we'll go for a cup of tea

Immediate bittersweet stab at recognition of a voice forgotten – how long? Her whole heart seemed to move with pity for the wee figure already making off toward a kettle. The still lamplight outlined his bald head and traced the grey nightcolour of his cheek where it moved to prepare another sentence of encouragement for her to come. It was a rough cheek, hairily whitened with stubble that had alternately fascinated and horrified her as a child; she felt its jaggy trail scratch a skirl of wild shrieking from an infant mouth, her eye stratched in excitement. *Too much excitement for the wean.*

Uncle George
Uncle George.

he was
He was walking ahead.
It's freezing. Come on and we'll get a heat.

She wanted to do something kind and wonderful for this, the swell of her heart now intolerable, but she couldn't think that. Not quickly enough, anyway. What was clear, though, was that it was now her due to be as gentle as she could for him. He had no awareness that he was dead and she would not let him know. That he should not suspect or have to hesitate for her, she spurred to movement then – a rush to reaffirm his short, bulky presence. They went jauntily and quietly, lured by the steamy warmth of the promised tea and its milkiness and sweetness. She knew he wouldn't live far away.

Men o the Mossflow

translated from the Chinese by
Brian Holton

Introduction

A Scottish equivalent of the Chinese novel *Shuihu Zhuan* (familiar to English readers as *The Water Margin*) might have looked like an amalgam of Hogg's *Three Perils of Man* and Scott's *Minstrelsy* – that is, it would be a sprawling, swaggering epic, told in language at once awesomely spare and vividly alive, spiced with bawdy laughter, and informed by a purpose of high moral seriousness. The origins of *Shuihu Zhuan* lie in oral tradition, but a great deal of sophisticated literary artifice has also gone into its making. Its putative 14th century author Shi Naian is the first great master of vernacular Chinese writing: this is the first work of genius to be written in the tongue that people actually spoke, and the language it uses is freshly-made, innovative, plastic and alive. Of the other hands the book passed through, none are more important than those of the brilliantly original critic Jin Shengtan, whose revised version of the novel has been a consistent best-seller since its publication in 1641. His recension tightened up the narrative to highlight the underlying implications of the story: if decent law-abiding individuals are squeezed between a corrupt government on the one hand, and organised thuggery on the other, what can they do? We join the story as rich kid Shi Jin, who is daft about martial arts, is discovering the consequences of befriending the hardmen who lead his local gang of outlaws.

*

Chapter III. Hou Maister Shi gangs by nicht tae Huayin toun an Controller Lu neivels the Wast Mairch Crusher.

Our tale tells nou o hou Shi Jin cried out
'But whit's tae be dune nou?'
and Zhu Wu, kneelan doun wi the ither twa capitanes, says til him

'Brither, ye're a man that's still unfylt, sae dinna get yirsel insnorled for our sakes. Tak a tow an bind the thrie o us up in it sae's ye can get yir reward: yon wey it'll no be our daein that losses ye yir guid name.'

'That maun never be!' says Shi Jin, 'for it wad seem like A'd been fleichan at ye tae come juist sae's tae cleik ye for the reward – an wad that no gar aa the warld lauch?'

'Gin daith it's tae be, you an me'll dee thegither: gin it's life, thegither we'll leive. Staun up an tak hert, for we'll no be lang o findin a wey roun this. Juist byde ye here an A'll gae speir ou hou it cam tae be.'

Sae up the lether gaed Shi Jin tae speir
'Whit's brocht ye herryan ma hous, at this third hour o the middle nicht?'
an the twae Ensigns answert him
'Dod, but ye're brazent, maister! We've Lucky Li here, that's the verra man that clyped on ye!'
'Hou cud ye sae sclander a daicent bodie, Lucky Li?' cries Shi Jin.
'Ah dinna ken a thing about it, but! A liftit Quarto Wang's letter in the wuids an A brocht it richt tae the burgh tae hae it read – the haill thing juist startit frae there.' says Lucky Li.
'Hou's there a letter back nou, whan you said there wisna ane?' cried Shi Jin tae Quarto Wang.
'Weill, A wis fou at the time' quo Quarto Wang, 'an A forgot aa about it.'
Wi a muckle rair, Shi Jin cried out
'Ye daft bruit ye! Whit'll we dae nou?'

Outbye, the twa Ensigns wis that feart that Shi Jin wad be owre handy for them, they didna daur breinge on intae the steadin tae cleik their men; inbye, the thrie capitanes wis pyntan wi their fingers like they wir meanan 'Gie them outbye an answer!': Shi Jin kent whit they they wir at, sae frae the lether he cried 'There's nae need for onie bother frae you twae: gin ye'll juist draw back a wee thing, A'll bind them in a tow ma ain sel, an A'll gie ye them owre tae tak tae the baillies.'
The twae Ensigns wis that feart, they'd juist tae agree: 'It's naethin adae wi us, this business – we'll juist hing on or they're brocht out in a tow~ an we'll aa gang in thegither for yir reward.'

Whan Shi Jin clam doun the lether an cam afore the haa, the firsten thing he did wis tak Quarto Wang tae the gairden roun the back an kill him wi ane straik, an the neisten thing he did wis cry on some o the haafowk tae pack awa the silks an aa the braw things o the hous an tae kennle thirty-forty torches up. At the mains, him an the thrie capitanes bucktt on their armour, tuik blades frae the weaponrack an pit them at their middles, an grippit their bills in their hauns. Than they kiltit up their gouns an set licht tae the theikit sheds in ahint the mains. Ilka cottarbodie wis set tae rowe up his things intae his pock.

When them outbye seen the fires lowan inben the haas, they gaed skelpan roun the back tae look, sae Shi Jin gaed tae the midmaist haa an set it in a lowe, an then he apent braid the yetts o the mains an, rairan an rowtan, out o't at a bang they breinged. Shi Jin wis at the heid of them, Zhu Wu an Yang Chun in the mids of them, an Chen Da at the hint-en, whan wi their cottars an their smaafowk they cam bashan out, eassla-wassla joukan, beltan wast an east. Och, but Shi Jin wis a muckle baist o a man tae! Whae wis there that micht kep or haud him back?

Ahint them the bleize wis weill alowe as they focht their wey out. On breinged Shi Jin or he cam up tae Lucky Li and the Ensigns, an fell roused wis he tae see them, for like fowk says,
'Whan twae ill-willers meets, byornar shairp's their een.'
The twa Ensigns hed seen that things wisna juist rinnan sae weill, an wis jinkin about tae rin awa, an Lucky Li wis set tae turn on his heel an gang as weill – but Shi Jin wis on him owre sune: he liftit his blade an wi ane straik he cuttit Lucky Li in twa. Chen Da an Yang Chun cam up on the Ensigns as they ran, an ilkane tuik juist the ae straik o his bill tae end the lifes o thae twa Ensigns.

Nou, gin the County Constable wis that feart he'd turnt his horse hame-awa at the gallop, hou wad the Fencibles daur advance? They ran for their lifes, the lot of them, skailt kens-whaur-awa. Shi Jin wis aye at the heid o the band, slauchteran as he gaed, an it wisna tae he wan tae the strenth o the Smaa Glore Hill that he drew braith or sate hissel doun in peace. An it wisna lang afore Zhu Wu an them wis commandin their smaafowk tae fell them kye an cuddy for a supper o congratulations – but we'll say nae mair o that.

A guid whein o days drew in, an here wis Shi Jin thinkan:
'This time A've kennlt a fire an brunt ma steadin doun, aa tae save thae thrie, an, tho A've some silk thing an some braw thing left tae me yet, ma coorse gear an ma wechty plenishins is awa entirely.'
He wis switheran in his hert, for whaur he wis juist wadna dae him. Tae Zhu Wu an the ithers he spak out:

'Ma dominie Leirsman Wang's awa servan in the Wardenrie o the Wastlin Mairches in Guanxi, an it's lang been a thocht o mines tae seek him out there. But, wi ma faither deean, A juist never got. This time, ma faimly's plenishins an ma faimly's steadin's baith feinisht wi, saw A'm set on gaun tae seek him out.'

'Dinna gang, brither' says Zhu Wu, 'but bide ye here at the strenth a day or twa mair an we'll hae anither crack about it. Gin ye're no willan tae tak tae the heather yir brithers here'll bigg up yir steadin ance aathing's caumed doun, an ye'll can be an ornar daicent bodie again.'

'Ah ken it's for freinship's sake ye speak' says Shi Jin, 'but ma mind's made up tae gang an A canna weill be kept. Gin A can airt out ma dominie A'll see an A get a stert out there, an A'll seek tae leive blythe an cheerie the rest o ma days.'

'But ye'd be chief o the strenth here, brither' says Zhu Wu. 'Is that no blytheness for ye? ... A dout the strenth maun be owre wee for ye, that ye'll no come doun aff yir hie horse!'

'A'm a braw lad, aefauld an unfylt' says Shi Jin. 'Wad A bemean the body ma faither an mither gied uis wi takin tae the heather? Dinna speak o't onie mair!'

It wis some days efter that Shi Jin concludit that he maun gae, an tho sair they besocht him, Zhu Wu an the ithers michta gar him byde. The cottars he'd brocht wi him he left at the strenth, for he tuik juist some odd bits o siller an the pock he'd rowed for hissel – ilkither thing wis left ahint him there.

Weill, he pit on his heid a Fanyang bunnet o white felt buskit wi a reid tossil, an ablow the bunnet a souple scerf o drumlie green bund intae the shape o twae horns; about his hass he'd a bricht yalla gravat o fine gauze; he wure about him a white serk of fine linen in ablow a double battlecoat that wis girdit at his middle wi a haunspang-braid pouchie-sash o ploum-reid cordit threids; he hed walkin-hose o bausent blue on his feet, an thae monie-luggit strae shuin that's sae guid for sclimman bens or scliffan throu the stour. He bucklt at his middle his guse-pen bladit sword wi the bress chymie haunle, he pit his pock on his back, an he grippit his bill in his haun, an than tae Zhu Wu an the ithers he gied his fareweills. Monie wis the smaafowk convoyed him doun the brae, an monie wis the tears Zhu Wu an them loot faa at the pairtin, afore aa thrie turnt back up the brae tae the strenth.

*

Our tale tells nou o Shi Jin, an hou he grippit his bill an gaed awa out frae the Smaa Glore Hill tae tak the gate for the Yanan road and the Wastlin Mairches o Guanxi. He'd tae eat whan he wis hungert an drink whan he wis dry, stoppan at een an awa wi the dawn. Mair as hauf the month he'd been on the road like this, wha he cam tae the toun o Weizhou.

'There's a Wardenrie here tae' he thocht tae hissel. 'Ma dominie Leirsman Wang wadna be here an aa, wad he?'

Sae intae the waatoun he gaed, an fand aa the streets an mercats ye'd ever think tae see, an on ane corner a wee teahous: in he gaed, fand hissel a place, an sate doun. Owre cam the Teamaister, speiran 'Whitna tea will ye tak, sir?'

'A'll tak steipit tea' says Shi Jin, an in nae lang time it wis maskit an set afore him.

'Whaur about's the Wardenrie here?' he speirs.

'Juist richt in front o ye – that's it yonder' answers the Teamaister.

'Wad there be a Leirsman Wang Jin in the Wardenrie that's no lang come frae the Eastren Capital, micht A ask?'

'There's an awfu number o Leirsmen in the Wardenrie here, an thrie or fower o them's cried Wang, but A wadna ken whae'll be Wang Jin' says the Teamaister.

An here, juist whan they wir at their crack, in cam a big lad, linkan intae the teahous wi muckle spangan steps: Shi Jin seen he'd the look o an officiar o the airmy, for his heid wis happit in a swastika-plet gauze scerf the colour o sesamum that wis bund ahint his heid wi twae Taiyuan rings o plaitit gowden wire; about him he wure a parrot-green linen battlecoat girdit at his middle wi a double 'policy an weir' belt o corbie-craw black, an on his feet he'd a pair o bricht yalla fower-gaured buits o 'earn's claw' sheepskin. He'd a roun face, muckle lugs, a straucht neb an a square mou, wi a lang gash-baird hingan doun frae his chafts: sax feet o lenth an ten spans o girth, intae the teahous he cam tae set hissel doun.

'Gin it's Leirsman Wang ye're seekan, sir' says the Teamaister tae Shi Jin, 'aa ye've tae dae is speir at the controller yonder, for he kens aabodie.'

Shi Jin wisna lang o gettin tae his feet an peyin his respecks, sayan 'Sit ye doun, sir, an dae me the honour o takin tea wi me, an ye please.'

Seean Shi Jin sae sterk an strang, an seean the look o a braw lad about him, the bodie peyed his respecks, and the twae sate doun.

'Gin it isnae owre bauld o uis, daur A ask yir name, sir?' speirs Shi Jin, an wi the norlan souch o Gansu or Shanxi in his tongue, the bodie answert him

'Masel, A'm a Controller in the Wardenrie. Ma faimly name's Lu,

an ma ain name's Da ... and whit's yir name, brither, gin A micht
speir it o ye?'
'A'm frae Huayin County o Huazhou, ma faimly name's Shi, an ma
ain name's Jin. Gin A micht speir o ye, sir: A've a dominie that wis
Leirsman o the Forbidden City Echt Hunder Thousan in the Eastern
Capital, an his name's Wang Jin. Ye wadna ken whether he's in this
Wardenrie, wad ye?'
'Brither,' says Controller Lu 'ye arena Maister Shi, the verra "Nine-
Gaired Dragon" o Shi's Toun, are ye?'
'Ay, that's me' says Shi Jin wi a bou. A bouan richt back, the
Controller says
           '"The soun o yir name's no like seein yir face
               For the sicht of yir face beats hearin yir name!"
'This Leirsman Wang that ye're efter – isna yon the Wang Jin that
gat the haterent o Hie Constable Gao in the Eastern Capital?'
'Juist him' says Shi Jin.
'Weill, A've heard o him, but he isna hereawa. A've heard he's
servan with His Excellencie Warden Chong the Elder, up Yanan
wey. It's H.E. Warden Chong the Younger that wairds our mairches
here: yon man o yours isna here.'
'Gin ye're Maister Shi, tho, ye've a guid name A've aften heard.
C'wa up the street wi me nou an we'll tak a dram.'
Sae Controller Lu tuik Shi Jin bi the haun an gaed out the teahous
door, lookan back tae tell the Teamaister
'A'll pey ye the siller masel.'
'Nae bother, Controller' says the Teamaister, 'Juist gang ye yir
weys.'

Airms cleikit, the twaesome gaed out the teahous, til forty or fifty
steps up the street they cam on a thrang o fowk staunan roun in a
ring.
'We'll tak a bit keek at this, brither' says Shi Jin, sae they pushed
throu the thrang an spied in the mids o it a bodie wi a dizzen
timmers in his haun, an spreid out on the grund afore him, a dizzen
or mair eyntments an plackets in ashetfus wi 'for sale' plackets stuck
intil them – here it wis ane o thae physicmongeran lads o watter an
lochside, that plays the run an the broadstaff juist tae sell their
mixters.
Shi Jin lookit at him, an kent him for his verra firsten dominie: it wis
Li Zhong, that they cry 'General Toober-the Tiger'! Intae the thrang
gaed Shi Jin, cryan
'Dominie! It's a lang while sin A seen ye!'
'Honest brither' cries Li Zhong. 'Hou cam ye here?'
'Gin ye're Maister Shi's dominie, come ye an tak a dram wi us an aa'

says Controller Lu.

'Haud on or A've sellt ma plaisters an gotten a bit siller, an A'll come wi ye then Controller' says Li Zhong.

'Whae's waitan on you? Gin ye're coman, come awa!' cries Lu Da. 'It's mait an claith tae's, Controller: A've nae ither fendin – gang ye on, an A'll seek ye out efter. Honest brither, awa you wi the Controller tae.'

Lu Da wis bleizan mad bi this time, an he stertit ruggin an ryvin at the onlookers, flytan at them an cryan

'Souk in the cheeks o yir erses, ye tinks, an piss aff out o here!'

Weill, whan they seen it wis Controller Lu they skelpit awa at his firsten rullion roar. Li Zhong, tae, seen hou wild an ramballioch Lu Da wis, but he dochtna say ocht, for aa he wis roused: he'd juist tae pit on a smile an say

'Wow, but yon's a spunkie chiel!'

An than he'd tae redd his gear awa intae his physic-pock, an pit his rungs an brodstaffs by.

Doun loans an roun corners gaed the thriesome, or they cam tae yon namely dramshop ablow the Stewartry Brig that belanged the fella Pan. A wisp wis stuck out afore the yett, an the pirlan dram-pennils wis flaffan an birlan in the wind as they gaed aa thrie up the stairs o Pan's dramshop tae choice out a trig wee chaumer an set theirsels doun. The Controller tuik hissel the heidmaist place, wi Li Zhong fornent him an Shi Jin in the laichest place. The barman chiel did them a service, an whan he seen it wis Controller-Lu, he speirit

'Hou monie drams will ye tak, sirs?'

'Get ye in fower horns tae stert wi' says Lu Da.

An whan he set out the fruits an the greens tae ease the drams doun, the barman speirit

'Whitna mait wad ye hae wi yir eattocks, sirs?'

'Whit are ye speir-speiran at?' cries Lu Da. 'Oniething ye hae, juist you bring it out – ye'll get yir lawin peyed! Ye dae naethin but mak a steir, ye tink!'

Sae doun gaed the barman an cam up wi hot toddies, an than aa kinkind o maits wis brocht in an spreid out owre the buird.

Nou, the thriesome hed taen a pickle drams an wir aa haein a bit crack, takan the meisur o their brodstaff-leir, an bletheran theirsels out intae the street, they wir that hertie, whan frae a chaumer throubye there cam the soun o fowk roaran an greitan an bubblan. Lu Da wis that roused, he juist soupit aa the ashets an the cups doun ontae the fluir. Up cam the barman, fleean in tae see whit wis gaun on: whit he seen wis Controller Lu in a fair tirivee o temper. Claspan his hauns, the barman says

'Gin ye lack onie thing at aa, maister of ficiars, aa ye've tae dae is tell us an we'll bring ye it!'

'Whit wad we lack!' cries Lu Da. 'Div ye no ken wha A am, that ye lat fowk mak sic a din o grietan throu yonder, distroublan me an ma brithers here frae our drams? Ye've shuirlie never gaed short o drink-siller throu ma daein!'

'Caum yirsel, maister of ficiar' says the barman. 'Hou wad we daur mak them girn an greit juist tae distrouble ye at yir drams, sirs?'

'Them that's greitan is a faither an his dochter that gangs singan roun the dramshops: they wadna ken ye wir at the dram-drinkin, sirs, an them greitan an girnan sae sair wi their trouble.'

'Here's an unco thing, tho' says Controller Lu. 'Cry ye them in for me.' An awa the barman gaed tae cry them in.

In nae lang time, here cam a quean o echteen-nineteen year auld, wi an auld mannie o fifty-sixty year auld ahint her, an the baith of them cairryan linkit chappie-sticks in their hauns. Whan they'd a richt look at her they fand that, tho she wisna aathegither o the bonniest, the quean wis still lousome tae see whan she lowtit doun in thrie deep deep curchies, dichtan her tears awa. The auld man made hissel kent tae them as weill.

'Whaur dae ye belang, the twae o ye?' speirs Lu Da. 'An whit's yir greitin an girnin for?'

'Ye mauna ken, maister officiar, sae A'll tell ye, an ye'll gie me leave' says the quean. 'We're Eastern Capital fowk that cam tae Weizhou here, ma mither an faither an me, seekan a bield wi our nainfowk, but never kennan they'd flittit awa tae the Southron Capital. Ma mither wis taen that bad in the guesten-hous, she passt awa, an me an the faither hes a weary gangrel life tae thole here, baith the twae o us.'

'There's a walthy merchant roun here cried Great Maister Zheng, "The Wast Mairch Crusher". He'd seen me an bi compulsion he gart the matchwyfe hae me bandit til him agin ma wull, ettlan A'd be his bydie-in. We'd nae thocht o the Letters Matrimonial that wis signed for thrie thousan in cunyie, but him, he lat the siller gae by, tho he held tae the contrack – it wis ma body he wis efter.

'Thrie months wisna by afore the mistress o his hous gat fell dour an turnt me tae the door. Nae comin back wad she thole, an she gart the keeper o the guestenhous staun guid for the herryin out o the thrie thousan that first A wis wadset for. An ma faither's that fushionless an saft, he canna pingle wi him that hes baith walth an wecht ahint him.

'Frae the verra stert we'd hed never a penny aff him, sae whaur wad we seek the siller tae pey him nou?

'There wis nae ither wey out. Frae the time A wis a bairn ma faither hed learnt me some wee bits o ballants, sae tae the dramshops we gaed tae dae the rouns. The feck o the wee pickle siller we tak in a day maun gang tae pey him back, wi juist a bittie owre for our keep. 'Thae twa days bypast, the dram-drinkan lads is that few an faur atween, we've mistrystit wi his siller, an A dout whan he comes seekan it we'll hae an aafu snash tae thole frae him.

'For thinkan on thae unhappy sorrows that we've nae wey tae tell, ma faither an me stertit tae greit an tae girn – we never thocht that bi mischance we'd distrouble ye, maister officiars. A beg ye tae lat the faut gae by, an haud hie yir worthy hauns abune us!'

'Whit's yir names?' speirit Controller Lu ance mair. 'An whitna guesten-hous are ye stoppan in? An whaur does this Great Maister Zheng "The Wast Mairch Crusher" byde?'

'A'm juist an auld bodie, the saicont o ma line' answert the auld ane. 'We're cried Jin, an the bairn's name's Emerant Lilly. This Great Maister Zheng, nou, he's Zheng the flesher that trokes in butcher-mait ablow the Dux Brig yonder – "The Wast Mairch Crusher" is his byname. Me an the lass is lyan at the Hous o Lu inben the foremaist eastren port.'

'Howt, man!' says Lu Da tae this. 'It wis aa this "Great Maister Zheng" A wis hearan, but it's nae mair as Flesher Zheng that fells the grumphies! The dirty bleck! He cuist in wi freins o our ain H. E. Warden Chong tae be their fleshmerchant, an this is the kin o cheatrie he's at!'

Than he turn his face tae Shi Jin an Li Zhong, sayan

'Byde ye here the nou, the twa o ye, an A'll gang an gie the tink a leatherin that'll be the end o him! A'll be back!'

But Shi Jin an Li Zhong clappit a haud o him, tellan him 'Caum yirsel, brither – ye'll can sort him out the morn.' Thrie times they tried, an five times mair, afore they gat him tae byde at peace. Than ance mair Lu Da spak out:

'Come awa then, auld ane! A'll gie ye the siller for yir keep, an ye'll can awa back the Eastren Capital the morn's morn. Whitlike's that?'

'Gin it wis possible for us tae gang back tae our ain toun, it wad be like haein ma faither an mither back in the warld ance mair, like mammy an daddy tae the fore again – but there's aye the keeper o the guesten-hous. Whit wey will he lat us gae: Great Maister Zheng's gat him staunan guid for the siller.'

'That disna maitter – A've the wey tae sort him out' says Controller Lu. Than intae the pouch at his side he gaed, fummlan for five-sax unce o siller that he pit on the buird. An he lookit tae Shi Jin an said 'A haena brocht muckle wi's the day: ye've siller, sae gie's a len o a pickle. A'll gie ye it back the morn.'

'White'er the cost, brither, A wadna speir for it back!' says Shi Jin as tae his pock he gaed tae tak out a ten-ounce siller lignate an lay it on the buird.

'Gie's a len o a pickle tae' says Lu Da tae Li Zhong, and Li Zhong brocht out twa unce o siller frae his puch. Lu Da lookit at it, seen the wee pickle that it wis, and said

'He's no sae gled tae gie, aither, this ane!'

An than he tuik the fifteen unce of siller an gied it tae Auld Jin, tellan him

'Tak this for yir keep, the twae o ye. Awa wi ye nou an redd up yir trammels, an A'll be roun the morn's morn tae mak shuir ye baith get up. An A'd like tae see the guesten-hous keeper that can haud ye back!'

Auld Jin an the dochter did him a service an gaed. Lu Da flang Li Zhong his siller back.

The thriesome drank aff a couple mair horns afore they gaed doun the stair. Lu Da cried tae the guidman

'A'll pey ye the lawin the morn, Guidman' and the guidman answert him

'Juist gang ye yir weys, Controller, for whit ye've hed's a smaa thing – an A'd never think tae see ye no come back wi the lawin!'

Sae out the door o Pan's they gaed, an on the street they twyned: Shi Jin an Li Zhong held awa tae their ain guesten-houses, but Lu Da – an it's o him our tale tells nou – he gaed back tae his ludgins fornent the Wardenrie, an gaed straucht tae his chaumer. He tuik nae denner, aither, but gaed tae sleep, bleizin mad. The guidman o the hous didna daur speir at him at aa.

Back tae Auld Jin, tho, tae tell hou he tuik his fifteen unce o siller back tae the guesten-hous an seen his dochter settelt for the nicht. Than he gaed furst tae an outlan bit ayont the burghdykes tae fee a cairt, an neist he gaed back tae redd up aa their trammels, clear the rent-dues, an pay the siller for their mait an their kennlin. Aa he'd tae dae nou wis wait on the dawin.

Naethin fell out in the nicht: the morn's morn faither an dochter wis up at the fift hour tae kennle the fire for their brakfaist, an ance it wis etten they gat aathing redd up tae gang. An juist whan the lift wis growan a wee thing bricht, here cam Controller Lu linkan intae the guesten-hous wi his muckle spangan stap, rairan at the tap o his voice

'Number Twae, whaur about's Auld Jin stoppan?'

'Maister Jin' cries the Number Twae, 'Here's Controller Lu come

seekan ye.' Auld Jin apent his chaumer door an said
'Sit yirsel doun inben, Maister Controller.'
'Sit naethin!' cries Lu Da. 'Gin ye're awa, than get awa! Whit are ye
waitan on?'
Sae Auld Jin led his dochter out, an wi their pockstangs owre their
shouthers they baith gied the Controller their thenks.
But juist when they wir set tae tak the road, the Number Twae
barred their wey, sayan
'Whaur are ye gaun, Maister Jin?'
'Are ye short for yir rent?' speirs Lu Da.
'Na, the rent wis aa peyed last nicht' says the Number Twae, 'but
they're awn Great Maister Zheng the wadset siller yet, an it's me
that's tae staun guid for it.'
'A'll be giean Flesher Zheng his siller' says Controller Lu, 'sae juist
you lea the auld ane tae gang awa hame.'
But wad the Number Twae lea them alane?:
Muckle roused, Lu Da streitched out the five fingers of his haun, an
he gied the Number Twae a skelp in the face that brocht the bluid
rinnan frae his mou, an than he gied him anither ane that knockit
his twae front teeth out. The Number Twae clam tae his feet an ged
aff like a fuff o wind tae seek a hidie-hole inben, an there wis nae
wey the keeper o the guesten-hous wis coman out tae stop them, sae
Auld Jin an his dochter gaed smertlie awa an out the burgh tae seek
the cairt he'd fee'd yestreen.

Lu Da, nou, hed a bit think tae hissel. He wondert whether the
Number Twae wad mebbe come rinnan efter them ettlan tae kep
them, sae he tuik a creepie frae out the hous, an set-hissel doun for
an hour or twae. Ance an Auld Jin hed hed the time tae gang a guid
road, he gat up an tuik the gate for the Dux Brig.
Weill, Flesher Zheng hed a double-frontit shop wi a pair o benches,
an fower-five big dads o pork hingan abune them. The man himsel
wis sutten doun ahint the counter, forenent the door, watchan his
dizzen butcher-laddies sellan the mait, whan in walks Lu Da, strecht
up tae the door, cryan 'Flesher Zheng!'
Seean it wis Controller Lu, Flesher Zheng cam skelpan out frae in
ahint his counter tae dae him service, cryan
'Forgie me, Controller, A didna see ye.' An cryan on his helpeners
tae bring a creepie, he bade the Controller sit hissel doun.
'A'm bidden bi His Excellencie's gracious mandment' says Lu Da
'There's ten pund o best butcher-mait wantit, it's tae be minced
smaa, an he's not tae see a drop o creish intil't.'
'Fine, sir' says the Flesher, an tae his lads he cries 'Yous anes choice
out a guid bit an mince ten pund o't.'

'A'm no wantan thae dirty tinks haunlan it' says Lu Da. 'Ye'll dae it yirsel.'

'As ye say sir. A'll juist dae it masel' says the Flesher.

An tae the bench he gaed an choicit out ten pound o best mait that he hackit intae fine fine mince.

The Number Twae o the guesten-hous, nou, hed bund his heid in a hankie an wis on his wey tae the Flesher's tae tell him aboot the business wi Auld Jin whan he spied Lu Da sittan at the bench bi the door. He didna daur come near, but stuid watchan frae in ablow the easins o a house a guid wey aff.

Neat an exack, the Flesher hackit awa a guid hauf hour afore he rowed the mait in a lilly-leaf an said

'Will A sen a man wi't, Controller?'

'Ye'll sen naethin!' says Lu Da. 'juist haud on – there's ten pund wantit an aa that's tae be juist creish alane, an he's no tae see a drap o lean intil't. It's tae be minced smaa tae.'

'But creish its lane!' says Flesher Zheng. 'A dout they maun be rowan puddins in't – whit guid's ten pund of creish?'

'His Excellencie gied his mandment' glowert Lu Da. 'Wha wad daur tae speir at him?'

'Gin it's a thing that'll get uised, then, A'll hack it, juist' says the Flesher, an he choiced out ten sonsie pund of creishie mait, hackit it intae fine fine mince, an rowed it in a lilly-leaf. It hed taen the haill mornin, gey near up tae the dinner hour.

Wad the Number Twae o the guesten-hous daur gang owre the road? Even the customers that wir wantan their maits didna daur come near them.

'Will A get ma men tae cairry it for ye, Controller, or will A sen it tae the Wardenrie?' speirit the Flesher, an Lu Da answert him

'There's ten pound o gowden girsle wantit tae, that's tae be hackit intae fine fine mince, an he's no tae see onie mait intil't at aa.'

Flesher Zheng gied a lauch an said

'Ye haena come here juist tae tak a len o me, hae ye?'

An whan Lu Da heard this he lowpit up, tuik the twae pocks o mince in his hauns, glowert at Flesher Zheng an said

'Ay, A cam here tae tak a len o ye!'

An wi that he flang the twa pocks o mince in his face, and – weill, it wis juist like a blatteran storm o mait!

Flesher Zheng wis that roused, an ire o wrath gaed hurlan in twae streams frae the howes o his feet richt tae his croun – the derk fire o anger in his hert bleized up intil a bricht lowe that cudna weill be slockent – frae aff the bench he claucht up a bane-scartan gully an on a sudden he lowpit tae't! Controller Lu hed smertlie leggit it intae the street bi this, tho. Whae amang aa the neibours or the dizzen warkfowk wad daur step forrit an stop them? The fowk passan on the street juist stuid whaur they wir, goavan an dumfounert wi fricht, alang wi the Number Twae o the guesten-hous.

With the gully in his richt haun Flesher Zheng claucht at Lu Da wi his left: Controller Lu tuik his chance, gat a haud o the Flesher's left haun, ran forrit, an gied him ae fuit in the wame that knockit him doun an sent him out intae the street wi a bang. Lu Da pit the fuit in ance mair, an trampit on his briest; than he liftit a muckle neive the size o a vinegar-pig, he glowert an he said
'Here's me, that stertit out servan His Excellencie Warden Chong the Elder whan first A listit for a Procognitioner in the Fift Circuit Airmy – it widna be for naething gin A wis tae cry masel "The Wast Mairch Crusher". But you, ye're juist a bit flesher bodie that drives the knife tae sell yir butcher-mait – ye're a man nae better as a tyke, an ye'd cry yirsel "The Wast Mairch Crusher"! Whit wir ye at, herryan Emerant Lilly wi aa yir joukery-pokery?'
An wi the ae neive he beltit him richt on the neb, sae the bricht bluid cam pouran out an the Flesher's neb wis shewit aa ajee – an it wiz juist like he'd apent an uil an sauce shop, for out cam scoushan the nippy, the saut an the sour, aa in ane!

Flesher Zheng wis fechtan tae get up, but he cudna. His sherp gully wis flung awa, a'n aa that he cud say wis
'A guid belt!'
'Ye granny-shaggan get, ye!' sweirs Lu Da. 'Wad ye answer back tae?'
An liftan his neive he gied him ane atween the eehole an the ebrou's end that ryvit his winker wide an gart the baa o his ee lowp out – an it wis juist like he'd apent a draper's shop, for out fell the reid, the black an the crammasy, aa in ane!

Aa the onlookers at aither side wis that feart for Lu Da, whae amang them wad daur step forrit an stop them?

Flesher Zheng cud take nae mair an wis beggan tae be lat aff, but Lu Da rairs at him 'Towts, man! Are ye guid for naethin? Gin ye wad fecht it out A'd lat ye aff – but nou ye're beggan for it, A shuirlie winna forgie ye!'
An wi ae neive he gied him anither ane richt on the brou – an it wis juist like he'd stertit the Full-Hous Land-an-Watter Deid Mass, for the chymies, the clatterbells an the haunbells gaed dirlan out aa in ane!

Whan he lookit, Lu Da seen Flesher Zheng wis streikit out sterk an stiff on the grund, with braith coman out o him but nane gaun in, an he wisna like movin. Sae wi fause intent Lu Da says
'Ye're lettan on ye're deid, ye tink! A'll belt ye again!' But bit bi bit he seen the Flesher's colour changin, an he thocht
'A wis juist ettlan tae gie him a guid leatherin – A never thocht tae feinish him wi thrie belts ... A'll shuirlie get the court for this, an A've naebody tae bring ma meat tae the jyle ... A'd better get out o this quick.'
Sae he stepit out, turnan as he gaed tae point at Flesher Zheng's cauld corp an cry 'Ye're lettan on ye're deid! A'll tak ma time, tho, an A'll settle up wi ye!'
An awa he gaed, cursan as he ran.
Whae amang aa the neibours or the Flesher's warkfowk wad daur stop forrit an hinder him?

Controller Lu gaed back tae his ludgins an in haste rowed up his claes an some o his gear – the fine stuffs an the siller, for his auld claes an his coorse gear he'd tae lea ahint him. An than he liftit his 'eebrou-lang' rung an gaed skelpan out the Southron Port, awa like a fuff o wind.

Weill, the fowk o Flesher Zheng's hous, an the Number Twae o the guesten-hous that cam tae gie him warnin, they tried a lang while tae save him. He michtna leive tho, sae – walaway! – he dee'd. The neibours auld an young made straucht for the Stewartry Buildins tae pit their dittays in, an there they waitit or the Sheriff-Principal hed taen his seat in the haa abune an gotten in aa their dittays. When he'd read owre them he spak:
'This Lu Da's a Controller o the Wardenrie ...'
An he didna daur gie onie direck order tae kep the ill-daer athout mair nor his ain ceivil authorite, the ill-daer bein an officiar or weir, an him bein Sheriff on the ceivil side.
Sae the Sheriff-Principal gaed straucht tae the Wardenrie in his sedan-chair. He clam doun an bade the sodgers at the yetts cry word in that he'd come, an the warden hed him bidden tae the haa. The Warden peyed his respecks tae the Sheriff-Principal, an said
'Whit cam ye for?'
'A thocht it best tae lat Yir Excellencie ke'n' offert the Sheriff. 'Lu Da, Controller in yir Airmy, hes for nae reason neivelled Flesher Zheng o the mercat tae his daith. A haena sent in a notandum, Yir Excellencie, for A dochtna hae him apprehendit on ma ain authoritie, him bean on the militar.'
This gied the warden a shog, an he thocht tae hissel

'This Lu Da, for aa he's guid wi the Martial Leir, he's got a coorse naitur. This time, it's the takin o a life, an hou wad A hide sic a faut? ... A'll hae tae lat him tak the Interrogator, an that'll mebbe dae it.' Sae tae the Sheriff-Principal he said

'This Lu Da, he stertit out as ane o ma faither the Elder Warden's officiars: he wis disponit here tae be ane o ma Controllers acause A'd nae helpeners here. Nou he's forfautit for a slauchter, ye can tak him an gie him the Interrogator, as accords o law. Sae be he clearly awns his faut an the sentence is set doun, ye maun lat ma faither ken afore ye gie decerniture.

'A dout the day ma faither needs this ane on the Border'll be an ill day tae see.'

'Efter speirin intae the grunds o this, A sall depone here sae's H.E. the Elder Warden kens, as accords o praticks, afore A daur gie out a hornin decerniture' says the Sheriff-Principal.

Sae he bade farewell tae the warden an wis cairrit frae the yetts tae the Stewartry Buildins, whaur he gaed in an ance mair tuik his seat in the haa. He cried in the captioneer Squad o the day, an subscreivit Letters o Caption in the case o the fautor Lu Da. Strauchtawa Inspector Wang tuik the brieves an led a dizzen or sae governmenters tae Controller Lu's ludgins, whaur the guidman o the hous tellt him

'He trailed out twa-thrie pocks, liftit his cutty rung, an awa he gaed. A juist thocht he'd been sent for, sae A didna speir at him.'

Inspector Wang lissent tae him, an whan he apent the chaumer door, there wis naethin tae be seen, for there wis juist auld claes an auld clouts there-ben. Sae he tuik whit there wis an he tuik the guidman, an he reinged aa owre the place seekan out his man. Frae north tae south the Stewartry he gaed, but never the caption cud he mak: he'd juist tae nab twae o the neibours an tak them back tae the Stewartry Buildins an repone there in the haa:

'Controller Lu is fugied tae airts unkent, in dreidour at his faut. The guidman o the hous an thae neibours here wis aa taen.'

The Sheriff-Principal lissent tae this, an tae the jyle he bade them, an Flesher Zheng's fowk he clappit in aside them. Crownrymen wir appointit an commands gien tae the Officiars o the Inbye Wards an the Baillies o the Outlan Wards tae double an treiple their speirins. Flesher Zheng's ain fowk seen tae the coffin an the kistins, layan the kist awa intil a cloister.

On the ane haun, the dittays wis pilin up in a muckle hott, an on the tither, men wis sent out at pains o the rod an time prefixt tae apprehend the fautor. The pursuers peyed their cautions owre an gaed hame, the neibours an onlookers gat the rod for Non luvandum an wir lat gae, an the guidman o Lu Da's ludgins an his neibours aa gat an Absolvitur.

Lu Da, tho, wis In Fugitation, sae Letters o Hot Trod wis sent roun for his apprehension in onie airt: a reward o a thousan in cunyie wis promist, an plackets wir tae be postit aa owre the place, giean out his years o age, his pairt native, an his description.

Aabodie wis dischairged efter the hearin, an Flesher Zheng's fowk gaed aff tae see the the murnin – but nane o them's in our tale onie mair.

We tell nou o Lu Da leavin Weizhou, an hou he gaed fleean east-awa an rinnan wast, skelpan ramstam throu stewartries an sherrifdoms, juist fair a case o

> Hungert men disna choice their meat,
> Cauld men disna choice their claes;
> Frichtit men disna choice their road,
> An puir men disna choice their wifes.

Lu Da bashed on his road wi dreidour in his hert, no richtlie kennan whitna wey tae tak: dumfounert aathegither, he ran for mair nor hauf the mollth or he wan tae the burgh o Yanmen in Daizhou.

In he gaed, intae the waatoun, an seen there aa the busy thrang o the mercatplace – fowk birlian alang throu the stour, cairts an horses clatteran up an doun, fowk buyan an sellan, an aa the hunder an twenty trades trokan their gear. It wis a trig laid-out place, tae, for tho it wis but a burgh-toun[3]. An sae he gaed about it til he seen a hiddle of fowk gaithert at a crossroads tae look at a placket. They wir that ticht packit thegither he'd tae squeeze in amang the press of fowk tae hear (Lu Da, ye see, kent nae letters, an juist hed tae lissen tae ither fowk readan out loud). Whit he heard wis this:

> Yanmen Burgh o Daizhou, as accords o the mandment o the Stewartry o Taiyuan, gies general chairge tae Officiars an Agents for allouance tae the writ o Weizhou in the apprehension o the the fautor Lu Da that neivelled Flesher Zheng tae his daith, forenamed bean Controller in the Wardenrie.
> 'Onie that wad gie concealment, ludgin, or buird in their hous is tae be airt an pairt forfautit. Onie that apprehends or brings him forrit will be giftit wi ane thousan in cuynie for reward …

Lu Da heard this faur an nae mair, for he heard ahint him a man cryan out 'Brither Zhang, whit brocht ye hereawa?' an he wis claspit bi his middle an hoyed awa frae the crossroads.

Gin this man hedna seen him an harled him awa or draggit him doun ...
It's tae be expoundit yet he hou Lu Da hed the hair o his heid shaved aff an his whisers scrapit awa, an hou, tho his killer's name wis chynged, he still steired aa the Salvator's saints tae anger. It wis aa sae

> A meditation-staff micht warsle out o jeopardie
> An a fastren-knife ding doun unrichteous men.

But in the hinner-end, an ye're tae ken whae it wis that pulled at Controller Lu, ye'll need tae see the neist chapter.

from Shoormal

Robert Alan Jamieson

POEMS IN SHETLANDIC

De

I am a bairn.
I am de.
I am in de.

Du is a bairn. Du stands at da hert
O da settlement. Dy feet ir bare,
Dir dirty, klestered wi gutter.
Dy body is cled wi coorse cloot.
Da reek o baests is apo dy skyn.
Hit is dy smell.
Du fingers da waa o dy hame,
Near da daek quhar da sentry staands.
It's a big roon crø, biggit be haand,
Møld underfit an owrehead girss.
Du touches dy hair, hit's aggelt an lang.
Du's never seen dy face, forbye atill da
Faces o dy bridders an dy sisters; du døsna ken
If du is 'beautiful' – but du feels it.

Da kennin is in de.
Du døsna seek 'knowledge'.
Feet in da gutter, du belangs.

Lion

My freend da lion his a waarm den.
Wi roar an grin, he bids da wind
Come in an fan his fire.
It døsna blaa oot,
But lowes still brichter,
Lichtin da mirk,
Still farder, still hicher.

We can aa øs dis lichthoose
I da broo, if we but open up
An coont da sowls itida mirk.
Dis nummers irna random,
Mind oot, dønna forgit dem,
Fir dey will be wir meid
Itida future.

We ir strang, no waek,
Pør, no wealty,
Soople, no stiff.

Let aa tochts be lichthooses,
Aa wyrds dir baems.
Hit isna as it seems,
Dis nummers irna random,
Dey ir wir meid.

T' Scallwa Castle

Quhitever shite drappt oot dy privvies
Still maer bed on ahint, inside de,
In da trots an haas an guts
O da Stewart clan at aaned de.

I canna celebrate dy stonn in ony tongue
Nor care ta rub da green fae yon bress plaet
Da National Trust sae carefilly hae nailed ta de.
Fir evry chisel swap, a bairn gret oot fir maet.
Fir every stonn lade t'dy foond, anidder stonnless
Grave wis fillt wi benklt brukkit bens o fok
Still young if de an aa dy hertless kyn hed
Only hed a tocht bit eence fir somethin idder
Dan dir gut-fat laanded swallys an dir privvy shite.

Gadderin Ler

We fan a lok a ghosts,
We twa freens, ae Seturday nicht.
Da wyrds o shadoos wir apo wir minds,
Da names o powre wir apo wir lips.
In wir heads lived squatters:
Idder fok's tochts.

Woman Wait

Ida hert oda voar, in a caald hoar-frost
Du left t'tak dy place amang da hellakrøss
'Lass, had de, had de', I gret as du fled,
An I cradled dy grey i me erm ida boxbed.

Bit cam dat hidmist soch o dine
At slokkit ony lowin taas o hope
I'd hunsed apo da hearth, e'en till da last,
As tødset dan, du slippit ertkent grace
An left dy braeth laek dalareek abøn dy face,
I rase an trukkt a heklin gait awa,
Sae ubadous t'ken dy løbet løf
Wid never maer warm.
Da voe wis swanklin at da craigs as
In a dwaam I lukkit Glunta, haddin
Athin in her swarm,
T'kom fae skoitin oot ahint da langmenn,
An flytit at her lachin face
Fir pullin de awa.
I knelt an gret agin da gable waa,
Wir flød an ebb noo dumba, faain in snaa,
An de still lyin but, still warm.
I coodna mak a soond ava
Save just t'utter, lurrin,
'Lass, had de'.

Prodigal

Quha can fill da føl's cup
Quhan he hads da thing da wrang wye up?
Or mak da craetir sit an sup
If he be bent on staandin up?

An quha can quheest his brøl
Quhan he kens owre late he's been da føl?
Or aid him fin da time he støl
T'fritter awa in ledli døl?

Misanters, aye, can be forgien
But no da wilful gait I'm gien,
Da witless raag I'm lately been.

Glossary of words and spellings outwith the Concise Scots Dictionary

Abøn: above
Aggl: to dirty or soil
Apo: upon
Benkl: to crumple up or dent
Brukk: rubbish
Brøl: bellow
Crø: (n) an enclosure (sheep-fold)
Dalareek: mist which gathers in valleys at night
Dumba: fine dust
Døl: grief, woe
Ertkent: widely known
Flød: flood
Glunta: the moon (fisherman's tabu-name)
Haas: the neck
Hellakrøs: the kirkyard, the dead therein
Hekl: to walk bent, and heavily
Hidmist: last
Hunkse: to push up (to make a burden sit better)
Ir, irna: are, are not
Klester: to adhere or stick
Langmenn: long strips of cloud
Ledli: indolent, lazy-looking
Lurr: to speak in a low voice, to whisper
Løbet: slightly warm, lukewarm
Løf: the palm of the hand
Meid: a landmark, used for navigation at sea
Misanter: a mishap or accident
Møld: earth, soil
Skoit: to look with a specific purpose
Støl: stole
Swankl: to splash gently
Trukk: to trudge or trample
Tødset: exhausted, brought to bay by pursuers
Ubadous: weakly, useless
Voar: the spring

Fionn MacColla

James B. Caird

ALMOST FIFTY YEARS AGO, in the spring of 1936, when I was a student in Paris, I gave a paper to the Cercle Breton on Scottish literature. In the course of it I remarked: 'Parmi les plus jeunes, dans le nouveau groupe de romanciers, Fionn MacColla est un séparatiste et un extrémist. Il espère que l'Ecosse deviendra Catholique et Gaelique, que la langue deviendra, encore une fois, comme elle l'était avant le onzième siècle, le parler non seulement du nord, mais aussi de toute l'Ecosse. Il veut que des rapports culturels et politiques soient établis avec l'Irlande. Dans son roman, *The Albannach,* il attaque avec une fureur amère le puritanisme et l'anglicisation qui ont fait tant de mal aux Highlands. Il décrit une région dépeuplée et qui perd peu à sa langue et sa culture, une race dont les instincts artistiques, dont l'humaité même sont écrasées par un puritanisme étroit et vindicatif.'

The Albannach, his first novel, had been published in 1932, and had been acclaimed by, among others, Edwin Muir, as a landmark in the Scottish novel. In a review published in *The Modern Scot,* Muir declared:

> The author of this book, *The Albannach,* has very remarkable gifts. He is, first of all, a born writer: he uses words sensitively, forcibly and exactly, and at times with great poetic power. His observation of character and physiognomy is extraordinarily subtle, his rendering of half-conscious feelings and sensations full of definition.... He has humour, passion, sincerity and an extremely effective turn for satire. *The Albannach* is a brilliant performance and should receive an unequivocal welcome from a country not remarkable for brilliant performances in literature.

How has *The Albannach* stood the test of time? As an undergraduate at Edinburgh University I found it intoxicating. Its bitter attack on a narrow, distorting creed, its satirical power, its lyrical evocation of the scenic glories of the Northwest Highland, its passionate advocacy of Scottish nationality – all filled me with enthusiasm. Since then I have come to regard it a little more critically. There is a certain amount of overwriting, the characterisation is uneven, leaning at times towards caricature, and the structure is unsure. Quite by coincidence, there was no sign of influence on either side, Neil Gunn published in the same year, 1932, a novel entitled *The Lost Glen*, which dealt with a similar theme, the resentment of a young Gael at the impoverishment and anglicisation of his countryside. Gunn's book, not one of his best, is melodramatic and hysterical in comparison with *The Albannach*.

When I heard that MacColla, or T. Douglas MacDonald, to give his real name, was actually living in Edinburgh, I determined to see him. It is extraordinary how many Scottish writers adopt pseudonyms: 'Fiona Macleod' (that dismal exponent of the Celtic Twilight, William Sharp), Hugh MacDiarmid (C. M. Grieve), 'James Bridie' (Dr Mavor), 'Lewis Grassic Gibson' (James Leslie Mitchell) are the most obvious. Does this suggest a split in the Scottish personality? Even Sir Walter Scott for years disclaimed authorship of the Waverley Novels. There is room for a thorough and detailed study of this phenomenon.

MacColla, or Tom MacDonald as I came to call him, had not long returned from Palestine where he had been lecturing in a Scottish Church college (at Safed) on history. He had put in a year at Glasgow University, studying Celtic languages, but for some reason or other had abandoned his Honours course. This I found puzzling, since he had the ability to have distinguished himself in any academic pursuit he took up. In Edinburgh he was living in poverty, subsisting on a small weekly sum he earned by writing a column on Gaelic affairs for the Scottish Nationalist Social Credit magazine *The Free Man*. Any researcher into this period in Scottish literature or politics will find back numbers of *The Free Man* indispensable reading. Hugh MacDiarmid, also experiencing a lean time in Edinburgh, was in a similar position. He contributed a weekly column entitled 'At the Sign of the Thistle'. In a small office, high up in India Buildings, overlooking the West Bow, these distinguished writers held court, and carried on passionate discussions with all who dropped in to see them. It was there, for instance, that I first met Robert Garioch. I took my courage into my hands, climbed the stairs to the top flat of India Buildings, and had the temerity to introduce myself to these men whose work I so much admired. This was the prelude to many meetings in pubs, in the Scottish Nationalist clubs in Shandwick Place and Coates Crescent, in University debating societies. They treated me with great cordiality. They both exerted contradictory influences on my outlook, since though at that time they were closely allied, they had diametrically opposed ideologies – MacDiarmid being a professed Communist and atheist (although I think he was more of a Deist), and MacColla tending towards Catholicism, and very much influenced at that time by Maritain. They were united, however, in their passionate devotion to Scotland, and to the cause of the Gaelic language.

MacColla had been born and brought up in Montrose, a town on the Angus coast – and in his youth had seen a lot of MacDiarmid, at that time a reporter on the Montrose local newspaper.

I am certain that MacColla was influenced by this connection, although later he angrily resented any such implication. MacDiarmid told me, for instance, that it was he who first drew MacColla's attention to the work of the neo-scholastics. Although later the two men drifted widely apart they each respected the other's achievement.

MacColla's father, who owned a shoe shop in Montrose, came from Ross-shire and was a Gaelic speaker. His mother, a Douglas, originated from north Mearns, that area south of Aberdeenshire stretching between the Grampian mountains and the North Sea, celebrated by Lewis Grassic Gibbon in his *A Scots Quair*. She spoke a pungent and pithy Scots. Thus MacColla was heir to two linguistic traditions, and this is reflected in his work. The prose style of *The Albannach*, like that of Neil Munro, has Gaelic inflections. He was to abandon this style in his later novels. In the two published fragments of his Reformation novel, *Scottish Noël* and *Ane Tryall of Heretiques,* he makes effective use of Scots. Both his parents were members of a strict Puritanical sect, the Plymouth Brethren, and this was of crucial importance for his development. In his short autobiographical work, *Too Long In This Condition,* he refers to his repressive upbringing. He defines the God of his parents as: 'horrible, hebraic, somewhat hirsute, bad-tempered, middle-aged ... with his outsize telescope always framed on me'.

The vehemence of his later attacks on Calvinism is, in large measure, a reaction against the strictness and joyless repression of his upbringing in childhood. In his polemical work, *At the Sign of the Clenched Fist,* he says:

> the concept of Necessity in human life and destiny (as in the doctrine of Predestination), the concept of a radically diseased humanity, the concept of the radical evil of human nature and even nature itself; these are not Christian.

In *At the Sign of the Clenched Fist* he makes the following outstanding claim:

> What the Reformation did was to snuff out what would
> otherwise have developed into the most brilliant national cul-
> ture in history.

After leaving Montrose, MacColla trained as a teacher in Aberdeen and was then appointed to a head teacher's post in Laide on
the seaboard of Western Ross. This was the basis of the community
and scenery described in *The Albannach,* and the beginning of his
long love affair with the Gaelic language. Here too he observed the
poisoning effects of a narrow puritanical sectarianism. In *At the
Sign of the Clenched Fist* he says:

> individuals of large acceptance and affirmation, if not liqui-
> dated, stifle if the accident of their circumstances should con-
> demn them to upbringing in an Evangelical sect or to residence
> within a territory where such a sect strikes the note of society.

After a few years of teaching in Laide he left for his lecturing post in
Palestine.

In Edinburgh, in the early 1930s, he lived from hand to mouth.
Many of his friends rallied round him. He stayed at various times
with Dr and Mrs Stanley Robinson in Musselburgh, a few miles east
of Edinburgh, and with George and Ann Scott Moncrieff in their
cottage in Peeblesshire. Helen Cruickshank, who gave so much help
to the Scottish literati in those days, and who was herself a poet of
some consequence, had rented an office in George Street which was
furnished with a divan and had a gas ring. For quite a time
MacColla slept and fed there, constantly on the lookout for the law
since it was strictly illegal to use office premises as a dwelling.
Hither he and I and some others would repair after the pubs had
closed to carry on our discussions over an illegally brewed cup of
coffee.

He was employed for a year or two by an institution that called
itself 'The New University Society' – an offshoot of Collins the
publishers, with an office in George Street, where he did miscellane-
ous literary hackwork, including the writing of a small textbook on
philosophy. Here he met the charming and capable lady who was to
be his wife, a Gaelic speaker from Islay, who was to bear him ten
children. She was the principal secretary of the firm. When war
broke out, MacColla went back to teaching – in the islands of
Benbecula and, later, Barra. When we were on holiday in Tiree in
the fifties, one evening my wife and I took the steamer, the *Clay-
more,* to Barra to visit the MacDonalds in their remote outpost. We
were given a cordial welcome and spent many pleasant hours before
returning to our island in the small hours of the morning. We were

astonished at the number of handsome children who materialised out of odd corners in the schoolhouse parlour.

Despite his enthusiasm for Gaelic and despite his Catholicism (he went over to the Church at the beginning of the war), on this Catholic, Gaelic-speaking island, MacColla was neither happy nor popular. In the 1960s he returned to Edinburgh, to a house in the Marchmont district, where he lived, a rather disappointed and embittered man, until his death in 1975 at the age of sixty-nine.

A word about his appearance. He was tall, dark-haired and walked with a kind of proud arrogance. He was dignified and even courtly in manner. He spoke clearly and distinctly with an unmistakable Scottish accent, with pure vowels and strongly articulated consonants – not for him the insensitive and exaggerated diphthongisation, and the absurd attempt to eliminate rhotism that were cultivated by so many anglicised Scots, particularly in Edinburgh. Despite his impressive air – that of a Spanish hidalgo – he had a wild sense of fun and a ringing infectious laugh when his sense of the ridiculous was aroused. In his later years he grew a longish white beard which gave him the appearance of an Old Testament prophet.

His embitterment and disappointment stemmed from his failure to receive recognition. Although he had written a number of novels, only two were published in his lifetime, *The Albannach* and *And the Cock Crew* (possibly his most important work), which, although written many years before, was not published until 1945. It is set in a Sutherland strath at the time of the Clearances, like Neil Gunn's *Butcher's Broom*. *Butcher's Broom* had appeared in 1934, when MacColla had written most of his novels. He had a suspicion, unfounded I think, that Gunn had stolen a march on him. *And the Cock Crew* is important, not only for its recreation of that traumatic period in Highland history, but for its analysis of the blighting effect of Calvinist theology on a fine, almost saintly personality. The central scene in the novel is the debate between the minister, Sachari, and the bard, Fearchar, about the Fall of Man and the part played in human life by music and song. Sachari maintains that pleasure in them springs from Man's utter depravity. Imperceptibly the argument becomes political – the right to resist injustice and tyranny. It seems that MacColla himself, in the person of Fearchar, is contending with Sachari, and incidentally with his own parents, opposing his vicious Calvinistic theories and proclaiming his Scottish nationalism, or, better, his Scottishness.

His unpublished work included *The Ministers,* published posthumously in 1979, and a kind of 'intellectual' thriller, *Facing the Muzhik,* which has yet to be published and which deals with the efforts of a body of Catholic missionaries, with headquarters in the Highlands of Scotland, to evangelise the Soviet Union. Perhaps the most important of the unpublished novels, provisionally entitled *Move Up John*, dealt with the coming of the Protestant Reformation to Scotland. MacColla regarded the Reformation as the single greatest calamity to have befallen Scotland. In *At the Sign of the Clenched Fist* he stated:

> the significance of the Reformation was the substitution of the Will for the Intellect, the Reformers' private interpretation of the Bible for the Authority of the Church, Wealth for Poverty as a spiritual ideal; it was equally a substitution of the Pulpit for the Altar.

Two fragments, the first and second chapters of this work, have been published, *Scottish Noël* in 1958 and *Ane Tryall of Hereticks*, which was included in *At the Sign of the Clenched Fist*. *Scottish Noël* is an account of an English invasion of Scotland in the sixteenth century, possibly part of Henry VIII's *Rough Wooing* – a stark, sombre battle-piece reminiscent of the battle scenes in *War and Peace*. It is set against a snowy landscape at Christmas time, and it strikes a note both of physical and psychological chill. It is a grim and moving narrative, displaying remarkable visual powers. It is one of the best examples of MacColla's writing. *Ane Tryall of Hereticks* is a dialogue in a rich, somewhat archaic, but thoroughly authentic, Scots between a panel of ecclesiastical judges and two men accused of heresy. It is weighted rather heavily in favour of the judges. It was presented as a play during the Edinburgh International Festival of Music and Arts in 1962, on a Saturday night. It was intended that, after the dramatic presentation, the audience should debate and discuss the questions raised. Unfortunately it was midnight and Sunday morning. The police marched into the premises and turned us all out. This sort of thing could only happen in Scotland. Robert Garioch, who was there, wrote a sardonic sonnet about it:

> I went to see 'Ane Tryall of Hereticks'
> by Fionn MacColla, treatit as a play;
> a wyce-like wark, but what I want to say
> is mair taen-up wi halie politicks
>
> nor wi the piece itsel; the kinna tricks
> the unco-guid get up whan thay hae
> their wey. Yon late-nicht ploy on Setturday
> was thrang wi Protestants and Catholics,

an eydent audience, wi fowth of bricht
arguments wad hae kept them gaun till Monday.
It seemed discussion wad last out the nicht,

hadna the poliss, sent by Mrs Grundy
pitten us out at twelve. And they were richt!
Wha daur debait religion on a Sunday?

The Ministers was posthumously published in 1979. It concerns an idealistic, young Church of Scotland minister in a Highland parish who has mystical experiences. These scandalise his parishioners and, even more, his fellow ministers. This was hardly respectable conduct in a man who should set an example to his flock. Like *The Albannach* and *And the Cock Crew,* as well as a great many other Scottish novels, *The Ministers* is concerned with the relation of an exceptional individual to the community in which he lives. This tension between 'the odd man out' and the community forms the theme, for example, of *The House with the Green Shutters* and *Gillespie,* although in these cases the 'odd man out' is, if anything, a force for evil and destruction and not a potentially regenerative agency.

The setting of the book is a West Highland crofting township with a declining seaboard population but with the urge to live almost broken, except for splutters of intolerant rancour and self-assertive spite. When the young minister's housekeeper discovers him practising techniques of meditation, 'falling asleep in body' and 'becoming a living soul', and finds that he has, as an aid to meditation, a series of reproductions of impressionist paintings, some of them female nudes, in his desk, the scene is set for a *cause célèbre*. The scene in the church where the ministers sitting in judgment on their unconventional colleague, is brilliantly described, with undertones of sardonic comedy. With three exceptions they are devout, well-meaning, even admirable men, but they cannot understand experience, above all spiritual experience, that deviates from the norm and has no place in the douce and respectable Kirk of Scotland. The ministers themselves are sharply differentiated. MacColla's presentation of them is not unsympathetic, but incisive and almost clinical, as in the case of the Reverend R. J. Macaskill, a native of the Isle of Lewis. He is stupid, belligerent, violently anti-Catholic, and fundamentally insecure. MacColla's rendering of Macaskill's Lewis speech, with his heavily aspirated ministerial 'howl' and his outraged falsetto bleat of 'nehket weemun', is accurate and brilliant. One meets his like, little 'popes' of their communities, from time to time in the Western Isles.

It is difficult to convey the quality of this novel. MacColla had always been interested in the phenomenon of perception, the relationship of the natural world to the consciousness that perceives and half-creates it. Accordingly the natural background of Wester Ross, which played such an important part in *The Albannach*, is mainly conveyed through the consciousness of MacCrury, the young minister. MacColla is particularly sensitive in indicating qualities of light in a landscape or a room. His work is also distinguished by exact and minute observation of physical peculiarities such as the two women on the road, 'drunk' with gossip and standing 'like a pair of stout elderly praying-mantises, their heads nodding slowly'. The book also generates intellectual excitement, although one suspects that many of the theories propounded by MacCrury, on e.g. the function of art or the interpretation of history, are the author's own. Like Raymond Aron, MacColla is opposed to the deterministic interpretation of history. He asserts the importance of reason and freewill. These occasional lengthy digressions on history and philosophy, stimulating and thought-provoking though they are, tend to impede the flow of the narrative. I helped to edit the book for publication, and these played an even more important part in the original typescript. MacColla is as in his previous novels, and like Neil Gunn, preoccupied and saddened by the decline of the Gaelic culture of the Highlands. An alternative solution, the industrialised little community in the area that he describes with such disgusted relish, is an alien and forced growth that only accelerates the process. It is not merely a question of more people in the Highlands, but of what people and with what values. *The Ministers* is, however, a much mellower work than the two previous novels.

MacColla could never decide whether he was an artist or a prophet. I feel that he thought that his polemical book, *At the Sign of the Clenched Fist*, was more important than his novels. He had superb descriptive skill and was capable of a fine narrative flow. He could write lyrical prose of a tough sweetness. He had a gift for satire and sardonic comedy. Yet often these qualities are cancelled by a dogged argumentativeness and tendency to embark on lengthy digressions. The whole question is ably discussed by John Herdman in the summer 1983 issue of *Cencrastus*. On the subject of influences he could be very sensitive. He angrily repudiated the suggestion that MacDiarmid had any influence on him. He recognised and appreciated the influence of Gaelic idiom on Neil Munro's style and also Munro's insight into Highland psychology, although he rightly pointed out that Munro's work was flawed by nostalgia and by a failure to face up to modern problems. MacColla had little sympathy for that other sensitive interpreter of Highland life, Neil Gunn. I think he resented the fact that Gunn had had over twenty novels published and that he had been given critical acclaim. His views on Lewis Grassic Gibbon who, like him, hailed from the north-east of Scotland, are interesting. In the short autobiographical work *Too Long In This Condition* MacColla refers to:

> the tremendous head of narrative steam he [i.e. Gibbon] is able to generate. But he is unkind to and misrepresents the Mearns peasantry – I am a Mearns peasant – my Douglas ancestors were there or thereabout for uncounted centuries.... What incensed me is that the admiration which should be shown for his literary merits is poured out on his supposed 'ideas', which, when they are not puerile, are incorrect ... the adulation poured on the wrong aspects of him now, constitutes him a cult figure, one whose defects are taken for virtues and held up to others as models.... Certainly of his famous trilogy it is painfully true, as Flaubert said of the latter part of *War and Peace*, 'il degrignole affreusement'.

This brings me to the novelists he most admired. He seldom, in his conversations with me, referred to the great English Novelists, and I don't think Scott or Galt meant much to him. He would refer admiringly to Stendhal, Flaubert and Proust, but his warmest admiration went to the great Russians, to Dostoevsky and, above all, to Tolstoy, of whom he remarked, with unconscious irony, that it was a pity that in his work the artist was so often sacrificed to the prophet. What about his views on Scotland, and on history? It must be admitted that he was partial and one-sided, with a strong Celtic bias. We have already discussed his views on the Reformation. He always contended that he was not in any sense a Catholic propagandist, but that he found that the Catholic faith most nearly accommodated his views. He deplored the narrow vision and Puritanism of, for example, much Irish and Scoto-Irish Catholicism. Certainly his analysis of the role of the Catholic Church in early Scottish history is accurate. From the time of the Wars of Scottish Independence in the thirteenth and fourteenth centuries, right up to the Reformation, the Catholic Church in Scotland was solidly patriotic and opposed to English domination, even at times contrary to Papal authority. But MacColla has nothing to say about the cultural and political contribution to Scottish life of the Scottish Episcopal Church, the church of Sir Thomas Urquhart of Cromarty, Bishop Leighton, of the north-western mystics, of Bishop Forbes and many others. This is all the more surprising in that, during the eighteenth century, the persecuted Episcopalians were patriotic Jacobites to a man, and MacColla was brought up in Angus, a strong Jacobite-

Episcopalian area. In his historical analysis, too, he tends to gloss over inconvenient facts, such as the Inquisition or the brutal repression of the Albigenses.

His Anglophobia, too, leads him to ignore the positive achievements of England in literature, architecture and art, not to speak of other aspects. MacColla failed to make the important distinction between 'the English' and 'the bloody English' (among whom I include Edward I, Henry VIII, and certain contemporary nobilities). He turned a blind eye to the incomparable richness of the English literary heritage. (The language of Shakespeare, Milton and the Authorised Version). He made disparaging remarks about the English language, which he himself used with skill and precision.

As a novelist he belongs to no recognised school. He is neither a Kailyarder nor a follower of the 'stinking fish' tradition of George Douglas Brown and others. He is diametrically opposed to the Celtic Twilight school, and he certainly does not, like John Buchan, adhere to the Stevensonian romantic tradition. Like Neil Gunn, that other very different interpreter of Highland life, he is very much of an individualist. He was a writer and thinker of distinction, a man of great integrity, passionately devoted to Scotland and to Gaelic culture. It is disgraceful that he should have suffered these long years of neglect, frustration, and the distortion of ideas by those who did not take the trouble to understand them. There is room for an intelligent and sympathetic full-scale study of his work.

Delivered at the conference Ecosse: Literature et Civilisation *at the University of Grenoble III.*

Sorley MacLean

IT HAS BEEN MY PRIVILEGE to have known MacDiarmid in the 1930s, before he had received the recognition due to him, and, at the same period, to have got to know men of such diverse personalities, views and talents as Fionn MacColla, Robert Garioch and Sorley MacLean, all of whom became my close personal friends. The old *Free Man* office at the top of India Buildings in Edinburgh's West Bow was a cementing influence. It was here that I first met MacDiarmid and MacColla, both of whom contributed a weekly column to the paper, and it was here too that I came across Robert Garioch. My friend, George Davie, who had an unerring nose for such things, had spoken to me of 'a young Edinburgh teacher called Sutherland, who was making effective poetic use of the language of the Edinburgh streets'. These were the days of 'Fi'baw in the Streets' and 'The Masque of Edinburgh'.

At least two of these *Free Man* contacts were to become connected with Sorley MacLean. He himself would agree with me that it was George Davie and I who first introduced him to *A Drunk Man Looks at the Thistle*. I cannot remember whether it was in Sorley's digs or in George's that we spent a whole evening reading and discussing the poem with him. I think it was George who introduced him to MacDiarmid in the flesh. The results we all know: the interaction of these two major poets was of very great importance for Scottish poetry. Sorley's relationship with Garioch was not as close as that with MacDiarmid, but they liked, respected and appreciated one another. Their first published work in book form was *Seventeen Poems for Sixpence,* a joint production issued in 1940 by the Chalmers Press (a handpress operated by Garioch). It was a splendid gesture of Scottish cultural identity in a dark period when it was threatened by eclipse.

But it was at Edinburgh University that I first got to know Sorley. He had graduated a few years before me, and, when I met him, in my second year, he was doing teacher training at Moray House. Again, I think it was George Davie who introduced me to Sorley. Like his elder brother, John, who was a distinguished classical scholar, and was later to translate *The Odyssey* into Gaelic hexameters, Sorley had a reputation for scholarship, having graduated with First Class Honours in English. He was also a perfervid Gael and a man of strong socialist convictions. I felt that he had absolute integrity and intellectual honesty, but, at the same time, too trusting and generous a nature. His glowing idealism and passionate commitment to a cause reminded one of Shelley, particularly the Shelley of 'Prometheus Unbound', who, indeed, was one of the earliest influences on his development. When he was aflame with enthusiasm for an idea or a poem, he was one of the most eloquent people I have ever met. In company he sat in silence, brooding over something or other (he had little gift for small talk), until a chance remark on a subject that touched him would arouse his interest. He would rise to his feet his eyes would flash, and a torrent of rhythmically cadenced, magnificent language would pour forth: a kind of vatic fury would possess him.

At that time our discussions would range widely over politics, both national and international. These were the days of Hitler, 'the brute and brigand at the head of Europe', and of the dreary, pusillanimous Chamberlain government. We were both affected by the myths of 1916 and 1917 and were both interested in and sympathetic to Irish nationalism, although I was struck by the remark of O'Leary the old Fenian quoted by Yeats that there were certain things a man must not do for his country. Pearse and Connolly played a prominent part in our discussions. Connolly, the socialist, above all appealed to Sorley's imagination, an appeal that has lasted, as his moving poem on the National Museum in Dublin shows. It is appropriate that in later life Sorley should have been honoured by the National University of Ireland.

We differed in our attitudes towards Scottish independence. At the time I was in favour of any non-fascist movement in that direction, whereas Sorley was committed primarily to a socialist remedy. The outbreak of the Spanish Civil War moved him profoundly. In more than one of his earlier poems he upbraids himself for not playing a hero's part in that conflict. He pays tribute to the poets, Julian Bell, John Cornford and Lorca who perished in it.

The conflict with fascism had its lighter moments. I remember vividly one summer evening in Edinburgh when Sir Oswald Mosley was holding a rally in the Usher Hall. He had brought a contingent of thugs, euphemistically call stewards, to deal with any opposition. A group of about a dozen members from the Celtic Society of Edinburgh University, including Sorley and myself, went along to the meeting. Most of them were stalwart six-footers. At one point in the proceedings Sorley rose to his feet to ask the question. 'What about your socialist pledges?' (Mosley had been a Minister in a Labour Government). Immediately four or five blackshirts materialized at the end of the row in which we were sitting, with the aim of forcibly ejecting Sorley. All the Celtic stalwarts rose to their feet and glared menacingly at the 'stewards', who at once retreated. Later there were wild scenes outside the hall, when a collection of irate citizens, including the inevitable shawlie wives from the Old Town, hurled insults and threw stones and pieces of lead piping at the buses that were to convey the blackshirts back to England. How far they were motivated by nationalism and how far by socialism it is hard to say.

As for literature, we ranged widely over Greek, Latin, French, English and Scottish poetry. Coming to more modern times we talked about Yeats, Eliot, Valéry, Pound, Lawrence, MacDiarmid, and the emerging MacSpaundy group, although Sorley's crofter radicalism, nourished on memories of the Battle of the Braes and Glendale, was poles removed from the affected English public school communism of these gentlemen. But we nearly always came back to MacDiarmid and Yeats, to whose work we were passionately devoted. Yeat's despairing love for Maude Gonne and the magnificent lyrics in which he expressed it particularly moved Sorley. In a sense they anticipated the anguished lyricism of some of his own love poetry, where he apostrophizes his beloved, 'You are the fire of my lyric – you made a poet of me through sorrow'. In one poem, indeed, he equates her with Maude Gonne and with Deirdre, Eimhir and Grainne. Sorley had written some verses in English – influenced by contemporary models – but he was dissatisfied with these, and was considering expressing himself in the language he had known before he had acquired any English and in which he still thought – Gaelic. He disapproved, however, of the facile lyricism and patterned nostalgia of much nineteenth century and early twentieth century Gaelic verse. What he was to achieve was both a step forwards – he brought Scottish Gaelic literature into the twentieth century – and a return to earlier models – in the use of syllabic verse form.

I regretted my ignorance of the language, since it meant that I was cut off from a major part of Scotland's cultural heritage. For an evening Sorley would read aloud to me, and expound a literal translation of poems by Ian Lom, Alexander MacDonald, Duncan Ban Macintyre and William Ross. He had a great deal to say, too, about the anonymous lyrics of the sixteenth and seventeenth centuries. My debt to him in this respect is incalculable. My eyes were opened to a whole new cultural dimension. Given the right audience Sorley was an inspired and inspiring teacher. He did a great deal for the teaching of Gaelic as Headmaster of Plockton High School. His continued and eventually successful struggle (along with the late Donald Thomson of Oban) to introduce the Learner's Paper in the SCE examination, is only one example of his activity in this direction. We must not ignore, either the help he gave Hugh MacDiarmid in his translations of MacDonald's 'Birlinn of Clan Ranald' and of Macintyre's 'Praise of Ben Dorain', not to mention the other Gaelic poems which were included in MacDiarmid's *Golden Treasury of Scottish Poetry*. His achievements both as Gaelic poet and propagandist for Gaelic culture have been recognized by his fellow Gaels, in that he has been accorded the almost unique distinction of having been elected for a second time Chieftain of the Gaelic Society of Inverness.

Sorley's first teaching appointment was to his old school, Portree High School. In June 1935, after I had my finals in English at Edinburgh, I spent a week or so in Skye. It was my first experience of the West Highlands. I was full of anxious anticipation as the train wound around Duncan Ban's shapely Ben Dorain, and as later I gazed out at the white sands of Alexander MacDonald's Morar and came in sight of the jagged impatient scrawl of the Cuillin against the dark grey slate of the sky. At the weekend he and I visited his home in Raasay. Raasay has played an important part in his life and poetry. His most formative years were spent there and it forms the setting for some of his deepest and most personal poems, such as 'Hallaig' and 'Coilltean Ratharsair'. We were rowed across from Braes in Skye by Sorley's father and some of his friends. That night we attended a ceilidh in the house of his grandfather, a venerable patriach with the liveliest eyes I have ever seen and the most infectious laugh I have ever heard. The night was spent in song and story, and I counted myself privileged to be there. It was a revelation of a way of life, a culture, that had persisted despite forces inimical to it, throughout untold centuries. For Sorley comes of a race of 'tale-bearers', transmitters of an incomparable oral tradition of song, of story, of historical memories. As well as MacLean he has Matheson and Nicolson blood, and he has an amazingly detailed knowledge of Skye, Raasay, and the Lochalsh area; of places, of houses, of the people and their forebears, down to the remotest genealogical ramifications. All of this, allied to scholarship, has made him the formidable figure he is. To go round Skye in his company is a rich experience. To him the sixteenth century is as real and vivid as the present day. This feeling emerges very clearly in that elusive poem, 'Hallaig':

Tha iad fhathast ann a Hallaig,	They are still in Hallaig,
Clann Ghill-Eain's Clann Mhicleòid	MacLeans and MacLeods,
na bh'ann ri linn Mhic-	all who were there in time of
Ghille-Chaluim:	Mac Ghille-Chaluim
Chunnacas na mairbh beò.	the dead have been seen alive.

But Sorley was not the only member of his family to be distinguished for his command of the Gaelic oral tradition. His younger brother Calum was one of the finest collectors of his generation of folk-lore and traditional tales both in Ireland and in the Western Isles of Scotland. He also wrote an original and stimulating book on the Highlands. One of the finest of Sorley's later works is the moving and tender elegy he wrote on Calum. In this poem the terms of reference, the values, are peculiarly, almost tribally, Gaelic: it might have been composed at any time during the past five centuries.

Later, when we were both teaching in Edinburgh, Sorley would read and translate his as yet unpublished poems to my wife and me in our flat in the New Town. We realised that these were no ordinary productions. In their blend of passion and intellect, their striking imagery, they bore the unmistakable imprint of poetic genius of a high order. When war broke out, he left pencilled translations of some of them with us: they are now in the National Library of Scotland. When news came of our call-up we spent an uproarious evening in the company of James Carmichael Watson and others. Watson was Professor of Celtic at Edinburgh and the editor of the poems of Mary Macleod. Soon afterwards he enlisted in the Royal Navy and was killed in a torpedo attack – a tragic loss to Celtic scholarship.

Our ways parted. I served in the United Kingdom and Europe. Sorley was posted to the Middle East, to the same theatre of war in which Garioch was captured to spend dreary years in prison camps. Sorley was severely wounded at El Alamein. These were anxious months in which we did not know what had happened to him. Fortunately the late Douglas Young and the Reverend John MacKechnie arranged for the publication of his poems. *Dain Do Eimhir* appeared in 1943, and it proved to be one of the most important works to be published in Scotland in this century.

Sorley was invalided out of the Army and resumed teaching in Edinburgh, where I saw a fair amount of him during my last year in the Forces, when I was stationed at Scottish Command HQ. Later still, when I taught at Peebles, we met frequently. By this time he had taken one of the best decisions of his life; he married Renée Cameron of Inverness. They complement one another. With her sense of humour, sound practical sense and sunny disposition, combined with an appreciation of the finer things of life, she is the perfect wife for Sorley.

During those Edinburgh years he saw a great deal of his fellow-poet, Sydney Goodsir Smith. Indeed for a time Sorley and Renée shared a house in Craigmillar Park (immortalised in 'Under the Eildon Tree') with the Smiths. Every time I saw him Sorley was full of amusing stories about Sydney – 'the Auk' – whose unconventional ways and witty conversation intrigued him.

Years later, when Sorley was back in the Highlands, as Headmaster of Plockton High School, our paths crossed once more. I was Her Majesty's Inspector of Schools for Ross and Cromarty, and, of course, Plockton was in my District. It was then that I realised fully the extent of his work for Gaelic education, and his dedication to the interests of his pupils. In many ways he followed the pattern of the old-fashioned Scottish dominie, capable of teaching, and teaching well, a variety of subjects. Staffing problems led to his taking classes at one time or another in English, History, Latin, French and Gaelic, in addition to the normal administrative duties attached to his post. He was a fearless fighter for what he considered to be the best interests of his pupils, undeterred by the authority of county councils and their representatives, or even, on occasion, the Scottish

Education Department. But unlike the old Scots dominie, he was not only interested in the 'lad (or lass) o pairts'. He was particularly helpful and sympathetic to pupils who had difficulty with their studies or had personal problems.

But these activities took their toll. There were years when the poetic impulse seemed to have dried up. Towards the end of his teaching career, however, and in the years of retirement, when he settled in Skye in a house (under Glamaig and facing Raasay) which had been inhabited by one of his ancestors, there has been a magnificent reflorescence of poetry, much more meditative, reflective and abstruse, less turbulent, than the early lyrics. Official recognition followed. He became Writer in Residence at Edinburgh University. He has received Doctorates from three universities. He has taken part in poetry readings in Scotland, England, Ireland, on the Continent, and in Canada and the USA. He is referred to respectfully (and this is a rare achievement for a Scottish writer) in 'quality' magazines and papers south of the Border. Throughout it all he has retained his integrity and – I use the term in a favourable sense – his admirable simplicity.

In some respects he is like the great Provencal poet, Mistral, although Mistral does not have the same astonishing lyrical power. They resemble one another in their attachment to their roots, familial and topographical, in their interpretation of the spirit and traditions of the countryside that had nurtured them, and in their successful use of a minority language in a declining state. It is a miracle that language spoken by a handful of people in a remote part of Scotland, at the north-western extremity of Europe, should have been the medium of expression of the greatest living poet in the British Isles.

Six Poems

by

Gerrie Fellows

Constructions

I

Above the street   a man in balance
takes the metal's arc   paring
his stance   pole by precise pole
down to a clipped breath

You and I and Marianne close
to the window   watching
him swing the bars   their
bandages of colour   out
over the late afternoon street
The movement of a hand   unclasping
from a taut construction
a part of what is possible

The long bars   components of a pause

A roof   caulked and healing
in the sun   like an upturned boat
inland   in a border town

II

A bar of light moves across
a green table

A step is washed with sun

In the yard   damp clothes
cling to the line
like summer leaves to a vine
with a sticky wrapped quiet

We knit the intimate thread
of our lives
into this moment
Ourselves
yet loss
an empty handedness

The tall avocado
at the narrow window
stretches   for light

You talk of a man working
body bent   steadying
flame to metal
intent on mending

How a life is sliced like this

What we hoped to make
is not made
Other things happen

III

Huddled
into the lee of a wall
wind battered   looking out
over a thin coastline
to exposed constructions
The stump of a gatepost
Plain houses   pinned
to scratched fields

The settlement closing
into the rain's wake
an inaccessible root
        surviving
        unguessed at

Ourselves
the strangers

The cars turning back
into the looped road
reflections   of rain
and earth

IV

A poverty
of description
drawn through
the fingers
to a thin clay
Or held
in the palm
and shaped
to a thumb pot
The hard blue
glaze of sky
over earth

Constructed
Reconstructed
Out of these materials
These selves

This is what the hands know

The certainty of the self
having no more need of proof
than had the pivot of the poles
in the hands of the scaffolder

Or the eye's knowledge of green
knowing no language   more
than its own immaculate spell

Clear voiced
in a moment beyond logic

V

The seaboard with its rage of water
is behind us   separated from us
by the stalks of the calendar
connected to us
through the cool glow of the pots

In this milk blur they shine across our talk

From a Window 22/7/86

In the back court
the morning after Glasgow Fair
three dustmen
who have somehow lost a dustcart
lounge against a pebbled wall
in the quick sunshine

It's the clatter of their laughter
that's drawn me   tousle headed
to pull up the blind
(We're all late this morning)
and stand   gazing down

Dark head   greasy curls   thin fair hair
the smoke   spiralling between them
three men in a kind of communion
At their elbows   forgotten
the sacks of used tins   tea-leaves
vegetable parings

High on the bleached wall   light
slaps at the flat vermillion blind
A woman in a cotton nightdress
opens the curtains

A blond man   lying on the lawn
the others draped against a metal fence
are still laughing

Young men   old enough
to be husbands   wiry
careless   in the bold sunshine

Will they grow old   battered   surviving
divorces   happy marriages   heart attacks
Using thick forearms to lift pints
Staggering home on Fair Monday
Pulling up the blinds
on a brief sunlit morning such as this
and gazing down   at other men
laughing   among the garbage

A Journey Through Sand

A red shirt will almost last the journey
ripping at the shoulders
where my rucksack straps
the sun's bleach   the blown sand
have worn it to a surface as thin
as butter muslin

The desert's yellow ochre settles
into folds and pores   Clothing   hair
have become a part of the same dull skin
Driven south
A grainy column

Here a figure glimpsed   through high dust
stunted scrub   might appear as a pillar
of eroded light

The body is brushed by heat
A snake moves   quick gold

There is no question of crossing to the other side
To the dark   almost coolness
of the cafe
              but never quite coolness
a thick blue shade

There is no question of crossing the sand
laid open to the sun's merciless noon applause
a ferocious stadium

I have grown still
I have learnt patience
I know how to wait   swaying
squat on my heels

Drink slowly
Swill the water round your mouth   Three times
will be enough   You'll get used to it
It's worse if you drink too much

But I gulp   unheeding   I know nothing
but thirst and water

Nightfall

I come home through late afternoon
A web of sky blowing dark   against
the stair   In the flat
the heaped garments brushed by shadows
The bedclothes   flung back

I dreamed I was piloting a car
of women through a foreign country
Traffic flung forward   against us
(Even the boys on bicycles straggled
across the lanes)   And I
could only hold the wheel   curving
through the storm of missiles   spun
at us   like snow in the headlights
Annihilating

I tidy the room   pick up
the strewn clothing   fold
a ribbon of jerseys into a drawer
Touch   in the soft wool
the glossy wood   cautiously
the faithful glimmer of being

Remembering how I woke
out of the acute dark   thinking
I'm still here

I go through to the kitchen
put on the kettle   stand watching
behind the tipped up circles of the dishes
the window   film with steam
and through it
night fall

Three Stages of Landscape:
(The occurrence of morning in Whiteinch)

I

Night of rain with a resonance of glass
a heartbeat   The irreducible sound
spun into the text of a compressed hour

The eardrum nags for cognizance
at a furled whisper   A voice carrying
the scraps of islands   eroded
particles of seashell   salt ocean

Gift and promise poised in the dark pause
Listened to   perceived   as a stillness
allows the audible breath
Or before dawn   the cessation of sleep

II

A flag of yellow light   opening
into the wider landscape of a wave   A late
grey wind   The seed rain's swept comb
plucking the flat charcoal to ash and silver

                Slate at a roof ridge
                Angle of red ochre
                A wind from the north
One gull   in flight draws an oblique tilt
into a sky the colour of butter muslin or
moss agate   bullied smoke

III

River into wing   slices its blind sail
into remembered light   My younger self
looking out over stitched black rails
from a house moored like a tall ship
to an uncertain quay   rickety with
voices   dreams   green water

The winter smoke ghosting to pure line
(The narrow thread of an escarpment
vanished into mist)

I was dispossessed by lack of light

A woman waiting for spring to open out
watching a sky form itself from the periphery
become baroque with rain   burled and gathered
                    visioning the north
          into a knot of cloud and cloth

A portion of moisture drawn inextricably
into the weave of endeavour

To Construct a Journey

                    A full moon
The headlights pick out sheep   The road
remembered   rain driven   glistens
shaping itself to a clearer speech

                    A plain language
with which to construct a journey
Its furrowed   late winter fields
The way the lines might run into the sun
Or shadow slip against a tractor's signs

A plough turning up artifacts worn
clear of ancient grief
                    What remains
is simply this neat   wire dissected land
The fenced animals bred for slaughter

The gently folded fields

At a gate   grass stitched
with tyre tracks

                    A wedding party
moving in the figures of tapestry
towards the long tables   the spilt wine
                        and fable   the feast
                        the danced pastourelle

                        And at its heart
the unrequitable   creature howl

On Reclaiming the Local

and

The Theory of the Magic Thing

Tom Leonard

The 'Glasgow operative' is, while trade is good and wages high, the quietest and most inoffensive of creatures. He cares comparatively little for the affairs of the nation, he is industrious and contented. Each six months he holds a saturnalia – one on New Year's Day, the other at the Fair (occurring in July) and his excesses at these points keep him poor during the intervals. During periods of commercial depression, however, when wages are low, and he works three-quarter time, he has a fine nose to scent political iniquities. He begins to suspect that all is not right with the British constitution. These unhappy times, too, produce impudent demagogues, whose power of lungs and floods of flashy rhetoric work incredible mischief. To these he seriously inclines his ear. He is hungry and excited. He is more anxious to reform Parliament than to reform himself. He cries out against tyranny of class-legislation, forgetting the far harder tyranny of the gin-palace and the pawn-shop.

(Alexander Smith: *A Summer in Skye* Ch. 16, 1865)

THIS PASSAGE COULD have been called 'The Problem of Them'. And so many urban poems, pieces of prose, and whole anthologies of either or both, have been produced for which 'The Problem of Them' would have been the most honest title. The works assume that those supposedly described don't read the literature that supposedly describes them. Smith here assumes that 'the' Glasgow operative will never be the reader: the operative is a predictable behaviour pattern, which pattern does not include reading the works of Alexander Smith. 'An' operative would *have* a behaviour pattern. 'The' operative is one. Readers of R. D. Laing might recognise the strategy. In a sense 'the Glasgow operative' is the Patient, while the writer has become the Doctor, the man-who-sees, the benign possessor of superior insight: in other words, a traditional image of the Poet.

This patriarchal image of the poet as detached diagnostic judge still dominates influential literary scenes. Most of Morrison and Motion's *The Penguin Book of Contemporary British Poetry,* for instance, is relentlessly judgmental. Separation is assumed – of the judging mind from the personal experience, of the poet/narrator from the beings who inhabit the world described. This is what is expected, this is what being a Real Poet is all about. The poet is a spectator at someone else's experience, be that someone else a he, a she, 'they', or the I of former (!) working-class days. This is to be 'objective', the professional tone, the invisible suit of office. The 'professional' exists through a language that acquits him of present

---

William Elder

from To The Defenders of Things as They Are (1870)

(First Supervisor of the Fountain Gardens, Paisley)

Why speak of peace, of order, and of law?
Teach mute subserviency to those who draw
The water, hew the wood, and dig the soil,
Whose piteous fate is hard incessant toil?
On land and sea, to work from day to day,
To heap up wealth, but which they may
Ne'er hope to share with those who rule
Their fate, and who in church and school
Teach obedience passive, doctrine fit for slaves.
To make men bow to tyrants, priests, and knaves,
Oh! when will mankind cease to heed such teachers?
Send to the 'right about' the glib and oily preachers
Of such a gospel, who, in the past as now,
Have taught the people 'twas their fate to bow
And be content and happy in that station,
Where 'God has placed them' to enrich the nation,
To work for kings, aristocrats, and priests so vile,
Who live at ease upon the 'holy' spoil
They wring from labour, and who feed and gorge
Revel in pomp, while others toil in mine and forge.

personal involvement: he is in control, through his craft. The ardently opinionated, the ardent in all forms, the raisers of voices, the thumpers on the table, the 'swearers', the passionate, those who burst into tears – these are all absent. This would be unprofessional, 'emotionalist', 'uncraftsmanlike'. To return to the Laingian reference, this would all indicate the presence of a Patient: and this is an anthology of Doctors.

Now you can trudge up and down nineteenth century literary criticism into the twentieth, from the introduction to the *Lyrical Ballads,* Coleridge via Germany, Arnold, Browning, Ruskin, Carlyle right through until you eventually arrive in the room that Mr Eliot is sorting out his objective correlative in, and had you lived through the period in question, and had had an attentive ear, you

---

Alexander Wilson
(1766-1813) from The Insulted Pedlar

Ae nicht short syne as hame I trampit
Beneath my pack, wi' banes sair crampit,
But owre a wee bit dyke I lampit,
      And trottin burn;
There to do for my ain bethankit,
      A needfu' turn.

Aweel, I scarcely had begun
To ope the evacuating gun,
I'll swear they hadna reached the grun,
      When frae the wud
A bellied gent, steps owre the run,
      Wi' 'Dem your blood!'

By whose authority or order
Came ye upon this corn-rig border
To rowe your filth and reeking ordour
      On me a Bailie?
Hence wi' your dirt, else by the Lord, or
      Lang, I'll jail ye.'

---

would have noticed as time progressed that the voices around you discussing the books you were reading, seemed to sound more and more sort of, ehm, 'objective'. The trouble was that after Wordsworth had been rrolled in Earrth's diurrnial urrn, and education was getting a bit universalised, the chaps hit on this super wheeze, namely how to turn your own voice into an object of social status. Nothing sinister, nothing undemocratic. All you needed to acquire this property yourself, was a fair bit of money. Now if your own voice has become an object that you share in common with other fellows who happened also to have a fair bit of money, how can this voice, as object, be other than objective? Now, when you open your mouth, you have the power to be im-personal.

The trouble with asking humans to enact the impersonal is that they usually do so by objectifying the humans around them. The humans around them won't behave like objects, so the 'impersonal' diagnostian has to construct mechanistic models of those humans that turn them into the objects they have refused to become. The models of depersonalisation are inevitably linguistic. That's why at the heart of politics is language, at the heart of language is politics. Always the converse happens to what is supposed to be going on. An address to a city-as-a-person, as for instance, Smith's address to 'Glasgow' in his best-known poem of that name, anthropomorphises beyond the personal conflict on which urban trade is actually based, to a single 'personal' unity which can be seen as 'natural' or aesthetically invigorating. The anthropomorphic functionalist image serves to create a bogus unified 'personality': it does so by leaving the streets clear of those whose opinions, if actually listened to, might spoil the image of a healthy and unified 'body' politic.

I think that in Britain the dominant literary tradition still 'taught' in educational institutions has been established by clearing the streets in this manner. A dominant value-system has been allowed to marginalise that which does not correspond to it, declaring it deviant and therefore invalid. It has been able to do so by the method of making the mode of expression of these dominant values literally synonymous with 'objectivity'. Now it is the mode of expression that counts: that device by which the persona is given the status of being detached, impersonal, above the battle. In speech it has been achieved through the fee-paying Received Pronunciation, buttressed by the Classics-based prescriptive grammar hammered into the pupils. These are the schools where, every single damned one of them, the British Army has its Officer Cadet Corps, where the young Inheritors of Objective Speech can take first steps in that training to lead into future battle those ordinary citizens trapped in the authentic expression of their own personal language.

The 'leaders' are separate from their language. Their language is a piece of purchased property held in common amongst themselves. Therefore, when they address you, their being stands at a tangent to what they have expressed; and when one attempts dialogue with

Edward Polin
from In The Days When We Were Radicals (1840)

(Paisley weaver and editor. The two verses here are from a
song in the satiric playlet *Councillors in Their Cups*)

In the days when we were Radicals,
   A short time ago,
We spouted much of labour's wrongs,
   And of the people's woe;
We held that Whigs, and Tories both,
   Had always tyrants been,
And bawled the people's rights were lost
    Those robbers vile between;
        And thus we ranted to the crowd
          With pleasant wordy show,
        In the days when we were Radicals
        A short time ago.

... And when we find that we shall need
   The people's aid again
We'll soon forget that Whigs we've turn'd,
   Although 'tis now so plain;
Our voices shall be raised once more
   As loud as e'er they've been,
To spout and sing our treason songs,
   And laugh at Prince and Queen.
        And thus again we'll gull the crowd
          With pleasant wordy show,
        As we did when we were Radicals
        A short time ago.

that expression, one addresses not simply a person but a closed
system of value. A closed system of value stands between the two
human beings in communication. To speak back, one must first of
all digest all the components of that system of value oneself, in order
that one can oneself stand at a tangent to what one is saying, and
reply to the person who has addressed you, from within the closed
system of value that stands between. In so doing, one will of course
have enlarged that closed system slightly, by the addition of one's
own contribution, while one exists personally unchanged outside it.
And all the components of that value-system will have been frac-

tionally altered, too, by the addition of one's own contribution. This, of course, is the Theory of the Magic Thing.

Like speech, like literature. Here the writer will be detached, at a tangent to the work produced, and the Magic Thing will be buried in the work itself. This Magic Thing will seem like an ordinary thing to the personae created by the man-who-sees, but to the reader-who-knows, this seemingly ordinary thing will in fact stand out as an inner Magic Thing, that places a value on the actions of those described. This value can be seen as the profit-value from the outlay on the personae created. As such, one might think that the personae have only been created in order that some profit-value might be reaped from them. From a functionalist point of view though what's important is that the profits reaped in any society from such trans-actions are not in a currency that might destabilise the prevailing monetary system. Hence the two basic functions of the application of the Theory of the Magic Thing are: –

(a) verification of a closed value-system

(b) control of the money supply.

This is a restatement of my criticism of Alexander Smith's quoted paragraph. Part of the verification of the closed value-system must consist in indicating that the lower orders don't have access to it. Classical music, literature, philosophy; a narrator couldn't casually mention without comment about conflict, that a working-class person happened to be listening to Beethoven. That is one of the things that the working class 'don't do'. The narrator would have to bring in some Magic Thing to cure the supposed conflict within the work, or, more likely, let the Beethoven stand as the Magic Thing that showed why the narrator couldn't go back to his poignant old roots. (I think some of Tony Harrison's work does this very clearly.) The truth is that having nodded through the value-system, it's almost impossible for the narrator not to sound either patronising (being functionally superior to his personae in the first place) or sentimental. But the profits paid out by the Magic Thing in this area show the imposed restricted nature of the behaviour from which they are derived: bathos, nostalgia, a kind of 'baffled poignancy' – or laughter at the expense of the described.

The most obvious area where the writer is usually patronising is in the depiction of speech – the apostrophes that indicate the 'and of the writer 'elping out the reader, indicating by sign the prescriptive norm from which the speaker is 'deviating'. He can't talk proper words himself, so the writer indicates where there's bits missed out, so you can better understand. It is important to grasp that such technique, of putting in apostrophes, has got nothing to do with indicating sound, since apostrophes themselves contribute nothing to the representation of sound. What they do indicate is a supposed deficiency of meaning which the reader, over the head of the persona as it were, must supply. The personae are trapped within the closed value-system that denigrates their use of language, while the writer communicates with the reader over their heads. For similar reasons any attempt actually to indicate specific speech sounds by spelling codes must avoid layers of puns etc. that provide nudges and winks at the speaker's expense: only by giving the speaker himself a consciousness that might include knowledge of them (i.e. that the speaker is at least partly the author) can this be valid. In this way the speaker can refer to the nature of the codes he is using and the language to which it refers.

Anonymous
On Three Children in the Eastwood Churchyard (1814)

Here lie the mouldering remains
O' three unskirsent, guiltless weans;
Wha never underwent that rite
Maks sinners mystically white;
Will ony zealot e'er presume
These early dwellers in the tomb
Wad nae admission gain in Heaven
Or that their sins were unforgiven?
Let him wi' care his Bible read,
An' to this precious text gie heed,
'Wha wad the bliss o' Heaven attain
Maun enter like a little wean.'

This again though is to side with the Patient against the Doctor, to accord their little bit of present-time consciousness that can have a behaviour pattern rather than just be one. It's that area of present-time consciousness that writers like Beckett and Graham give to their personae; and the personae in turn pass it on to the reader. It's a very political thing to do, since it seems to assume that the only – and equal – value that can be placed on any human being is in the fact that the human being actually exists. Insisting on the basic equality of consciousness means rejecting the closed-value system, handing the currency of valid being to all and sundry (increasing the money supply) and refusing to self-objectify individually or collectively.

It's in the reification of linguistic codes and their possession by dominant and powerful classes wherein lies real danger, now literally for the whole world. That reification will always contain as part of its mechanics the device to maintain the illusion that social conflict does not exist, or that such conflict as exists can be meaningfully recreated, and resolved, within its own perimeter. Self-expression outside that code becomes simply a mechanism of self-elimination. The dominant refuse to recognise that all language is an instrument of consciousness: instead, it is held as a symptom. Others don't 'have' a language – they 'are' it. In dismissing the language, one dismisses the existence of its users – or rather, one chooses to believe that they have dismissed themselves. The 'local' becomes that which can be bombed from 30,000 feet. After all, it had chosen to cede its existence even before it was destroyed.

This happens to the past as well as to the present, and it's happened to the West of Scotland as to everywhere else. The poems that accompany this article are from a projected anthology *Renfrewshire Poetry from the French Revolution to the First World War*. Much of the poetry I've selected is committed, anticlerical, republican; descriptive of work and poverty, with no separation between writer and persona, no 'distancing' of emotion; much of it is about drink, people who enjoyed getting drunk and people who saw the suffering it caused and wrote bitterly of it, with or without satire, and with no Salvation Army tambourines jingling at the end. There's Alexander Wilson, who emigrated to America and became a pioneer American ornithologist: before he left Scotland he had been jailed for his poem 'The Shark' attacking a local mill-owner, and forced to publicly burn his poem at Paisley Cross; there's his poem 'The Insulted Pedlar' satirising the arrogance of a local landowner trying to drive the poet off his land with a gun when the poet was doing a shite in the landowner's field. None of the stuff is cosy. It's got nothing to do with those execrable sentimental nights out with bathos-laden songs about the slums I left behind me. It's as likely to upset the same type of people today as it would have upset a hundred years ago. And by that I don't mean it's all anti-establishment. There's James Maxwell, 'Poet in Paisley' as he titled himself in the pamphlets he sold in the streets, thundering on in rhyming-couplets about how blasphemous poets might think they're smart now (1793) but they won't think that on their way to Hell. He was healthy. His mind was in his language, and he was entitled to his point of view. There's Robert Pollok of Eaglesham, whose huge 'The Course of Time' – a kind of Scottish Presbyterian 'Paradise Lost' – was, according to Eyre-Todd in *The Glasgow Poets*, to be found in most Scottish cottages and farmhouses throughout the nineteenth century. My own copy is described on the title-page as 'Seventy-Eighth Thousand'. There's poetry as a learning device: 'An Excursion Through The Starry Heavens' – a rhyming guide to the main-constellations by the Reverend Robert Boog, minister at Paisley Abbey for 49 years. There's poems reflecting deep personal depression, feelings of being gossiped about, the kind of work that those vanguardists with patronising attitudes to working-class people would think best forgotten as not showing 'them' in a positive enough light. The political poetry – obviously including Marion Bernstein's – remains a valid interpretation of current affairs.

But these poems are not held worthy of serious consideration. They name names, articulate opinions, would carry the conflict into the living-room. And for this they have been hospitalised in the oblivion such deviance deserves. But there's another view, and it's the view that I want to put across here. Such 'patients' are alive and well, and they have a multitude of things to say about the present as well as the past. Locality by locality, A to Z of behind-the-counter library stock, old newspaper by old newspaper, people must go on with the work of release.

Tales of Edgar and Virginia and other poems

Graham Fulton

Tales of Edgar and Virginia

     Truth
contorts.
Edgar with his headache sits
on a chair, by the table,
his thin left leg
crossed over his thin leg
in 1845, or thereabouts,
and hands clasped but
not in prayer
no sirree

      somersaults,
a vein gulps in the deep
of his big opium bone
as cousin Virginia
aged 14, perhaps,
stands beside the piano
droning a dirge by gaslight
with Ma's grimace on
the mantelpiece

     yes,
Virginia wears
Inquisition-red ribbons
in her sparrow-brown hair,
which is just as well
as they match
the gory grapes
she sputters, spouts
upon straining the highest note

because she has consumption
and they polka dot
her bodice, thud
on ivory keys

        his
brain
storms, boils, erects,
as he bundles her up to bed
supperless, up
the stairs of their happy home
in the Industrial North
upon which their marriage
remains unconsummated
and a doctor is
sent for (come

        quickly
please
it's an emergency)
and you'll have to iron
your own shirts,
clip your own toenails
from now on, Eddie,
until you find yourself
out for the count
in a Baltimore poll-booth
under sawdust, and peculiar
circumstances, no doubt

Stunting

Whacked   dimpled
baby moon ball
bounces on the green
green   again   Monsters
with white knees
and backs crash
from rough
alongside terrified clean rodents
They snatch
and drop the ball
into a fat bag

slip secret agently
into new rough
sniggering   and farting
into short enormous trousers
with deep squirming pockets

The golf man wanders puffing   puzzled
The train from the sea to Glasgow plods by
The monsters pick
stringy fruit pith
from their mouth
urinate briskly
hotly
behind itchycoo
spit chocolate spits
in the pram
pushchair
electric
fire dump
sell the same ball
back to the same man
before it gets
too dark

The tarpaulins groan on the building sites
The smokes from the factories wheeze by
There is much left
to look forward to

drunk ramming taxis

vaulting strange
dustcart rust
and tumble driers

Bits of Sweet Home

A down and out
incredibly
slumped
between

two cars
a red one   a dented one
with windscreen wipers
nodding dog
fizzy cassette
in the William Hill's
the bookmakers
car park   for staff only

Flaking green grim statue
of ornithologist and poet
Spray fresh bench
in pretty place
spray paint lift
in pretty scheme
Shampoo sachets
flat crisp packets
bobbing in the chlorine
A woman

going over
on her ankle
on the library steps   chutney
in the gutter   twiglets
in the slush   Pinocchio
in the graveyard
strung
winter
river lights
bill-posted shutters
of the old gone fire brigade station

The gone thread mill
The gauntlet
of shoeshops
to the horizon

Smoke-choked pub serving bar lunches
with tabby cat carpet   cubicle splish
fruit machines
durex machines
Four foot man dodging
elbows   out of the corner

of the eye disgust
collecting still-warm
lip print
glasses

for a little living

spittle glaciers
sliding
down
the
insides
to the bottom
of what
is bottomless   eating
something which might
be something
very nice to eat
like a toasted
sand
wich
like the one you get
at the pensioners coffee morning

winning
a bet with himself
or with someone else
unseen   slumped between
the next two cars   or the next two
the next two   next two   two

Postcard from the Knackers Yard
The River Clyde landing on Gallipoli. April 25th, 1915.

Scorched
heathen canvas,
scene of the crime.
A thicker
than

Turkish
water colour slaughter
painted by insane,

commissioned
hands.

Sir Ian full
of snuff and port.
Pontoons stacked with
bum-fluff meat,
immortal altar

Saps in sepia
shimmying
on virgin blood,
cherry red
coat cement.

Whistling God
save the King,
first one
heaving
fusilier,

Then two thousand,
swaddled
in quilts
of horror
and steel.

The Unmasking Scene

Tinted purple and
                in synchronisation
with an upright piano

                Mary Philbin unmasked

Lon Chaney

                to reveal a wire
trussed nose and
                a receding hairline

which were essential

credentials for an

artist in the Twenties
            until my mantis baby
with varnished toenails

            gave me her halo to stop me

growing out of my trousers

            and asked me where it
all went wrong
            to which I offered

'spineless and spiteful or

            something or other'

and she gave me her popcorn
            to stop my tummy rumbling
and I enquired what

            I required to be an

artist in the Eighties

            for I realised she had
an answer to everything
            and she replied with a sigh

'a vicious streak is

            fine and dandy

a fucked-up life can
            come in handy'
and she searched for her toothbrush

            to help flush the dreaming

while I sent postcards

            to my brylcreem friends
until the leeches

were delivered and

Lon disappeared

beneath the Seine

Pupil Dilating

On a useless
evening
Danny Kaye
is bubbling
spaghetti hoops

are bubbling
nearby
I think of
plastic binoculars
dropping   splitting   on
a cruel Scarborough kerb
on a useless
evening
greasy
with chipshop
conspiracy
stuttering
wooden ghost train   motorbike
and shooting gallery crack
on a bubbling
evening
Danny

Kaye
is useless
the pieces
          behind me
slow   slow   smashed
in a mess
of seams   high heels
stitches on the shirts
of dodgem squatters
with vodka heads
and testicles

and trembling
funfair mongrels
with Hans Christian Andersen
tinder box teeth
on a trembling
useless
evening
sharpened

on stick
stick of rock
with SCARBOROUGH through it
and plastic binoculars

R. D. Laing and Scottish Philosophy

Ronnie Turnbull and Craig Beveridge

LET US BEGIN with a personal comment and an acknowledgement. We began to read and discuss Laing in the late sixties and
early seventies. We were students, and encountered Laing as one of
a group of radical theorists who were then fashionable in leftist
circles. But Laing, in a way which we could not then have articulated adequately, was a puzzle, for he was Scottish. And everything
in our education had made us believe that nothing of significance
now originated in Scotland. History happened elsewhere, the ideas
we lived by came from elsewhere. Laing was a rebuke to that
crippling self-distrust. We are grateful to him.

The Divided Self was published in 1960, shortly before the
appearance of Foucault's *Folie et deraison* (1961). Together with
Foucault's study, Laing's critique of conventional psychiatry was
instrumental in initiating an important debate about psychiatric
practice, its conceptual apparatus and socio-political functions; and
it made Laing one of the *lumières* of new leftism.

But if Laing is widely recognised as an important theorist, to date
there has been no attempt to explore with any seriousness the
cultural background of his thought. The available studies – such as
Friedenberg's volume in the *Modern Masters* series, and the *Laing
and Anti-Psychiatry* collection edited by Boyers and Orrill – make
next to no mention of the Scottish background, and fail entirely to
examine the possibility that Laing's ideas might be locatable within
Scottish intellectual traditions. The reason for this, of course, is the
assumption, which has only recently begun to be challenged, that
Scotland is a cultural wasteland. Laing cannot be inserted into a
Scottish tradition, because there are here no intellectual traditions,
to put the view simply. So in addressing the question of the local
roots of Laing's thought it will be necessary to explore a dimension
of recent Scottish intellectual culture which is still largely unknown.

Of course, there is a common journalistic way of placing Laing which *does* emphasise his Scottish origins (this has been employed in the *Guardian,* the *Times Literary Supplement* etc.). On this view Laing upholds a Scottish tradition of interest in divided or schizoid personalities, a concern which is taken to reflect the pervasiveness of a distinct and profound schism in both the Scottish psyche and Scottish society. Within this reading, Scottish culture is defined in an entirely negative way, identified as something freakish and pathological.

Such interpretations, which conveniently require no close knowledge of Scottish cultural traditions, seem often, in fact, to be motivated by crude anti-Scottish prejudice. This is apparent in the following extract from a *Guardian* feature on Laing. Commenting on what he sees as Laing's shifting intellectual allegiances, the author writes:

> Clearly Dr Laing is himself somewhat divided, as are so many Scotsmen. Highlands and Lowlands, cold rationalists and Calvinist fanatics, Glasgow and Edinburgh, teetotallers and dramdrinkers. Perhaps *The Divided Self* should be seen in a tradition that includes such other works by Scots as Stevenson's *Dr Jekyll and Mr Hyde,* and Hogg's *Confessions of a Justified Sinner.*
>
> (Richard Boston, 'The Divided Self', *The Guardian,*
> 3 August 1976.)

Predictably, our own intellectualettes have not been slow to echo this view. Alan Bold, for instance, presents Laing's work as an investigation of the 'internal division' which, so he would have us believe, is definitive of the Scottish world. (A. Bold, *Modern Scottish Literature,* Longman, 1983.)

The aim here is to do justice to the totality of Laing's work, and to relate this achievement to a specific cultural milieu. The significance of Laing's Glasgow University training has recently been indicated by George Davie in *The Crisis of the Democratic Intellect.* Davie draws attention to the 'German-Hegelian' orientation of the Glasgow philosophy department, a tradition which survived down to the sixties, and the phenomenological concerns of certain of its members (most notably J. J. Russell). When the department succumbed to the Oxbridge analytic regime, Davie argues, the Glasgow philosophical tradition survived in the work of psychiatrists such as Laing:

> The departure of Russell did not mean the extinction of the phenomenological interests within the Glasgow Arts area of

studies. Suppressed within the Philosophy Department, Russell's project of using phenomenology to reanimate the intellectual life of Britain reappeared among Glasgow psychiatrists, and was realised in practice with striking success by Ronald Laing.

(George Davie, *The Crisis of the Democratic Intellect*, Polygon, 1986, p. 176.)

This goes some way to dispelling ignorance about the intellectual roots of Laing's work. We would like to complement Davie's account by considering the ideas of a number of recent Scottish thinkers who have affinities with Laing. This will allow, we believe, the development of a new perspective on Laing's achievements.

Science, Knowledge and Persons

The main focus of many recent Scottish contributions to theory is the development of a culture in which science has achieved intellectual pre-eminence. Specifically, here we frequently encounter challenges to the claim that scientific reasoning represents the primary mode of human cognition, and anxiety about the ethical and personal consequences of the triumph of the 'scientific worldview'. There is a stark contrast here with intellectual developments in England, where philosophers, taking the hegemony of science for granted, have sought to achieve an approximation of philosophy and science. In Scotland scepticism about the scientific outlook has entailed an often fierce hostility to developments like the subordination of philosophy to science as the logic of scientific inquiry.

One central argument of these Scottish thinkers is that empiricism or 'the naturalistic viewpoint' involves an arbitrary and illegitimate restriction of the concepts of experience, knowledge and reality. This has, for instance, been a major theme in the work of the philosopher and theologian John Macquarrie, who is co-translator of the English edition of Heidegger's *Sein und Zeit* and the author of a popular account of existentialism. Macquarrie presents one of his recent books, *In Search of Humanity* (1982), as a 'plea for a wider concept of knowing' than that which is inscribed in the dominant Cartesian epistemological tradition. Knowledge of natural fact is only one mode of cognition. We ought also, he urges, to take seriously such modalities of knowledge as conscience, that intimate form of acquaintance which discloses the gulf between the empirical and the actual self. Our understanding of cognition has been restricted, too, by the belief that knowledge demands detachment from its object. Certain forms of knowledge involve a coming together of the knower and the known. 'In many subjects, and not least in the study of humanity itself, the idea of detachment is a hindrance.' Knowing another involves an attempt at union with and participation in the world of the other.

Macquarrie draws on Heidegger, Buber and Polanyi, among others. A major influence on his work is the thought of John Macmurray, professor of philosophy at Edinburgh from 1944 to 1958. Macmurray is now a neglected figure (none of his books is currently in print), but he may yet come to be recognised as one of the most interesting and fertile of recent Scottish thinkers.

Of particular relevance to the present discussion is Macmurray's critique of conventional discourse on knowledge, reason and objectivity. Like Macquarrie, he rejects the view that knowledge is exhausted in intellectual cognition, arguing, for instance, that the artist has a deeper, more intimate knowledge of the world than the scientist. He also contests the idea that reason should be identified with detached, passionless reflection. Reason is not intellection, but rather a matter of objectivity: 'reason is the capacity to behave in terms of the nature of the object'. He goes on to criticise the conventional opposition of reason and emotion, since emotions, like thoughts, can be objective, i.e. appropriate to the reality to which they refer. At the same time, Macmurray sees no grounds for distinguishing feelings and thoughts in terms of the supposedly 'subjective' nature of the former, since the latter are also, in the same sense, subjective.

> If our feelings are subjective because they occur in us, why not our thoughts which as surely occur to us? If our thoughts are objective because they refer to objects, then our feelings, which refer to objects in their own fashion, are objective also.
>
> (*The Self as Agent*, Faber, 1969 edition, p. 202)

The thrust of Macmurray's position, then, is that we are profoundly mistaken to disesteem our valuations and feelings about the world, to dismiss them as 'irrational' and 'merely subjective'.

The restriction of the notions of reason and knowledge which the triumph of empiricism has entailed is leading, such thinkers believe, to ethical decay, the undermining of human responsibility and the atrophy of our lives as persons. Thus H. J. Paton's committed account of Kant's moral philosophy was intended to counter the challenge to the moral life which was posed by the spread of the scientific *Weltanschauung*. (Paton, one of that distinguished line of Scottish Kant scholars which includes Kemp Smith and Pringle-Pattison, was professor at Glasgow and Oxford.) The prestige of scientific reasoning, Paton felt, is a dangerous threat to the claims of a less narrow conception of reason to demonstrate the possibility of fundamental ethical principles. 'It is a serious matter both for the individual and society if men are to be told that there can be no objective moral principles because these are not the same as scientific generalisations.'

According to John Macmurray, we are faced in the twentieth century with a '*crisis of the personal*'. This constitutes the fundamental issue of the age, which it is the duty of all serious philosophy to address. The decline of religion, he argues, is both a symptom and an agency of the impoverishment of our lives as persons, for religious forms of life have served to inculcate the practice of self-criticism, to foster the interior life, and to uphold the categories of personal responsibility and personal merit. The waning of religion therefore signals a profound and alarming cultural development. This unfashionable perspective is worth quoting at some length in Macmurray's own words:

> The decline of religious influence and of religious practice ... betrays, and in turn intensifies, a growing insensitiveness to the personal aspects of life, and a growing indifference to personal values. Christianity, in particular, is the exponent and the guardian of the personal, and the function of organised Christianity in our history has been to foster and maintain the personal life.... If this influence is removed or ceases to be effective, the awareness of personal issues will tend to be lost, in the pressure of functional preoccupations, by all except those who are by nature specially sensitive to them. The sense of personal dignity as well as of personal unworthiness will atrophy, with the decline in habits of self-examination.
>
> (*The Self as Agent*, p. 30)

These thinkers have been concerned to emphasise the full range of experience which constitutes subjectivity, and to resist the disestimation of areas of experience and reality which fosters a diminution of humanity or personhood. 'I must trust my experience,' wrote the theologian John Baillie, 'my sense-experience, my social experience and my moral experience.'

It is important to guard against the impression that these 'personalist' theorists are proposing some form of withdrawn inwardness. Personal life, they emphasise, has an inextricable interpersonal or communal dimension. Macmurray writes: 'the Self is a person, and ... personal life is *constituted* by the relation of persons'. Macquarrie wishes us to see our lives as the 'task of becoming a person', but, he adds, 'it might be more accurate to say that the goal is to become a person-in-community, for no person exists in isolation, though a self may try to do so, and in so doing diminish its own personhood'. For Ronald Gregor Smith, the Glasgow theologian and Buber translator, 'it is as persons along with other persons that the essence of true humanity consists.... True humanity is community.'

Laing and Scottish Personalism

A foregrounding of the phenomenon of personhood; an insistence that knowledge is not exhausted in scientific cognition; hostility to the disestimation of important aspects of human experience which the triumphs of science have encouraged – these parameters of recent Scottish thought largely define the nature of Laing's intellectual career also, as we will now indicate.

In *The Divided Self*, Laing's critique of conventional psychiatry centres on the failure (itself, he suggests, an instance of madness) to approach the patient as a person. 'We shall be concerned,' he writes, 'with people who experience themselves as automata, as robots, as bits of machinery, or even as animals. Such persons are rightly regarded as crazy. Yet why do we not regard a theory which seeks to transmute persons into automata or animals as equally crazy?' The depersonalisation of the human being in established theory means that the task of creating an authentic study of persons has hardly yet begun.

Macmurray had insisted that the self cannot be understood as a substance or an organism, but only as a person. Laing quotes him to this effect in the opening chapter of *The Divided Self*; Macmurray is in fact the only thinker whose ideas are discussed there. The influence of Macmurray on Laing, and the similarity of their discourse, have been pointed out by Philip Cornford, in 'John Macmurray – A Neglected Philosopher' (*Radical Philosophy* 16,1977) and 'Psychological Influence' (*The Times Higher Educational Supplement*, 8 August 1986).

Behind attempts to account for human behaviour in chemical, mechanical and biological terms, Laing argues, lurks the belief that only via such approaches can scientificity be attained. 'There is a common illusion that one somehow increases one's understanding of a person if one can translate a personal understanding of him into the impersonal terms of a sequence of it-processes.' However, the 'objectivity' thus attained is pseudo-scientific, and the 'knowledge' generated by depersonalisation must be considered dubious. Laing proposes an approach which, in contrast, emphasises on the one hand the person's desires, hopes, fears, intentions, projects, his/her own conception of their being, and on the other the social world in which persons exist. As he writes in *Self and Others*, 'we cannot give an undistorted account of "a person" without giving an account of his relations with others'. This principle yields one of the key ideas of Laingian psychiatry: that we require 'confirmation' by others, and that where others systematically disconfirm our worth and our nature as agents we can be destroyed. In this sense a depersonalising psychiatric practice represents collusion with the patient's madness.

The relationship between psychiatrist and patient must be a personal one, centred on 'the original bond of I and You'. The model of detached observation imported from natural science is here misplaced. (We may recall here Macquarrie's remark that 'the ideal of detachment' can be a hindrance.) The goal is understanding, not explanation. Laing comments: 'I think it is clear that by "understanding" I do not mean a purely intellectual process. For understanding one might say love.' In order to understand, it is necessary to enlist 'all the powers of every aspect of ourselves'. Though such involvement must represent, from the viewpoint of 'scientific' psychiatry, a departure from rationality and objectivity, it is a procedure which can be fully justified in terms of the philosophy of Macmurray, in which knowledge and rationality are not restricted to intellection. Indeed, from a Macmurrayan perspective, it is a 'scientific' psychiatry which is irrational and subjective, since it constitutes a failure to 'behave in terms of the nature of the object'.

Laing's main political work is *Reason and Violence,* a study of Sartre's *Critique de la Raison Dialectique,* co-written with David Cooper and published in 1964. Critics have complained of the book's obscurity, and there may be some irony in Sartre's comment that it is 'un exposé très clair et très fidèle de ma pensée'. Nevertheless, the 'personalist' emphasis of Laing's earlier works can be clearly identified here too. The project is to achieve a mitigation of Marxism's determinist moment by allowing for the reality of individual freedom and intentionality. 'What contemporary Marxists forget is that the man who is alienated, mystified, reified, and so on, remains none the less a man.' Sartre is praised for tracing 'the life of a person to its own ultimate issues'. For, Laing writes, 'it is only through the discovery of a freedom, a choice of self-functioning in the face of all determinations, conditioning, fatedness, that we can attain the comprehension of a person in his full reality'.

On the evidence of a remarkable recent essay entitled 'What is the Matter with Mind?', Laing's thought is now taking on new emphases (in *The Schumacher Lectures,* edited by Satish Kumar, London, 1980). If in the early books Laing is resisting the illegitimate extension of natural-scientific paradigms to the study of persons, now there is a much fiercer hostility to the scientific outlook, and concern about its ethical consequences. Here Laing echoes ideas prominent in the work of other Scottish thinkers, such as Baillie, Macmurray and Macquarrie if in much more polemical tones.

The main theme of the essay is that science excludes from its sphere of investigation much of our ordinary reality.

> We know that meaning, value, quality, love and hate, good and evil, beauty and ugliness, exist in some sort of way, which is not a number or quantity, or a thing.... The natural scientist explicitly excludes that subjective morass, he leaves all that behind, he sheds all he can of it, before even embarking on his voyage of scientific discovery.

Science debars value,

> love and hate, joy and sorrow, misery and happiness, pleasure and pain, right and wrong, purpose, meaning, hope, courage, despair, God, heaven and hell, grace, sin, salvation, damnation, enlightenment, wisdom, compassion, evil, envy, malice, generosity, camaraderie ...

(a list, it is worth noting, which contains a surprising number of religious categories).

But the scientific perspective is not a primary or pure or neutral apprehension of reality. As Laing writes in *The Divided Self,* it is not neutral 'to see a smile as contractions of the circumoral muscles'. Science in fact transforms primary experience. It involves, in Laing's memorable phrase, a *de-realisation of reality*, through an ablation of ordinary experience, an exclusion and devalorisation of whole fields of human experience which are perceived, except from the scientific perspective, as real. Reality and objectivity are denied to all those phenomena present to consciousness which are not amenable to quantification and experimental control.

> All sensibility, all values, all quality, all feelings, all motives, all intentions, spirit, soul, consciousness, subjectivity: almost everything, in fact, which we ordinarily take to be real is derealised, is stripped of its pretensions to reality.

The victory of this way of seeing signals a major cultural mutation. For where ethics is divorced from fact and value from knowledge, where the conviction that 'all our subjective values are objectively valueless' gains ground, we witness the undermining of human responsibility towards being.

'If I am older, I am now also younger'
It might be objected that the parallels between Laing's thought and that of other recent Scottish theorists are more or less fortuitous

(improbable though this would be), and that the conception of a strong local cultural influence has been overstated. In reply we would draw attention to two elements in Laing's biography.

Our argument receives confirmation, in the first place, from the fact that in the 1950s Laing was a member of a Glasgow discussion group which had a marked existentialist and personalist orientation, and which, indeed, included certain of the other figures we have referred to above.

This informal circle was sometimes called 'the Abenheimer group', also 'the Schorstein group', after the two Jewish thinkers who had emigrated to Glasgow – Karl Abenheimer and Joe Schorstein. [Abenheimer's essay on Karl Jaspers was recently published posthumously in *Edinburgh Review* 74. This issue carries his 'Existentialism and Psychotherapy'.] Ronald Gregor Smith, theologian and translator of Martin Buber, appears to have been the dominant intellectual presence in the group, which went into decline after his death in 1968. John Macquarrie, like Laing a former student of C. A. Campbell's Glasgow philosophy department, was another member. A very significant proportion of the group's membership, in fact, were theologians or churchmen. Gregor Smith had little patience with analytic philosophy, and it was Continental thought which dominated the group's meetings. Thinkers discussed included Kierkegaard, Heidegger, Jaspers, Buber, Bultmann, Tillich, Sartre and Unamuno. Laing was a participant before moving to London, and read to the group drafts of *The Divided Self*.

Of the group's intellectual ethos, Jack Rillie, another participant, writes: 'Baillie, Macmurray, Buber were all in the conversational stream'. While acknowledging that not all members would have been happy to be termed 'personalist', Rillie observes that 'the predominant existentialist interest of the members certainly inclined it in that direction' (personal communication).

A second feature of Laing's biography, concerning his early life, also deserves emphasis here. Like many of the other Scottish thinkers referred to in this essay, Laing enjoyed a religious upbringing. In a *Listener* essay published in 1970, he wrote of this in the following way:

> I grew up, theologically speaking, in the nineteenth century: lower-middle-class Lowland Presbyterian, corroded by nineteenth-century materialism, scientific rationalism and humanism ... I remember vividly how startled I was to meet for the first time, when I was eighteen, people of my age who had never opened a Bible.... For the first time in my life, I could see myself being looked at rather as I imagine a native may see

himself looked at by an attentive, respectful anthropologist. I could see myself regarded with incredulity by an eighteen-year old French girl, a student from the Sorbonne, as some idealistic barbarian still occupied by issues of religious belief, disbelief or doubt, still living before the Enlightenment, exhibiting in frayed but still recognisable form the primitive thought forms of the savage mind.

(R. D. Laing. 'Religious Sensibility', *The Listener*, 23 April 1970)

If these words hint at a resolution of the conflict between 'Lowland Presbyterianism' and secular rationalism in favour of the latter, and an approximation to the worldview of the girl from the Sorbonne, Laing's more recent work, as we have seen, with its appreciation of the significance of religious categories, suggests a rather different balance of forces. What is clear, in any case, is the tension between religious culture and *Aufklärung,* a contradiction which made acceptance of any purely scientific and secular philosophy impossible. Laing's roots in a strongly moral-religious milieu should thus be seen as a key to his intellectual trajectory.

In 1964, in the preface to the Pelican edition of *The Divided Self,* Laing wrote: 'If I am older, I am now also younger.' It is possible that Laing could today repeat these words with a different investment of meaning, given the emphasis of his recent work, in acknowledgement of the values he learned in his youth. Perhaps we could say of Laing's thought, too, as Walter Kaufmann has written of Buber's, that its problematic can be defined, ultimately, by the question: 'what does the religion of my fathers mean to me today?'.

(We would like to thank Jack Rillie for kindly providing us with information about the Abenheimer group. This article draws at various points on our essay, 'Recent Scottish Thought', which is published in the Aberdeen University Press *History of Scottish Literature.*)

A Preface to
The Anthology of Prefaces
PLUS THREE CRITICAL COMMENTARIES

Alasdair Gray

'EVERY PREFACE,' says William Smellie at the start of his preface
to *The Philosophy of Natural History* published in Edinburgh in
1790, 'Every Preface, besides occasional and explanatory remarks,
should contain not only the general design of the work, but the
motives and circumstances which led the author to write on that
particular subject. If this plan had been universally observed, prefaces would have exhibited a short, but a curious and useful history
both of literature and authors.'

This plan, of course, was never universally observed but it has
been widely observed. Few great writers have not placed before one
of their books or plays a verbal doorstep to help readers leave the
ground they usually walk on, and allow them a glimpse of the
interior. Prefaces are advertisements and challenges. They usually
indicate the kind of attention the book requires, the kind of return it
is meant to give. It has been possible for at least two centuries for
anyone who enjoys a good library to collate, at very little expense of
intelligence, the best part of this pithy little history of English
Literature by those who created it. If I am the first to turn Smellie's
suggestion into a book it is because former critics have been blind to
a useful task which would not stretch their brains. To wheedle a
sufficient advance from my present publishers I take English to be
the language of more nations than England, more islands than
Britain, more continents than Europe. I also assume that English
literature is what folk thought it before it was taught as a special
subject in universities, namely: poetry, great translation, drama,
religion, legend, history, essays, travel, biography, political, moral
and natural philosophy (now called science) and criticism. Despite
the old prejudice that novels cannot be fine literary art because most
readers enjoy them, I include prefaces to novels. I include prefaces
to a few books which, influential in their day (e.g. Harrington on
flush lavatories and Culpepper's *Herbal)* are now ignored. But

Alasdair Gray

prefaces by poets, playwrights and storytellers outnumber those of other writers, since imaginers like Shakespeare, Bunyan, Burns and Hemingway wrote for all the sorts of people they knew, not for a specially educated class of them. This lets them make good sense to later centuries.

By preface I mean any author's preamble entitled *preface, prologue, introduction, introductory, apology, design, advertisement* or *explanatory* which can be detached from a work without damaging it. This excludes the great prologues to *Piers Plowman* and *Canterbury Tales* which are necessary foundations of the books' architecture. Most verses in this collection are prologues to stage plays. In the case of *Tristram Shandy* and the 2nd edition of Burns' *Poems Chiefly in the Scottish Dialect* I use dedications because these are good samples of the authors' styles and seek to avoid the usual sycophancy of the form: the first by being ostentatiously fluid, sweet and cunning (he was an English parson) the second by being ostentatiously bold, cunning and manly (he was a Scottish farmer). I had meant to exclude pseudonymous prefaces but would eliminate Defoe, all of whose preambles are lies. So I include the pseudonymous, and in the case of Swift and Stevenson put a factual and pseudonymous preface side by side. I also break my rule of giving one preface per author in other places. The reader will usually see why.

The prefaces are ranged chronologically to display sometimes gradual, sometimes quick changes in English over the centuries. Before the coming of printing they are placed in the supposed order of writing, thereafter in the order of the publication. Marginal notes in small type tell something of the author's lives, the events which prompted their books, and the political and emotional choices shaping their style. Most authors' preambles have been magnificently crisp. Milton's preface to the second edition of *Paradise Lost* is four sentences, so is the conjoined Notice and Explanatory to *Huckleberry Finn*. I seldom use a long preface to a less important work when an author has put a brief one before his best. This makes it possible to print, without cutting, good prefaces which are essays and manifestos.

There are four pleasures I hope you will find in this book. I list the nastiest first.

1 THE PLEASURE OF SEEING GREAT WRITERS IN A HUFF

Prefaces to first editions try to forestall criticism, those to later editions frequently counterblast it. Authors usually defend themselves by explaining their intentions or choice of subject and method, but some resort to unfair tactics. The conservative monk who wrote *The Cloud of Unknowing*, the sturdy corrupt journalist who wrote *Moll Flanders* were very different men, but their preambles indicate that their books will be abused or misunderstood by the vicious. The commonest defensive tactic is the lofty intimation, the second commonest is its counterpart, the poor mouth. Both are symptoms of intelligences unhealthily exalted or depressed by their social standing – a frequent British disease. In his preface to *Utopia* Sir Thomas More loftily intimates that he writes for the discerning few, not the multitude. He had good reason to say so. *Utopia* was written to introduce King Henry VIII and the literate part of his nobility to some old-fangled notions of tolerance, social welfare and equality under law. It was written in Latin, circulated in manuscript, and not printed till after his death. Yet his snooty example is followed by several great writers who want to be enjoyed by as many readers as possible. Listen to Wordsworth: 'Those who have been accustomed to the gaudiness and inane phraseology of many modern writers, if they persist in reading this book to its conclusion, will, no doubt, frequently have to struggle with feelings of strangeness and awkwardness ...' He certainly enjoyed constructing that sentence but our amusement is partly at his expense. The Americans are better at critic-deflecting irony because they treat their readers as equals. See Twain's *Notice* again and the last sentence of Hemingway's introduction to A *Moveable Feast*. I will give no examples here of the poor mouth preface, but refer you to Charlotte Bronte's preface to her sister Emily's *Wuthering Heights*. (This last, by the way, is my only exception to the rule of having each preface written by the same author as the book.)

2 THE PLEASURE OF THE BIOGRAPHICAL SNIPPET

Some prefaces blend declarations of faith with a personal experience, so we discover Shelley writing and sunbathing on a platform of green turf high among the ruins of the baths of Caracalla, and Shaw conversing gallantly with a London prostitute, and Synge with an ear to a chink in the floor, eavesdropping on the kitchenmaids in the room below. These feed our love of gossip.

3 THE PLEASURE OF THE ESSAY

Preface-essays vary as greatly as authors. Pope's preface to his *Iliad* translation illuminates Homer – and incidentally Virgil – for those like me who have no Greek or Latin. Scott's preface to *The Lady of The Lake* explains a historical stage which should interest more than the Scots. Lawrence's preface to his translation of *Cavalleria Rusticana* is one of the best essays on modern literature ever penned. An essayist's remarks, of course, only please when they confirm our settled opinions. As a Scottish socialist who thinks a federation of British republics a necessary step toward the creation of a humane democracy I am delighted by Shelley's statement in 1820 that, 'If England were divided into forty republics, each equal in population and extent to Athens, under institutions not more perfect than those of Athens ... each would produce philosophers and poets equal to those who (if we except Shakespeare) have never been surpassed'; also by Mandeville's remark a century earlier that small, peaceful, self supporting states are the best homes of happiness; also by Pope's information that Homer's language was not based on one district in the Greek archipelago but on usages from all of them. Those who find such statements comic, unconvincing or irrelevant will find plenty of remarks to support their own prejudices.

4 THE PLEASURE OF HISTORY

Great literature is the most important part of recorded history. We forget this because we are inclined to see great works as worlds of their own rather than phases of the world we live in. No wonder! At first sight the differences in style between Chaucer, Shakespeare, Dickens and today's newspaper make their differences look more important than their connections. It is almost impossible to imagine a passage of history in any solidity and fluidity for more than a few years even when we've lived through it ourselves. But we may get some experience of a civilisation over several centuries from the book of extracts which lets us see, on adjacent pages, language changing from decade to decade in the words of authors who usually know they are changing it. The taste, rhythm and meaning of a statement is the taste, rhythm and meaning of life when it was uttered.

I sometimes lapse from the high seriousness of my historical purpose by including, mainly from the modern times, prefaces from work which is less than the greatest but which informed or entertained me. The marginal notes will not always explain why.

Lastly, this will be a useful book for those who enjoy talking
knowingly about other books without reading
them. Conscientious parents and teachers
forbid it to children and students.
It could help glib ones pass
examinations on no
basis of insight
at all.

THE CLOUD OF UNKNOWNING
Author anonymous (circa 1350)

This is written in an age of great revolutions. Plague has killed at least a quarter of the labouring population, and a much larger part of the population of the monasteries, which makes religious folk fear that those most devoted to God have most displeased Him. There is schism within the church and heresy outside it, and official attempts to impose wage restraints have caused revolts among the peasantry. This Prologue is a plea and a warning: a desperate plea that readers of the book will turn their backs on the bad job of the world, a warning that a careless reading of it will harm them. A consciously conservative, contemplative priest is advertising for like souls to accompany him on a hard dangerous inner journey to the true source of light and life. His slow, careful, rather anxious sounding sentences, in the English of the Wycliffe bible, blend the terms and cadences of communal prayer with the devices of a vernacular legal document which intends to leave no loophole for misunderstanding. While believing his book is on the most important business possible he desperately wishes it not to arouse controversy.

LEVIATHAN or The Matter, Forme & Power of A COMMON-WEALTH, ECCLESIASTICALL AND CIVILL
by Thomas Hobbes of Malmesbury (London, 1651)

This is written in an age of great revolutions. A deadly efficient English puritan army, originally formed to protect the rights of the smaller landlords and richer burgesses, has tried and decapitated the second King to rule all Britain, allowed and dismissed a couple of republican parliaments, and in the year this book is printed defeats an invading army of Scots and Irish led by the third King of all the British, who barely escapes to the Continent with his life. In this Introduction a consciously late Renaissance, late Protestant Englishman who feels capable of grasping *everything* is challenging like minds to join him in a universe which is harder and drier, but also simpler and more excitingly intelligible, than they had hitherto noticed. Like Milton, his contemporary, he fears neither God nor government because he is sure he can justify both. His conscious influences are not the Bible, Homer, Virgil and Ariosto but Euclid, Bacon, Galileo and Descartes. He is so enraptured by recent improvements of the printing press, the musket and the clock that he does not believe he is using a poetic metaphor when he describes men and their nations as different sizes of mechanical doll; he thinks he is being modern and scientific. In this he resembles our own theorists who are so awed by developments in the computer industry and their ability to comprehend these, that they tell us that people are essentially computers. The prose of Hobbes is better than theirs because the notion that we are the same kind of thing as our insensitive constructions is new to most of his readers, so he needs to be terse and clear. The long sentences of the Introduction keep stimulating us with spiky little aphorisms in the Baconian style, but jauntier and more persuasive than Bacon, because for all the scientific pretension of this metaphor he is using the sort of wit Donne uses when he describes the body of his mistress as an ocean full of undiscovered lands.

LYRICAL BALLADS by William Wordsworth
(London, second edition, 1802)

This is written in an age of great revolutions, agricultural and industrial, French and Napoleonic. Britain is threatened with invasion. The wealthy part fears insurrection. A poet of thirty-two with a small but adequate unearned income is introducing a middleclass readership to verses whose main form is popular folksong, main diction is plainer than they are used to, main theme is the lives and surroundings of agricultural labourers. He also wants to reject the suggestion that he is a democrat with a taste for low life without appearing to take note of it. He tries to lose potential antagonists by obscuring his subject, predicate and object in a fog of modifying and qualifying phrases, phrases which add little to the sense but convey a strong desire to be genteel because he seems to be continually adjusting his dress. This is prose which gives the prosaic a bad name. It would be a good essay in composition to set students of English the task of editing out all language in this preface which is purely self-defensive, because it contains a message. He feels that since the death of Milton, poetry has been tied by stilted diction to a narrow class of passions and subjects, but now his own mind and art are reflecting again what is glorious and sombre in nature and the largest part of humanity. He is announcing the start of a new age in his own person, and is terribly embarrassed, because a great many have been doing that recently and been mocked, reviled and sometimes arrested for it. So he buries the message under complicated, erudite dictions where only friends will have the endurance to dig it up. Meanwhile he is writing a proper defence of his poetic task, a long poem called *The Prelude* which will be published after his death half a century later, when nobody living thinks his poems provide revolutionary insights.

Postscript 7 May 1995

I wrote the above over ten years ago before starting serious work on the anthology, hoping it would raise a publisher's advance to let me do so. This explains the rapid jocular tone. I did get an advance, and started working seriously, and found this stretched my brain more than I expected – stretched it so sorely that relaxing from the anthology to write works of fiction felt like being on holiday, besides being financially unavoidable. Last month I signed a new contract with a London publisher, promising to deliver the finished work in 1998.

'There's Blood Running from the Old Wound'

THE PROPHETIC VISION OF 'NEUE SLOWENISCHE KUNST'*

Charles Stephens

Some statements by 'Neue Slowenische Kunst'

ON ART AND POLITICS

'Politics is the highest and all-comprising art, and we who create the contemporary Slovene art consider ourselves politicians.'

'Laibach'

ON THE RELATIONSHIP BETWEEN ART AND IDEOLOGY

'The Theatre of Scipion Nasica exiles religion and ideology into the mirror image of art, and thus abolishes them.'

'The Theatre of Scipion Nasica'

ON THE RELATIONSHIP BETWEEN ART AND SOCIETY

'To discover and evaluate history anew, return the power to institutions and conventions, as well as diminish the distance between artistic expression and the collective consensus.'

'IRWIN'

ON THE AVANT-GARDE

'It [the Theatre of Scipion Nasica] proclaims the avant-garde to be the ultimate genuine style of the modern civilisation *which is coming to an end due to the defeat of revolutions.*'

'The Theatre of Scipion Nasica'

ON THE FUNCTION OF TERROR

'Terror obtains the function of production power which extorts discipline and the adaptation of the masses to the existing productional relations and apparatus. Systematic terror becomes a constitutional instrument of authority.'

'Laibach'

ON ART AND THE INDIVIDUAL

'Neue Slowenische Kunst is based on the principle of a conscious abandoning of personal taste, judgements, conviction ... free depersona-

* First published 1988

lisation, the willing adoption of the role of ideology, the unmasking and recapitulation of the regime "postmodernism" … '

'Neue Slowenische Kunst'

THE FIRST OPPORTUNITIES for British audiences to see 'Neue Slowenische Kunst' were in Edinburgh under the umbrella of the Richard Demarco Gallery. The Theatre of Scipion Nasica (TSN) performed, until shut down, for six nights at Demarco's George Heriot's School venue during the second week of the 1986 Edinburgh Festival. Between May 9 and May 30 of 1987, 'IRWIN' displayed their 'Was ist Kunst' show in Demarco's Blackfriars Street Gallery. This presentation was accompanied by an exhibition of Marko Modic's photographic documentation of 'IRWIN', of 'Laibach's' 1987 Ljubljana concert and of performances by 'TSN' of their productions 'Maria Nablocka' and 'Baptism'. It was very fitting that NSK should first emerge in Britain under the aegis of the Richard Demarco Gallery. It was Demarco who first presented Paul Neagu, Joseph Beuys, Tadeusz Kantor and Marina Abramovic to British audiences. These artists are all, nowadays, recognised to be superb practitioners of Performance Art and NSK are worthy successors to this impressive tradition of talent from Central and Eastern Europe.

In their own statements, NSK proclaim the explicitly political, and indeed revolutionary, nature of their intentions. They announce, stridently, the primacy of ideology in all that they do. It would be a mistake to overlook or attempt to ignore this aspect of their activities. Beneath the rebarbative and alienating surface of the public interventions is a formidable 'ideological' interpretation of the condition of art and of European man in the late twentieth century. Neglect of this fundamental dimension of NSK's activities will lead, very rapidly, to incomprehension and frustration. NSK does not intend to be taken at face value. It should not be so taken.

It is not an accident that a group, of artists such as NSK should emerge from Yugloslavia and from Slovenia in particular. Invaded and occupied in the early 1940's, firstly by Italy and then Germany, Yugoslavia became part of the front line of the Cold War from 1948 onwards. To this day [1988] many standard NATO wargames are premised upon a Warsaw Pact invasion of Yugoslavia as an opening gambit in World War III. In 1988, Yugoslavia hangs suspended, quite literally, between East and West, just as it once shivered in the 1930's and 1940's, between the Swastika and the Hammer and Sickle. Within the memories, contemporary experiences and future hopes and fears of its people, all the key questions of present day Europe vibrate at high frequency. Yugoslavia is a kind of laboratory of Europe, a country hanging with his legs dangling over the abyss of the times. Within this remarkable country, there is Slovenia. Slovenia, of all the Yugoslav republics, is closest to Northern Europe by its geography, its culture and its history. For centuries a part of the Hapsburg patrimony, Slovenia has lost little of its cultural inheritance. Its capital Ljubljana, also called 'Laibach' by German speakers in the past, is a place which has considerably more in common with cities such as Prague, Vienna and Cracow, than with Belgrade, Sofia and Bucharest. One small fact of its cultural history is eloquent of Slovenia's place in the historic culture of Central Europe. The first performance of Gustav Mahler's daemonic Sixth Symphony took place in the Concert Hall of Llubljana in 1906.

NSK are not emerging into the daylight of European culture from some quaint corner of 'Eastern' or 'Balkan' Europe. They are coming, like a sharp knife, right out of the European heartland. NSK are a living part of the world of Kafka, Schoenberg, Musil, von Hofmannstahl, Wittgenstein, Klimt, Kandinsky and Schiele. In their work, the tradition of this great and tragic artistic culture is still alive and still fighting. The story of NSK is that of the Avant-Garde in the era of 'the defeat of all revolutions'. Its project is the response of the artist to the collapse of the utopian vision of Christian Europe and its submergence by Totalitarianism. The assessment of these 'ideological' questions by NSK is the key to the strategy, the appearance and the meaning of its art.

NSK is eloquent and aggressive about the 'political' nature of its activities. On the one hand it invokes the rhetoric and the memory of the idealism of the Russian Revolution and of the Surrealist manifestoes. On the other, it deliberately deploys the images, icons and language of the art of Nazi Germany and Stalinist Russia in all of its public statements. What is more, NSK knowingly uses revolutionary iconography in the full knowledge that the prospects for liberating, utopian revolution in contemporary Europe, particularly in the east, are bleak to the point of hopelessness. NSK also brandishes, without comment, excuse or explanation, slogans and imagery reminiscent of Nazism in a country, Slovenia, where such things are unsayable and unthinkable. It is scarcely possible, without the heaviest framing of irony or satire, to associate oneself with such material in any European country, East or West, without courting, at best ridicule and suspicion, and at worst execration and condemnation.

NSK thrusts this material down the throats of its audience and so generates outrage and scandal. The explanation of this apparently perverse, mischievous and self-destructive strategy is that NSK is stating, unequivocally, that a genuine political art has become impossible in the twentieth century. By means of its deployment of a blend of revolutionary and totalitarian imagery and rhetoric, NSK is announcing that, in the twentieth century, all art which has attempted to work with political premises, such as those enunciated so stridently by itself, has inevitably fallen between the twin stools of the failure of Revolution, as happened in Russia between 1917 and 1925, and service to a totalitarian state, as was the order of the day in Nazi Germany and Stalinist Russia during the 1930's and 1940's. In other words, there has been a choice, for any twentieth century artist or thinker who sought to square themselves with the political domain, between the futility of Andre Breton and his associates and the self-seeking or jejune prostitutions of figures such as Ilya Ehrenburg or Martin Heidegger. As far as NSK is concerned, other art, and they have in mind, the a-political or non-political 'Modernism' and 'Post-Modernism' of western Europe and North America, is either ignorant and therefore impotent, or else knowing and therefore corrupt. In the opinion of NSK, this condition of crisis and tragedy in the relationship between art and politics is a lethal and, may be even, a terminal one. It is a predicament which NSK seeks to confront and to overcome.

As NSK see it, this desperate situation is the result of a rupture in the historic culture of Europe. This discontinuity has occurred, in their analysis, as a direct consequence of the failure of revolution and the triumph of Totalitarianism in the twentieth century. The political violence and terrorism of the 1930's and 1940's has, in the understanding of NSK, severed what had been a coherent and vital link between art and a genuine utopianism. This crucial symbiosis between art and utopia had previously existed in various forms which included the Catholic Christianity of the eleventh and thirteenth centuries, the Protestant Christianity of the seventeenth century, the radical scepticism of the eighteenth century Enlightenment and the Nationalism and Liberalism of the nineteenth century. The advent of communism, Fascism and all of the other tendencies towards Totalitarianism during the twentieth century has, in the analysis of NSK, destroyed all possibility of a viable political, practical movement of reform or revolution such as might make a decisive transformation in the conditions of life. All that remains is defence, fear, control or capitulation. The vitality of art in the past has, in the view of NSK, been dependent upon the possibility that life on earth might be changed for the better in a moral, spiritual, aesthetic as well as a material way. The severing of the symbiotic link between art and political possibility has therefore precipitated a crisis in which either destruction, or else a new beginning, must intervene.

This is a paraphrase of the historical vision which inspires NSK. It is the source of its momentum and the inspiration of its ferocity. NSK seeks to alert Europe to her historic predicament. In its own words, NSK, has taken unto its shoulders 'the terrible revolutionarity of the prophet'. This is the reason for its deployment of the imagery of revolution and totalitarianism. The iconography of NSK reveals its diagnosis of the cultural condition of Europe and the task which lies ahead if it is to reveal its vision to the citizens of Europe. Such a task will not be a comfortable one.

In order to achieve their self-appointed task of prophecy and renewal, NSK has adopted two complementary strategies. On the one hand, it has mounted a systematic critique of, assault on and subversion of the hallowed institution of the Avant-Garde. On the other hand, in close synchronisation with this 'cultural terrorism', NSK has deployed what it calls the aesthetic of 'Retro-Grade'.

In the twentieth century all 'progressive' and 'advanced' art has been, almost by definition, considered to be Avant-Garde. Conservatives have consequently always attacked the Avant-Garde with undisguised hostility. It would therefore be an unnerving moment when a group, looking and sounding very much like an Avant-Garde group, emerged whose basic premise rested upon the relentless undermining of what would appear, in Western European eyes, to be its sole raison d'être, namely its very Avant-Gardism. That moment has arrived and NSK is that group.

The very idea of a group of artists working together, in particular a group such as NSK [whose talents and skills cover the whole range of artistic expression: painting, graphic design, architecture, theatre set design, acting, dance, photography, music, performance] is intrinsic to twentieth century Avant-Gardism from the Blaue Reiter to the Bauhaus to the New York School. Manifestoes, statements, proposals, programmes and position papers flow out from Neue Slowensiche Kunst as they did once from the pen of Andre Breton. So far so good. It is at this promising moment that the iconoclasm begins.

The strategies of scandal, so beloved of Avant-Gardists, are vigorously deployed by NSK, but there is a difference. It is supposed to be an aesthetic commonplace that the strategies of shock and scandal were used up and worn out during the 1960's, and yet NSK have managed to do what has not been done since the Dadaists and Surrealists were in their prime. However, unlike the classical Avant-Garde, NSK are not attempting to 'épater les bourgeoises', nor are they seeking to widen boundaries or open up frontiers. In their statements and manifestoes, some of which are quoted above, NSK reject freedom of expression and scorn the concept of the autonomy of the artist.

Such attitudes as these are the very antithesis of Avant-Gardism. What is more, NSK are vehement about their support for the State and claim that they aspire to to give a mirror-like expression to the needs and aspirations of the State. They firmly reject any suggestion that they are critical of the State, and come near to claiming that they are the State, not an alternative to it. NSK are scathing about 'professional' dissidents and have no desire to leave Slovenia. Exile in the West is not an option, or even a dream, as far as they are concerned. They are financed by the Slovenian and Yugoslav governments, who consider them, with good reason, to be a considerable asset to contemporary Yugoslav culture and an enhancement to Yugoslavia's image in the world. NSK are 'official' art. They are not bohemians.

It is difficult to imagine anything which could be more corrosive to the old ideals of Avant-Gardism than a group, such as NSK, who appropriate all of its rhetoric and its techniques and then invert, or maybe pervert, the inner ideology which they are supposed to serve. The Emperor Scipio, from whom the Theatre of Scipio Nasica derived their name, was notable for one action. He closed all the theatres in Rome because he considered them to be corrupt and frivolous. It would not be difficult to imagine that the theatre wing of NSK chose their name out of sober sympathy and stern fellow feeling rather than from any sense of humorous irony. I suspect that if they had their way, they would emulate their imperial precursor and close down the galleries and theatres of 'Modernism' and 'Postmodernism'. For the time being, they must be content with striking a series of hammer blows against such 'decadence' by means of the vehicle of their art. NSK is a blow pitched against the body of 'established' twentieth century art. It is, in a quite literal sense, an offense.

'Retro-Grade' is the aesthetic 'ideology' which NSK seeks to articulate by means of the problematic 'avant-garde' apparatus of group, manifestoes, confrontation and scandal. The aesthetic of 'Retro-Grade' has been most clearly expressed in 'TSN''s performance of 1986, 'Baptism' and in the paintings of 'IRWIN'. Superficially, 'Retro-Grade' seems to exhibit the random eclecticism and stylistic promiscuity which is so typical of much Western European and North American Postmodernism. Such deceptive appearances are pleasing to NSK. However, whereas the plagiarists and pillagers of Postmodernism are distinguished by a comprehensive ignorance, or disinterest in, the past and in patterns of historical development, NSK has a tenacious grasp of the realities of the historical culture of Europe. As I have argued above, this perception leads NSK to an apocalyptic vision of contemporary Europe, a place which they perceive to be trembling between the twin unknowns of destruction and 'new beginning'. 'Retro-Grade' is not an indiscriminate borrowing from the past. It is a conscious reiteration, by means of the images and styles of certain phases in European art, of the historical process which has brought European culture to the apocalyptic predicament which, according to NSK, confronts it in the final part of the twentieth century. By means of this re-presentation or 'Retro-Grade', NSK gives visual form to its 'ideological' preoccupations.

The visual impact of 'Retro-Grade' is stunning by consequence of the formidable artistic skills of 'IRWIN'. The painters of this anonymous group recreate the images of the past by making new images rather than by 'quoting' or 'collaging' in the Postmodernist manner. There is something else which makes 'Retro-Grade' something utterly different from nostalgia and eclecticism. 'IRWIN', who provide the visual material for all aspects of the activity of NSK [for example, the stage design for the 12 sets and 70 scene changes of the 'Theatre of Scipion Nasica''s performance, 'Baptism'] do not just choose any old artist that they fancy from the past. Their choice is deliberate, eloquent and intellectually astringent. 'IRWIN' re-enact their understanding of the culture of Europe by choosing to rework the work of artists such as these. Kasimir Malevich, the Suprematist, pioneer of abstraction, mystic and great master of art during the early part of the Russian Revolution; Franz Marc and Emil Nolde, German Expressionists and mystagogues; Wassily Kandinsky, a Russian and a Theosphist, and also, like Malevich, a pioneer of Abstraction; Yves Klein, native of Alsace-Lorraine, Rosicrucian, philosopher, painter of Blue paintings and pioneer performance artist; Joseph Beuys, genius of ritual and master of the philosophy of nature. 'IRWIN' also deploy the styles and motifs of traditional Slovenian art ranging from the numinosity of the thirteenth century icon to the dark, turbid romanticism of nineteenth century Nationalist painting. Inevitably, the familiar iconography of Revolution and Fascist or Communist totalitarianism occurs frequently in their image-making. There is nothing arbitrary or random in this choice of artists and styles. Like NSK itself, these artists and these modes of art come out of Central or Eastern Europe, the place where the history of the twentieth century has been experienced most intensely. All of them have been deeply involved, implicated or tainted by the upheavals of Revolution and of Communist and Fascist Totalitarianism. They depict and represent those threads of European history which NSK seeks to re-articulate. 'Retro-Grade' is therefore the iconography of NSK's vision of the dynamic of European culture and history.

The signs of religious imagination and hieratic aspiration are pervasive in the work of NSK. Such 'spiritual' or 'transcendental' allegiance distinguishes NSK sharply from the 'regime' of Postmodernism which they are seeking to 'unmask'. The art of Beuys, Klein and Malevich, all of whom were touched by some form of mysticism or utopian religious vision, is an insistent and active presence in the work of NSK. The paintings of 'IRWIN' are mounted in dully gleaming golden frames. Often the images are made in the shape of a cross, echoing Malevich, but also invoking the presence of Christ and of everything that the Christian revelation has meant for the culture of Europe with regard to the relationship between the State [the secular Empire] and the soul of mankind. In a quite deliberate manner, 'IRWIN' invokes the icon as the ultimate image of European art. In so doing, they pose the great question: is the future of Europe to be that of Rome, of the totalitarian State, or of Christ, the symbol of the final repository, in the language of European culture, of all resistance to the demands and tyrannies of the State.

The theatrical performances of 'TSN', and of their successor 'Red Pilot', are imbued with an hierophantic and ritualistic atmosphere which strains towards the expression of something which might transcend the seemingly hopeless impasse of a century which has seen the 'defeat of revolutions', as NSK puts it. 'FIAT', the title of the new production by 'Red Pilot', seen at the Riverside Studios between July 28 and August 8 1987, is a word rich in association. It can mean will or dictat, the expression of pure force. It is also inextricably linked with the Book of Genesis by the phrase 'Fiat Lux'. Here, in one word is the epitome of the European vision of NSK: the struggle between the brutal violence of power and the light of vision and creation. NSK have said that 'Red Pilot' are the 'religious' section of their campaign. They should be taken at their word.

The logo of NSK is eloquent of the fact that, beneath all the rhetoric, posturing, fascistic demagoguery and cultural terrorism, something very pure and very powerful is waiting to be released, in NSK, but also in the soul of Europe. At the centre of the logo is a cross, bound with rope and made up of axes, which is reminiscent of Italian fascism and of Ancient Rome, but also, a stark expression of the perennial symbolism of atonement and sacrifice. The background to the cross of bound axes is the black cross of Malevich, used also by Joseph Beuys. Both of these artists articulated the exact antithesis of all that Totalitarianism has stood for in the twentieth century. Around the cross is a halo in three parts: thorns, an industrial cog and a pair of antlers. In these we are reminded of the Crucifixion and also the barbed wire of the concentration camp and the Gulag; the power and force of the industrial process and its machinery which have created the Totalitarian State, and the forgotten, mysterious past of European paganism, of the shaman and of the land itself. Antlers are deployed frequently by 'Laibach' and also in the productions of TSN and 'Red Pilot'. It is no coincidence, that Joseph Beuys, an artist much respected by NSK, was much preoccupied with the stag and on many occasions made drawings of that animal and also gave voice to Stag noises in his performances.

At the base of the logo are three burning torches bound together by the orbits of an atom. The energy of fire and of the atom are forces which work for destruction and for renewal. Flame is a central image in the work of NSK and the ambiguity of its potential is a metaphor for their own purposes and their understanding of the state of the world in which they find themselves. The concentration of imagery which is found in the logo is an eloquent metaphor for the 'ideology' which hides behind the problematic surface of NSK. NSK is concerned with nothing less than the fate of the soul of Europe. Crosses, axes, thorns, cogs, antlers and torches, in all the complexity of their symbolism and iconography, are the tools which they use to give form to their prophetic vision. In one of their manifestoes, TSN reveal their true intentions:

'The Theatre of Scipion Nasica understands the Utopian instinct, as an innate and not as an acquired value. The instinct as a value granted by birth, is the striving of a moral entity. Therefore, in creating its style, the Theatre of Scipion Nasica cannot seek the right for its existence in an actor, a space or a formal production, but only in culture and civilisation whose traumatic experiences are being recapitulated by the theatre through its retrospective productions.'

NSK is an attempt at exorcism of the culture of Europe and a commitment to a new beginning for that old world. If they succeed in their objective then it may be something like it might have been if Malevich and the Suprematists rather than Rodchenko and the Constructivists had come to lead the Russian Revolution. There again the logic of 'Retro-Grade' would seem to dictate that the future will be quite different from any past that we have known. A hint or two of that future might perhaps be glimpsed in the work of NSK over the next few years. NSK are telling its audiences that the old wound of Europe is not yet healed. They are also telling them that healing is the only alternative to catastrophe. In a real sense, NSK are heirs to the artistic and philosophical vision which was given body and form by Joseph Beuys. They are advancing into the world of which he was a pioneer. No-one can tell what they will find there.

After the Rains

Janice Galloway

think
it is too warm here and my heart is racing think
where was I
I was
in the bus shelter. Dripping in there with the rest of them out of the
rain. It must have been about 25 past 10 because the bus to the
Cross had just drawn up and the brakes were still squealing and
when they stopped there was a sound of nothing. We were all
listening, aware of the difference. Simultaneously, carefully: we
were listening silently together, trying to fathom what it was. That
was what began to give it away: the fact that we could hear
ourselves being silent. A child outside ducked suddenly and looked
up, suspicious. One gesture. Herd realisation fluttered in the shelter
like a trapped bird. We thought, paused and realised afresh in the
same single second. It had stopped raining. It had stopped raining.
after nine solid months it had stopped raining
We peered with all our eyes and curled pieces of ourselves beyond
the perspex. Tentative, testing from under our rain-mates and
overhanding hoods for our various private proofs. For mine, I took
the nearest of the currant bushes to the stop, one of a grove planted
by the council to represent nature in the concrete island of the
estate. It was dripping yet. I watched. It was dripping yet but
but
but I could swear the drops were less assured now, visible seconds
lurching between one
drop and the next as I watched.
Not all of us had the patience or the time for such nicety, though.
There was a muffled grunt that could have been apology as a large
woman bulked past on her way out of the shelter and into the
middle of the road, her face bravely upturned to the sky to see for
herself. She made sure for all of us.

Then we were all out with her, all over the road, our talk buzzing, strengthening to outright exclamations of surprise and congratulation. In a burst we were new people. It was like Hogmanay: it was better for we didn't need the drink to open to it.

warmth in my chest
like warm soup to remember it

Spontaneously, without the false prop, we were speaking to perfect strangers, smiling and laughing and clapping them on the back. Folk normally so wary, so shy of ridicule it hurt, we blossomed for each other. We marvelled and cracked jokes while the bus sat like a ruin on the road. Its passengers had joined us, helping the older folk down off the platform. Reckless with enjoyment, one man held up a bottle of lemonade and shook it, his thumb over the neck, to splash it about like celebration champagne. There was laughing and cuddling and general pagan revelry.

The driver was out with us too. Even given the festival mood, that was remarkable since he was usually such a bloodyminded big bastard. He made a hammy mime of looking at his watch. He had had his look. The rain was off. Now he was finished. He announced it: if anybodys goin to the Cross they better come wi me cos Im away. No-one minded. Yes, we would come, goodnatured to spite him. We started to drift back

was it then?
it was then I saw

As I was straggling on, I noticed something in the corner of the shelter: a wee girl, huddling in on herself and keeking out from between her fingers? I craned out from an upstairs seat for another look as the bus started to move off. She was still there, indistinct behind too much hair. I should have been more curious, maybe done something, but the bus took me and my excitement eclipsed her.

The very road was interesting now the rain had stopped. Commonplaces about the weather became significant as we noted with genuine feeling it was turning out nice or drying up. We knew a change
the change
had begun. In places the tarmac was surfacing. Normally, there was

a two-inch film over the whole road, but the hydraulic emergency pumps were working away as steadily and greedily as always, noisily swallowing rivers ful when no more was falling to replace it. Boys were out on the crest of the road, right in the middle of the traffic path, for the novelty of standing on it without the water tugging at their shoes. They were kicking the planks away too. Sometimes people put planks across between pavements to try-and get over keeping their feet drier or because they were afraid of the current. The police did what they could, of course: it was selfish, dangerous and illegal. A plank accident on this very stretch of road had killed one person recently, and cost two others at least one necessary limb each. It was like a prayer touching all of us, a thanksgiving ritual to see those boys kicking the planks away. Someone sang a hymn. The rest of us pointed and waved at them, and at everything else newly emerged from behind the veil of drizzle, rubbing with cuffs at the windows streaming with our too close breath and the wet from our clothes. The chatter on the bus seemed abnormally loud: it wasn't just that we had more to say, but that the white noise of the rainfall was no longer fuzzing everything. The extra dimension to sound as well as that to sight must have been too much for some, though. A few around me were in tears and a low whimpering and groaning came up from the lower deck. Maybe they found it too sudden, maybe even painful.

we should have spoken about it questioned more
we were too pleased with ourselves
too smug

Only half an hour after the rain stopped the sky had lightened considerably. At the Cross, almost every office and shop window was framed with workers looking. Looking out to rediscover un-filled spaces between surfaces. I could see rows of them from my bench seat at the corner of the pedestrian precinct. I was

what was I doing?
just looking too just taking it all in
looking up
it was when I was looking up

Then quite suddenly, without warning, the sun came out. It tore a great rip in the cloud curtain and came out in one movement, one flaming presence. Colour flushed back immediately with shocking, breathstopping vividness. With a catch of emotion, we realised how much of it we had forgotten and how ashen everything had been for so long. The low light, the constant smurr– we had encouraged it. Black and white television had enjoyed a revival; there was a fashion for subdued lighting in our homes – as though we were afraid too much brightness would make the continual rainlight more depressing. We had not fought. But now we took the courage to look and everything blazed; the yellow, the green, red and orange glaring noisily and gloriously in our eyes. As one, we made a long intake of it, then sighed. From all over the Cross and all over the town purred a sigh of relief and wonder. The sun had come out.

the sun had come out

Those of us in the street spurred to motion again, some hurrying to see into the window of the television showroom for affirmation. We were only ordinary folk and untrusting of the evidence of our own eyes. For a moment or two, all we could see was a cookery demonstration, then a news flash. It told us the sun had come out. A cheer. The cookery demonstration continued to mix and fold itself behind the printout. Then it disappeared altogether and a man came on to explain with radiating lines and velcro symbols about the weather. We got another news flash. It said that scientists were confident this was the end of the rain for some considerable time. There would be a full report later. We were satisfied and turned away from the TV to shine our faces upward, crunching our eyes against the unaccustomed brilliance cracking the sky above our heads.

our scalps began to get warm then

Shop workers clustered in doorways and filled their display windows with face tilting toward the sunlight. As if it had been waiting for this moment, it appeared then: a massive, seven-coloured arch fanning above us, pouring itself above the buildings and the town, looping and glittering to prickle ready tears. We applauded. We all applauded the rainbow and its promise. We were radiant.

By the afternoon it was hot. I hadn't moved much: the length of the street, a little shopping, then back to the bench at the Cross to watch the day unfold along with others who had the time, the reward of the jobless. The streets were misty and dry patches squared out on the paving. None among us could have foreseen such a difference in so short a period. City Bakeries sold out of sandwiches as people lunched al fresco. Bright dots of tee-shirts began to appear among the crowds. Sloughing off rainclothes allowed us to look at ourselves afresh and become dissatisfied with what we saw. Those that could went to change: light trousers, summer dresses, short-sleeved shirts with bleachy angles poking out. Some improvised, rolling up trouser legs as though they were at the beach in a jokey but serviceable imitation of bermuda shorts, fit for the steamy tropic the Cross had become. Almost everyone wore a hat, sunglasses or visor against the glare. It came from more than unaccustomedness, this sharpness against our eyes. More news flashes confirmed the suspicion: it was indeed a freak heatwave and the temperature was rising by the minute. A thermometer in the travel agents window bled steadily upward and made a talking point for all watchers as we rolled up our sleeves and loosened collar-buttons.

I went to the riverside walkway
cooler there
then it was later did I fall asleep
I must have slept
but I woke and

It was later afternoon when I returned. The Cross was much less crowded; many had drifted off out of the punishing light. There was a crowd under the canopy of the Co-op looking out from its little shade as they waited for their bus home. The newsagents on the corner shut and the women who worked there walked across the road to join them with the keys jangling into the stillness. As I watched them walk across, I saw something pale and puffy billow out from under their feet. It took me a minute to place what it was. It was dust.

dust

Dust rising up from gutters that had churned with running water for so long. It was scarcely credible. My head thumped as I thought about it and with the heat and windlessness of the street. Workers who had poked from their doorways earlier to seek the sun now did the same for air. It must have been hell in the shops – all that glass. A very plump woman who owned the flower shop appeared at her open door, wheezing and gasping, the effort of her lungs making her very red about the face and chest in her short summer-frock. Some shops were near to closing now and a few individuals were out lowering shutters, keen, I supposed, to get out of the thickening air. Numbers swelled at the bus stop, waiting.

waiting

They sweated and sighed, pearls of their moisture oozing to drip and melt on the slab pavement. It was very still, the absence of the hiss of rain had left a vacuum. The pumps had cut long silence.

no flies there was no thrum of flies

It was sickly quiet and the air seethed with expectation. Something *something was coming*

it was coming then
Then there it was. A stretching sound, like a mass intake of breath:
a sort of inrush of air that came not from us, the people, but from
above our heads. Then that low rumble along the horizon, hollow-
ing the ear across the line of the sky. It was the sound of men
clearing their throats. Now an earth-rippling crack: we looked up.
Overhead, the rainbow, evanescing more wildly, was criss-crossed
by countless others, all arching and diving at crazy angles over and
through and around themselves, filling up every corner of the clear
blue so none remained as a touchstone for the sky. Immediately, a
huge rushing surged in my head, spreading from ear to ear as
though some invisible hand were unzipping the hair from the skull.
I threw up my hands defensively. I could see others were doing the
same and some had fallen down on their knees.

too late
too late for that
A few children danced incongruously about on the pedestrian walkway, either from stupidity or delight at what they saw and it
occurred to me we were not all seeing or hearing the same. It was
certain we were all inhabiting something far outwith the normal
run, but *not the same thing*. The faces around me behind the glass in
doorways and on the road varied so extremely.

high sudden screaming
Then all heads turned from their own pain to find the source of a
single shrill scream. It was the florist. She appeared to be trying to pull

a shoot

no

several green shoots
she appeared to be trying to pull several green shoots and leaves
from her dress as we watched. More and yet more leaves burst out
despite her efforts, and I realised suddenly they were not attached to
her dress. They were attached to her elbow, to her arm. I looked
harder. They were her arm. *They were her arm.* Greenery surged up
her neck and into her hair, buds clustered then filled out and burst
into riotous bloom in a pink halo all around her head. Huge roses
ripened at her armpits and elbows, camelias and magnolias fanned
out of her cleavage.

She had stopped struggling with it now and enough of her face
remained to let me see she was smiling. She was welcoming the
beauty of the garden, of the flowers she had become, smiling at the
perfumed loveliness that was herself. I felt a twinge of outrage, but
as I looked again at the woman's smile and at her childish delight

and I was moved with compassion. I had to admire it too. The scent was overpowering.

it carried all the way from the other side of the road.

Her assistant was next. Formerly a girl of about seventeen, now a living display of hyacinth and spring ferns. The grocer in the next doorway was gazing down affectionately at a cabbage foresting the front of his overall. He saw me gaping over, hesitated then pointed at it shamelessly with his carroting digits. The reaction of the crowd to his bravado was enthusiastic. Some cheered and one old woman tottered over for a closer look, muttering endearments. Another hurtled from the back of the bus crowd to give himself room: a checkout boy I recognised from Tesco's. A pregnant bulge at the front of his coat elongated as he stood, squaring out to make a full-size trolley complete with front wheel to balance the projection from his body. As though pleased to have joined the elite, he lowered his shopping into it with great dignity.

Behind him, the electrical goods manager of the Co-op came out to display a shiny transparent door in the centre of his wide barrel chest, and turned from side to side to show off the gaily-coloured washing tumbling inside in graceful whorls, beaming amid the congratulations of his proud neighbours. All the while the sun grew hotter.

it is too warm here

I began to walk the length of the street to find some shade for myself where I could more comfortably continue to watch. I had begun to see a pattern in it and wanted to see it unfold. I thought I knew what would happen, though some might have longer gestation periods than others. Loud snortings and scufflings emitted from the bookies as I went past ducking in to the doorway to avoid soft collision with a squashy bundle emerging from the Wool Shop. It was taking off.
too fast
a whisper of warning
mouthing in my head, half-formed. Perhaps I recalled the child in the shelter from the morning. I was waiting then too. Realisation prickled its beginnings up the back of my neck. I ran round the corner and saw the truth of it.

An enormous pulsating grub writhed reflexively in the gutter, its blind bulbous tips waving in what looked horribly like appeal.

Beyond this nerveless thing, the pavement crawled with three-headed phantoms, blocking my progress. Where features should have been was only tight, smooth skin, blanket grey and eyeless. The phantoms hovered helplessly and fell as another of their kind fumbled from the council offices, apparently in an extreme of agony, and would have cried out as it spattered down had it had a mouth to scream. I spun back against the wall of the Employment Exchange to get out of its way, then rebounded as quickly at the ripping cold of it against my skin. Even in this heat, frost had feathered the windows and a faint mist of frozen vapour issued from the open gate and its maw of jaggy ice teeth. I knew nothing would come out of there.

It was sure now.
There would be others like this too. Not flowers, not harmless eccentricities, but other things.
terrible other things
A foul, pitiful screeching that pierced to my bowels forced me to turn. I was facing the butchers. The howling and the bloody trail at their doorway
I would not look in there
I did not want to see
I began to run again   faster
curiosity pushed my glance down despite the urgings of reason
my hands were very pale and whitening still
they were stark white

I kept on running.

The Seaside Photographer

A. L. Kennedy

I CAME to the library and I don't know why.

There's an old man behind me and he's breathing like a big cat asleep. It's breath that should come with running, with pulling back at the anger before you fight, with making love. This man is blue round his lips and gasping from sitting in a chair and reading the morning's paper.

I came to be in the library and I don't know why. The air is full of reading and you can't and I didn't think of that before I got here. I just came to be in the library, not knowing why.

This was a good day. The umbrella has stayed in my bag, telescoped and rolled up tight. Dawn started slowly today. And I was up to see it rise: the milky blue dawn, clear and almost chill, that brought in a hot, sweet afternoon. It is now a very gentle evening and, if I could see them, the clouds would be blushing or burning, or sculling off with the sun towards the West. Whichever would be most appropriate.

When I don't have a book of my own, I read Ed McBain. Whatever they have with his name on, I read until it's time for me to leave and each of the unfinished pieces has collided and combined. There are severed heads in airline holdalls and burnt up bodies tied with wire. When I read them, I like the characters and the way that he talks about Spring, but afterwards it's the pathology that clings. There'll be a reason for that, but I don't know it.

Twice I've ever seen you with a book. The first one you put on the window sill in the sitting room when I came in. That was a Western with a desert coloured cover and its price in pence and shillings on the front. You gave me the second one later, when I couldn't get to sleep; it was an Alistair Maclean, I think, quite new. I didn't like it and I still couldn't sleep.

You keep watch in the night, you always have. I remember your coughs and creaking; you slipping into the toilet to have a smoke and shadowing out to the back and look at the night. I knew. I heard you. You never slept. McBain might not have suited you, might not have been just right, but I wish I had given you something, then, to save you from the dark.

For me, it happened today, this good day. I woke, having dreamed a little, and washed and spent hours full of the small things to do with me. I worked. Also, I answered the telephone. It told me how different your day had been. This day and how many before it.

I wanted to call you and say things, or say nothing and hope that you would know.

I don't understand what I should do.

I have you in my head and it's all lies. Not memories; lies. You are walking through the snow with your black umbrella, striding with it furled, wanting to show me the bears, or the parrots. I am in the shadow of your overcoat; my hand in the pocket of your overcoat, down among the tickle of cellophane and peppermints and I am warm. It feels like Good King Wenceslas and I'm wishing for a blizzard to come, to let me step in your footprints and still be warm. Later, at the bus stop, I can wrap both my arms around one of yours and let it lift me up. I can swing.

But this leads me to other places, now; to a path between woods, under sugarloaf cones of orange lamplight and warm rain where I walked with my fingers laced in other fingers and our hands in the pocket of his rain coat while he talked. It was the last night we could have before he went away. My third time ever and every time with him.

There is nothing to keep them apart, these lies: year on year on year and each one becomes another. Except that I see his face as I can see it today and your face is fifteen years out of date. You are not much in my dreams. But I do love you.

Then, I thought you had everything you wanted. You'll remember once, I asked if you were rich. It wasn't out of greed, not even curiosity, I was sure in my heart that you were a millionaire. I just wanted to hear you say it out loud. I didn't know that you would always give, whether you were able to or not. I didn't know what you did when I wasn't there. To me, you could not have been anything but happy and certain and wanting to give, because you were made like that. A while ago, I watched another man turn to walk away on a Summer street and if it had been a child of mine, running too near the edge; there is always an edge; it would have been the same. He moves like joy, without knowing, and God must surely bless him and the sun must surely shine, but maybe not, so you want to call him back and say it, in case you can't say it again. Am I right that it was like that with you? You were as happy and certain as anyone else, as me, and, when I asked, you laughed and said you weren't rich really, not really at all.

And you had no power.

I realised that sooner and younger and you know I blamed you. I thought you had made a decision: that you could make that decision: and it was your fault. When you said they should call off all the wars and work it out with the gloves on, up in the ring, it was you that I saw. Your hair in a glossy black crew cut, with the flag a discreet block of colour on the shine of your white vest; high boots and long shorts, the Saviour Of Our Nation. Of course, you hadn't fought for years: since before I was born, but you still had the build and the faith in your muscle. I believed in your faith. The honourable hero, you would swallow your pride and never shoot first, but you would shoot.

Then I stood next to you in your kitchen and leaned the way you were leaning, over the window, over the edge. I made it so our shoulders were touching and feeling the warm through your shirt made me shiver as we looked out the back. Through the window, it was icy mist and your cigarette threaded out to join it and there was dead quiet out there, like the ghost of a dawn.

My mouth was still tasteless with sleep and my eyes kept yawning back and trying to close and you said to me,

I thought you were going to stay longer,

and kept on looking out. I couldn't think of any words.

So my father led me away, past the bed that we would have made later and that would have been still warm from where I'd slept. I knew that you weren't going to stop him, that's why I never asked. I never even cried.

You couldn't stop your daughter's husband, like you couldn't stop the wars.

I'm sorry. I don't think as sorry as you.

The things that made you, I'll never see. You told me all about London, before the war, when you were the Champion of the Works; the Black Country apprentice, taking all comers on. There was the time when the man got caught in the overhead belts and went up and round and was dead before they got him down. You didn't talk much about it, but I remember. Everyone else had gone to bed and I was up late, listening, when you said about the white hot bar and the way it just touched the chest of this one man and went straight on through. You looked at his back and saw daylight before he fell.

After that, you stopped yourself in case you gave me dreams. You didn't. I felt the same way that I did when you took me down to your work. A Sunday, no one else there and, I don't know how, but you let us in and the whole place was as if it belonged to you. Every one of those machines, you understood, and you could set all that heaviness in motion at a touch. You could conjure up whirling and screaming that filled the shop and set strange new components slithering out: still hot. You pattered me along the corridors left between the machines and all of it was waiting for the switch, to set up a roar, with the bitter smell of sweat and metal stirred up everywhere we stepped.

For that afternoon, you were the master, the owner and conductor and magician and that, more than any of the rules we'd broken, was, I think, why you made me promise not to mention where we'd been.

Because you were not the master and the magic did you harm. You still have the little dips bitten into your skin from when spatters of boiling metal flew too fast for you to catch them in your shirt. How many evenings did you come home grey faced and heavy and fall asleep with your dinner half eaten; cold and spoilt on the tray in your lap? Out of all those evenings, how many times when I was there did you have to have me sitting beside you with the needle, to work the black steel splinters from your hands? Each time I saw it hurt you, I wished that I could stop and the needle would turn slippery in my grip, but I had the smallest fingers and the sharpest eyes. They were other hands that drew the splinters from your eyes and you were lucky that time, but you have too many scars to be a master.

I don't know what made you how you are. I wasn't there on the day you decided there were changes you could no longer make and now you would stay with turnups, stay with flannel for underwear and after Heath you would stop voting and each year would put you closer to your past.

Now there is a change for the worst. I don't understand how these things happen. Perhaps you took too many punches and they hurt inside your head, perhaps the little sparks of iron that caught you were finally too much, or perhaps it was always being patient, only letting it show with the tap and tap and tap from your nervous foot in the dark of the room. All these cancers you collect through time; they are in you, but not of you and yet they are part of what people think of, whenever they think of you. They are as real as you. Each one of them could be a reason, it could be none of them, it could be all. Whatever the cause, you are blind now. Suddenly.

I have no magic for you and there is nothing I have learned to make. If, in this world, I could, I would write you whole and well. I would write you smiling through windy sunshine and strolling with your wife, the thin boards of the promenade beneath you reaching up to a seaside photographer. I would wish myself unborn and you as you were in a holiday picture. A picture I have lost.

As it is, you are more and better now than ever you were then, a more beautiful and perfect, breathing man. Nothing should dare touch you, not a thing. Only, the years and the years' hardness; they were out and waiting for you from the start.

All I can do is write you words you cannot read, feel the words between us, love you.

Nationalism and the Philosophy of the Unthinkable

George Davie

A response written in 1969 to Government and Nationalism in Scotland, *a set of seminar papers published by Edinburgh University Press.*

I found the seminar very interesting and illuminating but I think that the papers and discussions would have been more effective if they had given more attention to the question of what Nationalism is in contrast to Devolutionism. The important point here, I think, is that, whether or not the Nationalist alternative is felt to be practicable, it is essential to bear it in mind, if our discussions are to make sense. It seems to me an evident proposition that one will not be able to think clearly about the prospects for Scotland within the Union, unless one can at the same time imaginatively bear in mind the contrast with the prospects for Scotland outside the Union. Unless one takes seriously what must seem to many the unrealistic alternative, it is surely hard to make sense of the alternative which most people perhaps judge the realistic one. When a writer, typical of the last generation – Professor J. Y. T. Greig in his *Life of David Hume* – proclaimed that modern Scotland was unthinkable apart from the Union, his words betrayed a point of view which takes it for granted that modern Scotland does not bear thinking of at all. But over and above it being theoretically essential to bear in mind the question of Nationalism, there is also certain practical importance about it too. No doubt public opinion polls show that a very small percentage of the Scottish people – only, I think, some 15 per cent – is committed, on principle, to Nationalism. But as against this one may note that in the crisis-points of political agitation a genuine Nationalist note is often surprisingly effective. During Mrs Ewing's election at Hamilton one of the chief slogans, I believe, was 'Put Scotland back on the map'. Now there is no question that this propaganda point, with its reference to an independent re-appearance on the international scene, has nothing to do with an Ulster-like form of devolution and everything to do with a re-assertion of independent sovereignty.

If the Seminar, in the course of its deliberations, had thought more seriously about the historical and continuing role of the University, under the auspices of whose Social Science Faculty the discussions were held, the participants would quickly have been made more aware than they, in many cases were, of the factor of national pride and aspirations in Scottish life. On the broad view of the last two hundred and fifty years, it seems clear that one of the chief ways in which this national aspiration found a certain due outlet and satisfaction, under the conditions of the Union, was the signal contribution of the country to the severer disciplines of the scientific and philosophical kind – a contribution which has made our own University world famous.

It is here, in the international intellectual field that Scotland in the last two centuries has made its impact and the absence of any paper or contribution on this subject was a very grave lack in the Seminar. More than anything else, it might have brought home to the participants that they are dealing with a nation which has made a distinctive and fundamental contribution to the civilization of our own times. Indeed, in order to understand the national motif in Scotland it must be borne in mind that we in Edinburgh University – in coping with the Scottish intellectual inheritance – are not just involved with a museum piece which can be safely left to inspire the researches of historians. On the contrary right down to the third and fourth decades at least of the present century, the intellectual genius of Scotland was still very much alive in its distinctive themes; and the life of our University, down to the present day, is still perhaps chiefly interesting and memorable through the drama of this continuing impulse to keep alive the tradition of distinctive Scottish universalism in research, in an atmosphere where sympathy with it is too often imperfect and where sometimes an apparently alien set of values complacently attempts to over-look it.

Impelled by Riches

Gael Turnbull

impelled by riches, not poverty
one gulp of air is all we have

making relation of unequal things
according to the interval, according to the context

morning, already heat haze, watching
an Indian woman, Tumamait or Shamash,
down from the hills near Santa Ynez
within glitter of the Pacific surf –
the scorched air thick with scent
of anise, eucalyptus, sage –
her eyes, under tatar eyelids, dark
as wells without reflections, caverns
into a past and distance beyond us

and at dusk, blurred by falling snow,
five of them from off the tops,
largest creatures in this land,
only a few paces from our door
in winter coats, some still with antlers,
as in cave paintings, charcoaled, ruddy,
massive in shoulder, turning their great heads,
not cautious but aloof, part of the storm,
their eyes unseen upon us

in a flowing contour, pulsing forward
gripping upon itself, compact of detail

the song patterns of many birds
'much too rapid in variation
for the human ear to distinguish'
and certain butterflies 'transparent scales
with opaque particles to scatter the light
creating the same blue as the sky overhead'

and under volcanic pressure and temperature
in the deepest rifts of the earth
'living organisms that thrive'

and by the shore of an open bay
watching the crests of the long rollers
from the full reach of the Atlantic
as they move in from over the horizon
in unwearied sequence to some rhythm
familiar beyond definition, to remember
the eyes of a man by a road somewhere
in the southern bush who said, when asked
how many years he'd lived, just 'much'

amid a plankton of expiring suns
finding laughter even in the void

called to house by neighbours insisting
'something has to be done' about
a cheerful lass, pregnant five times
(though lost two) before twenty-one
by different fathers, first of whom
beat her then left for an older woman
while the other is bisexual and in prison
for selling heroin (but incompetently
as the bailiffs are due next week)

and of the children (she has gone out
no one knows where) the eldest cowers
mute behind settee with the middle one
(in hospital last year: unexplained bruises)
while the youngest, a toddler, has fallen
against only heat in the house, a one bar
electric fire (the guard was broken) and
as I wait for the ambulance, their puppy
of six weeks dribbles into my left shoe

ply against counterply, keeping the tension
shaping the explicit from the possible

taken by a stroke three weeks later
which left him unable to speak or write
except for the occasional syllable
impossible to understand in spite of effort –
otherwise lay, had bowels and bladder emptied,

squeezed her hand, took sips of liquid,
sometimes waved one arm at the ward
or opened his eyes and shook his fist
until heart and breath faded out

and at the crematorium in the middle
of several miles of derelict and open ground,
there was a pile of rubbish lying outside
including floral sprays with violet ribbons
still wrapped in their plastic covers
abandoned from a previous funeral
that the wind suddenly tumbled across
the car park towards us and which no one
appeared to notice or find remarkable

take hold anywhere and all shall follow
between what might and is then beyond recall

imaged in words, as news from nowhere,
awakening to what might be, in a dream
of where a dustman 'while the sun
flashed back from him at every step
as if clad in golden armour' strolls
towards us on some casual morning
'with that somewhat haughty mien
great beauty is apt to give' to bring
discarded things to whatever lasting place

and from beyond the curve of the world
out of a storm of light and spray
Columba's boat steers to us and that island,
burial place of kings, who comes a stranger
to the land that he made his, claimed him,
watched by two lads, dumbfoundered,
sprawled on the machair – in the pigments
of that painting which still hangs
within a stroll of where I came to birth

as a thread between thumb and finger
as a boat between wind and tide

who remember that one day we shall not
and not a word but sound till heard

'Impelled by Riches' is part of a longer construction, 'Impellings'.

A Note on 'The Politics of Experience'

From the Psychopathology of Everyday Life to the Pathology of Normalcy.

R. D. Laing

THERE IS a very fine edge between what Freud called the psychopathology of everyday life and what Fromm called the pathology of normalcy. The early Freud seemed to envisage a normal psychophysiology, as it were, which is frequently invaded by psychopathological processes in otherwise 'normal', that is, healthy people. In the later Freud (from *The Future of an Illusion* on), the 'norm', the usual, the average, comes to be seen as 'off'. Civilisation, at least, capitalist industrial society of the first part of the twentieth century is seen as having taken a course, such that adaptation to it requires such inhibition and repression (Freud), and other actions of self on self to manufacture successful conformity to it, that 'health' becomes an ideal, but hardly a real possibility. I gave expression to my version of this sensibility most sharply in *The Politics of Experience* published in 1967 based mainly on lectures and talks given over the past decade from 1956. This work struck a chord in many people, and became in the USA the book with which I am most identified.

Karl Abenheimer thought I had gone completely 'off'. So did many others.

Elliot Mischler, a sociology professor at Harvard, got a US Federal Government Grant to look into whether I had gone psychotic, and published several papers in which he concluded that I might have, but the evidence was inconclusive. Professor Sidney Jourard told me that at least eighty per cent of psychiatrists in the United States in the late sixties thought I had crossed the line, clinically, on the evidence of that book. In the USA I still (1989) hear that I am in a mental hospital, that I have committed suicide. Now, of course, I am dying of AIDS. I have had the uncanny experience several times meeting people who know I am not me, because I am dead. A detail like death wouldn't deter a Glaswegian. 'Didn't you used to be the R. D. Laing who used to live off Great Western Road?'

Thoughts about the pathology of normalcy are bandied about at cocktail parties and dismissed as '*Arabesque chic*', etc. They induce a whole range of responses from contempt to terror.

I hope I was not saying anything 'new' in *The Politics of Experience*. One could marshal an anthology of quotations from every spiritual tradition on the mind of man in the last two to three thousand years. Think, of Hindu sages, including Gautama Buddha, the Socrates of Plato, the Old Testament Prophets, Jesus... Their terms like ignorance, delusion, evil, sin, etc., refer to the usual, normal, average state of mind, not to special, exceptional, abnormal, unusual, aberrations of the norm, of healthy normalcy.

In *The Politics of Experience* I wanted to present old wisdom in a fresh way. I was not repeating by rote what I had learned – I was bringing to bear on the present what I had been taught at Sunday school in the light of my life.

You can look on *The Politics of Experience* as my attempt to synthesise Scottish Presbyterian Celtic Calvinism and elements of Hasidism. Those who have not the faintest inkling of what I might mean by this remark will have no idea why Eric Fromm told me he so much admired it, why it helped to make me friends for life with Rollo May, why I got a standing ovation at the Baylor University, Texas, on the strength of it, and why I can say that the two most important people behind it were Joe Schorstein,* whose father was an Hasidim, and the Very Reverend George McLeod.†

---

* 'Few books today are forgivable. Black on the canvas, silence on the screen ...' comes from Joe. He said it, with a sigh of appreciation, after he had read *The Politics of Experience* in ms.
   'Can I use that?' I asked him, at once. 'Delighted,' he said.

† McLeod was seen by some hovering in the heavens between the Vatican and the Kremlin. He chuckled at the image. Read *Only One Way Left*. (There is a pun on 'Left'.) '... Wyclif frequently translates "to glorify" as "to clarify": to make God clear to men. A boy threw at stone at the stained glass window of the Incarnation. It nicked the "E" in the word "HIGHEST". Thus, till unfortunately it was mended, it read, "GLORY TO GOD IN THE HIGH ST".'